Sisters of Sinai

Also by Janet Soskice

Metaphor and Religious Language
The Kindness of God

Sisters of Sinai

How Two Lady Adventurers Found the Hidden Gospels

JANET SOSKICE

Chatto & Windus
LONDON

Published by Chatto & Windus 2009

8 10 9

Map by Reginald Piggott

Extracts from *Period Piece* by Gwen Raverat reproduced by kind permission of the Raverat Estate
and Faber and Faber Ltd. Extracts from the diaries of T. R. Glover reproduced by kind permission
of the Masters and Fellows of St John's College, Cambridge.

First published in Great Britain in 2009 by
Chatto & Windus
Random House, 20 Vauxhall Bridge Road,
London SW1V 2SA

www.rbooks.co.uk

Addresses for companies within The Random House Group Limited can be found at:
www.randomhouse.co.uk/offices.htm

The Random House Group Limited Reg. No. 954009

A CIP catalogue record for this book
is available from the British Library

ISBN 9780701173418

The Random House Group Limited supports The Forest Stewardship
Cou   l our titles
th   C logo.

Nec Tamen Consumebatur

Yet it was not consumed.

Exodus 3.2

Contents

List of Illustrations

Acknowledgements

My thanks are due to the Master and Fellows of St John's College, not only for the assistance their predecessors gave to Agnes and Margaret and to Solomon Schechter, but for permission to use extracts from the diaries of T. R. Glover and to reproduce an image of the portrait of Professor Palmer. Thanks are also due to the University of Birmingham Archive for permission to use the letters of James Rendel Harris.

One of the advantages of writing a book such as this one is that it obliges the author to seek out specialists in so many areas not her own – in this case historians and biblical scholars, keepers of coins and keepers of pots, archivists, philologists and travel guides. I would like to thank here: Dr Martin Allen, Keeper of Coins, and Dr Lucilla Burn, Keeper of Antiquities, both at the Fitzwilliam Museum; Rene Aris of the University of Heidelberg; Elizabeth Bell of the Ardrossan history library; and Professor Sebastian Brock (who generously read some very rough drafts). Also Professor John Emerton, Professor Sidney Griffith, Mr Rolf Haaser, Professor David Holton, Professor David Armstrong, Professor Geoffrey Khan, Dr Emma Loveridge and the Reverend Andrew Macintosh (for superb Sinai guiding), Dr Scot McKendrick, Head of Western Manuscripts at the British Library, Dr Jane McLarty, Robert Murray S.J., Dr Mary Roussou-Sinclair, Professor David Thompson, Deidre Wildy, Dr Dirk Jongkind and Dr Peter Williams. Fr. Jean-Michel de Tarragon O.P. was generous in showing me the splendid photographic archive, and historic photographic equipment, preserved by the Dominicans of the *École Biblique* in Jerusalem.

Robert and Gillian Siwek, descendents of the Gibson line, were generous in sharing family photos and reminiscences, as were Margaret Barwise and Mr and Mrs Miles Burkitt, descendents of Francis Burkitt. Mr William Campbell of Edinburgh shared with me his findings in Smith family history.

At Corpus Christi College, Cambridge, I would like to thank Gill Cannell of the Parker Library, Iwona Krasodomska-Jones of the Butler library and Robin Myers, modern archivist. Professor Stefan Reif and his successor as Head of the Taylor-Schechter Genizah Research Unit, Dr Ben Outhwaite, have been generous with photographs and enthusiasm for this project.

Thanks are also due to friends: John and Gabriel Cornwell and Professor Gemma Corradi Fiumara for encouragement throughout. Bridget Tighe accompanied me on various journeys in the footsteps of my adventurous subject, and read an early draft. The same labour was kindly undertaken by Hilary Clay and by Dr Alessandro Falcetta, New Testament scholar, biographer of James Rendel Harris and most generous of correspondents.

I am indebted to Clare Alexander for suggesting that I write this book and to the wonderful publishers she put me in touch with: Rebecca Carter, Clara Farmer and Juliet Brooke in London, and George Andreou in New York. It has been a delight to work with all of them.

Special thanks must go to the members of Westminster College, past and present – and to numerous of their alumni for encouraging reception of my early efforts on Agnes and Margaret. Above all, I am indebted to Margaret Thompson, their Archival Admistrator, for her assistance and encouragement from first to last.

To the monks of the Monastery of St Catherine at Mount Sinai, especially in the person of the Librarian, Father Justin, I am grateful not only for assistance to me, but for the work of preservation and scholarship they carry on with such diligence 'to the greater glory of God'. I hope that more visitors may be encouraged by this book to visit St Catherine's and Mount Sinai.

Finally, to my daughters Isabelle and Catherine, who read various drafts and who, in the case of Catherine, was from time to time editorial assistant, abundant thanks. My husband, Oliver Soskice, immersed himself in this project with me from its first instance to its final inking. My gratitude to him knows no bounds.

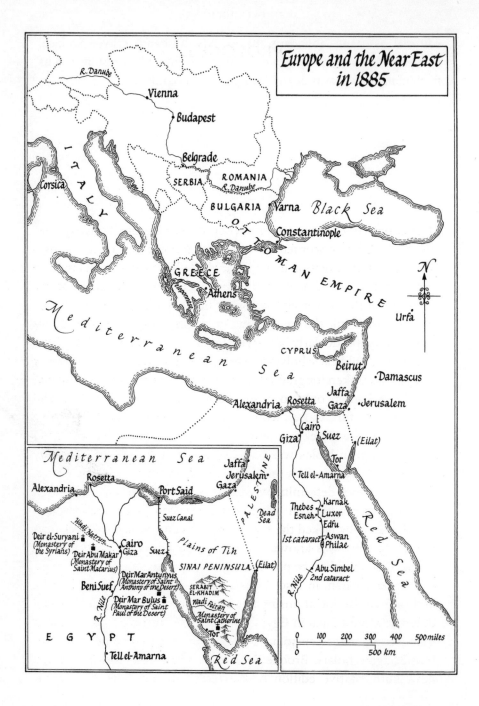

Europe and the Near East in 1885

R. Danube

Vienna

Budapest

Belgrade

SERBIA

ROMANIA

R. Danube

ITALY

Corsica

BULGARIA

Varna

Black Sea

Constantinople

OTTOMAN EMPIRE

GREECE

Ioannina

Athens

N

Mediterranean Sea

Urfa

CYPRUS

Beirut

Damascus

Jaffa

Jerusalem

Gaza

Alexandria

Rosetta

Cairo

Suez

(Eilat)

Giza

Tor

Tell el-Amarna

Inset map:

Mediterranean Sea

Alexandria

Rosetta

Port Said

Jaffa

Jerusalem

Gaza

PALESTINE

Dead Sea

Wadi Natrun

Suez Canal

Deir el-Suryani
(Monastery of
the Syrians)

Cairo

Giza

Suez

Plains of Tih

Thebes

Esneh

Karnak

Luxor

Edfu

Deir Abu Makar
(Monastery of
Saint Macarius)

SINAI PENINSULA

(Eilat)

1st cataract

Aswan

Philae

R. Nile

Beni Suef

Deir Mar Antunyus
(Monastery of Saint
Anthony of the Desert)

SERABIT
EL-KHADIM

Abu Simbel

2nd cataract

Deir Mar Bulus
(Monastery of Saint
Paul of the Desert)

Wadi Faîran

Monastery of
Saint Catherine

R. Nile

Red Sea

E G Y P T

Tor

Tell el-Amarna

Red Sea

0   100   200   300   400   500 miles

0   500 km

PROLOGUE

The latter half of the nineteenth century was a time of anxiety over the Bible. This concerned not only the Scriptures' factual claims – such as that the Creation had been subjected to a Universal Flood and the Israelites had fed on manna in the desert – but also bore upon the integrity of the text itself: was what had percolated down through the centuries still the same now as it was in the beginning? This uncertainty particularly affected the trustworthiness of the New Testament. Biblical scholars had long been questioning the accuracy of what was taken for granted in every pew. But from the 1850s what had been known only to a few became disturbingly public, 'and propaganda for those who wanted to beat the Churches'. Specifically, the Greek text on which the King James Bible and many other European bibles was based was widely known to be highly imperfect. 'You stand on the authority of Scripture,' said the critics, 'but you cannot determine what was originally written.'[1] Although scholars were agreed in calling for a revision of the standardised Greek text, they lacked the manuscripts against which to check it. A fine early copy was known to exist in the Vatican Library, but its keepers did their best to prevent anyone from seeing it. The impasse was broken when, in 1859, Constantin von Tischendorf disclosed a biblical manuscript of unsurpassed antiquity, which he had tracked down at Mount Sinai in Egypt. On the basis of this and the Vatican manuscript, whose custodians eventually relented somewhat, two Cambridge scholars, Brooke Westcott and Fenton Hort prepared a new, authoritative edition of the Greek of the New Testament, which a revision committee released in English translation on 17 May 1881.

There was intense public interest in the new arrival. A bribe of £5,000 was offered (and refused) for an advance copy. On publication, the text was telegraphed immediately to the United States; and, in England, the Oxford University Press alone sold a million copies on the first day.[2] Wagons waiting to take away copies for distribution jammed the London streets surrounding the printing houses.

Not everyone was pleased. The scholars declared themselves content with the Greek, but in the new translation many cherished phrasings had been lost. Most Englishmen, it was agreed, would have rather seen a revision of Shakespeare than of the King James Bible.[3] But despite a mixed reception, it was hoped that, with an authoritative Greek text in place, uncertainties could finally be put to rest and sceptics confounded. Thus it was with considerable interest, and not a little anxiety, that in the spring of 1893 a public sensitised to the disruptive consequences of biblical manuscripts received news from the Holy Land of a major find that was almost as old as von Tischendorf's.

CHAPTER I

Cambridge, 13 April 1893

On 13 April 1893, the London *Daily News* brought an extraordinary story – fresh from its Berlin correspondent. Two ladies, a Mrs Lewis and her sister, Mrs Gibson, had travelled to Mount Sinai in Egypt and discovered an ancient manuscript of the Four Gospels. Although Sinai had been searched for written treasures many times since von Tischendorf, the present discovery had 'remained hidden from former investigators'. Professor Rendel Harris of Cambridge, on first hearing the news, had set off for Mount Sinai where, for forty days, he and the two ladies had sat in the convent deciphering the manuscript, and they were now on their way home with the results. 'It is a palimpsest manuscript,' wrote Professor Harris in a letter to a German friend (the source of the Berlin correspondent's scoop), and 'When Mrs Lewis first saw it, it was in a dreadful condition, all the leaves sticking together and being full of dirt.' She had steamed its pages apart with her camp kettle and, finding that the underwriting of the manuscript contained a very early text of the Gospels, had photographed the lot – some 300–400 pages. As to who this Mrs Lewis and her sister might be, or what credentials they might have for the study of ancient books, the *Daily News* said nothing other than that both were fluent in Arabic and Greek and that Professor Harris had instructed them in the photographing of handwriting.

A further letter from Professor Harris, posted from Suez and published that very day in the *British Weekly*, had the same exciting story, but an equally frustrating lack of explanatory detail. It was left to the *Cambridge Chronicle* of the following morning, in its coverage of the breaking story, to say that 'as our readers are aware, Mrs Lewis is the widow of the Rev. S. S. Lewis' – sufficient information to identify the two ladies to the insular world of 1890s Cambridge.

An undergraduate, cracking open his *Cambridge Chronicle* in the Central Coffee Tavern, might recognise the Reverend S. S. Lewis as the very recently deceased Latin tutor at Corpus Christi College, and suppose his widow to be one of the two remarkably similar-looking ladies often to be found awaiting him at the college gates.

The shopkeepers on the King's Parade could report to customers that they were indeed well acquainted with Mrs Lewis and Mrs Gibson, for few Cambridge ladies had Paris frocks and bonnets, let alone a private coach and coachman. The two were alike in most every way – trimly built, not in their first youth, but fine-looking and energetic, with brown eyes and chestnut hair piled on their heads *à la mode*. They would often stop by for gloves, hats or hose, ordering their goods in brisk Scottish accents, and not occasionally countermanding each other as they spoke. The two ladies had been prominent features of the town for the last few years as well as good customers, recently fitting out a grand house they had built for themselves at the foot of Castle Hill.

Members of the town's Presbyterian congregation remembered well the first appearance amongst them of the two sisters in January of 1887, both wrapped in furs and one in deep mourning. They were twins and alone in the world and, it was said, very learned. Their father was reputed to have settled an enormous fortune on them, on condition that they never live apart from one another.

The residents of the fine, newly built houses of Harvey Road recalled Mrs Lewis and Mrs Gibson living briefly there while the large – some said pretentious – house at Castle Hill was being built. It was reported that they had astonished their neighbours by taking exercise on parallel bars in their back garden – in their bloomers – and that their new house avoided the cause of this distress by incorporating a tower with gymnastic ropes so that the two sisters could exert themselves in privacy.

Many knew that the two ladies were keen travellers, but few

imagined they would venture as far as the Sinai, a region known to be rugged and dangerous and where only ten years before, the university's Professor of Arabic had been murdered by bandits.

Just as surprising as the destination was the reason for the two ladies' travels. Apparently they had been searching quite purposefully for ancient manuscripts of the Bible, such as the one they had found. But on what basis, many in Cambridge might ask, were they doing so? Learned they might be, but they were not scholars and they had not a university degree between them. The hunt for early copies of the Bible was a difficult scholarly pursuit and dangerous furthermore, especially for ladies, since you could hardly know what – or whom – you might meet in the untravelled Levant.

For most people, the Bible was still an unquestioned compendium of truth, its immutable word conveyed supernaturally through the generations. This remained so in recent decades, despite the war that had erupted over the Bible in particular and religious faith generally – a war in which Cambridge was one of the battle fronts. Scientists were in the ascendant in the university (once dominated by ministers in training) and Darwinian ideas (as well as actual Darwins) were swirling about. A young American visitor to the city in the 1880s wrote back to her family to report that George Darwin, Professor of Astronomy and son of the eminent Charles, had not been to chapel in a dozen years. She had it from a reliable source that he was 'an *argonaist* [sic]. I think that is the word [Agnostic?]. But it means an infidel who does not try to make other people infidels. So many of the people here are that kind.'[4]

Even in Cambridge these free-thinking ideas were relatively new. Darwin's theories, readily generalised, had led to the notion that everything – from the shape of barnacles to the beaks of birds – had been subject to long processes of development, and if barnacles and beaks, then why not human institutions and artefacts – even religions and the Bible? This added an apparent scientific rationale to the views of certain religious radicals that the Bible as we know it emerged not contemporaneously with, but generations (even centuries) after the events it was meant to chronicle. There was thus avid popular interest in any new manuscript finds that might push reliable testimony back to earlier dates. And now it appeared that Mrs Gibson and Mrs Lewis, two rich but otherwise unremarkable Cambridge ladies, had made a signal discovery.

In the senior combination room of Christ's College two men who knew rather more than most about the expedition in question, a Romanian rabbi named Solomon Schechter and his friend and colleague William Robertson Smith (successor as Professor of Arabic to the Sinai murder victim), considered the newspaper coverage and reflected that something had gone amiss in the transmission of the facts of what had happened at St Catherine's Monastery. Almost certainly there would be hell to pay.

Similar thoughts were going through the minds of the inhabitants of Castlebrae, the large house at the foot of Castle Hill. The *Daily News* article erred in many respects; for one thing, Mrs Lewis and Mrs Gibson were not in Egypt, but already back in Cambridge recovering from their arduous camel ride across the Sinai peninsula and a rough sailing from Suez to Marseilles. As they received the press reports that were catapulting them into the public eye, they recollected first setting out for Sinai just a year earlier: how Rendel Harris had persisted in teaching them the art of photography; how, on the day before their departure, they had stayed up late in their rooms in the Charing Cross Hotel, making sure the photographic apparatus they had bought for themselves was in order. They recalled their initial nine-day crossing of the Sinai peninsula and, walking ahead of their camel caravan, their first sighting of the walls of St Catherine's, its bearded monks in black robes and stove-pipe hats hallooing from the parapets some ninety feet above (monks who were rumoured to have thrown stones at unwelcome visitors in the past), and wondering what sort of welcome awaited them. Now, with friends relaying, almost hourly, local rumours and with garbled newspaper reports reaching them from as far afield as Rome and New York, they sensed that they stood not at the end, but at the beginning of something rather daunting.

This is the true story of two sisters who, like the biblical Moses, made a discovery at Mount Sinai that would transform their lives. As in Moses's case, the miraculous turn in their circumstances would come about only after trials (including some on the Nile) had proved their worthiness, and would lead them to places they could scarcely have imagined.

CHAPTER 2

The birth and upbringing of the lady Bible-hunters

On 11 January 1843 twin girls were born to a Scottish lawyer named John Smith and his wife, Margaret. Mrs Smith died only two weeks later, and her husband resolved never to marry again and to bring the twins up by himself. The older (by one hour) was named Agnes and the second twin Margaret, after their mother. Their father never once spoke to them of their mother, and they had no other close relations.

The Smith family lived in Irvine, a quiet, conservative and civic-minded town of some 6,000 about thirty miles south-west of Glasgow

Irvine in the early nineteenth century

on Scotland's west coast. A contemporary account speaks of the 'Dutch quaintness of its principal street . . . a strange medley of crow-stepped gable ends, thatched cottages, last century mansions with outside stairs, and new buildings of banks and shops and residences of well-to-do burghers'; it adds that 'at most hours of the day a cannon ball might have been fired along the High Street without peril to life or limb'.[1] A stone bridge over the River Irvine connected the town to the harbour hinterland, where there was intermittent industrial activity – a ship-builder making tea-clippers, a lime works and a boiler-maker – beyond which lay the lonely marshes of the estuary.

Irvine had once been an important port, its merchants exporting coal to Ireland, importing wine from France and smuggling whiskey from the Isle of Arran that was just visible to the west on clear days, but gradually the harbour had silted up. While nearby townships, anticipating the surge of trade from America and the colonies, seized the moment to construct the deep-water ports that Glasgow manu-facturers required, the Irvine city fathers could not bring themselves to spend money on improving the sea approaches, with the consequence that, just at the moment of a huge boom in shipping, the port of Irvine became a backwater.

Apart from shipping, the main source of employment for Irvine's citizens had been, until recently, hand-loom linen-weaving. Robert Burns worked in Irvine briefly in the 1780s as a flax-dresser, manually beating the fibres in preparation for weaving, before his partner's tipsy wife burned down their shop and propelled Burns towards his poetic calling. But by the 1840s Glasgow merchants had largely mechanised the linen industry, thereby hugely diminishing the numbers it employed. Soup kitchens had to be established for a 'large body of the handloom weavers . . . destitute of employment and in very necessitous circumstances'.[2]

Irvine during the decades of the twins' childhood was, in short, the kind of town that people, especially ambitious young men, were 'from', drawn by the economic dynamism of Glasgow or possibilities for enrichment in America or Australia.

Yet not all its citizens were distressed, and one who was indeed quite wealthy was the twins' father, John Smith. He was a self-made man and the beneficiary of Scotland's parish school system, which enabled clever boys from modest backgrounds to enter the professions. By the time he was married, aged forty, he had built up a legal practice and was the owner of a fine stone house. He was widowed only a year later.

Agnes and Margaret adored their father, and despite his emotional austerity in never mentioning their mother, he was a good and loving parent, active in the town and especially in anything that concerned his daughters – President of the Burns Society, Captain of the 'Irvine Company' of the Ayrshire Rifle Volunteers, and a force on the board of Irvine Royal Academy throughout the twins' time as pupils. John Smith educated his daughters more or less as if they had been boys. He taught them to argue and to reason, and gave them considerable freedom to roam around the quiet streets of Irvine and to travel on horseback through its surrounding fields and lanes.

Smith approved of education, independence of mind and foreign travel. Railway travel was in its early days; the 1840s saw train lines spreading across the map of Britain and the Continent, making travel possible for the affluent middle classes as never before. John Smith and his daughters were amongst the first beneficiaries, both because they loved to travel and because Smith had had the prescience to invest in the railways.

Finding that his daughters had a gift for languages, he early entered into a pact with them: for each foreign language they should learn, they would be taken on a visit to that country. On this happy plan, and with a twin as a constant practice partner, the sisters mastered French, German, Spanish and Italian while still quite young.

School was the Irvine Royal Academy, a short walk from home. This forward-looking establishment educated boys and girls together, teaching them the same subjects and in the same classrooms. In this, the sisters were most fortunate. Girls' education in Scotland was generally better than that in England, on account of the Presbyterian requirement that each human soul be able to read and understand the Bible, but since a young woman's earthly future lay not in a profession but as a wife and mistress of a household, most parents still considered that their daughter's apprenticeship for later life should properly take place at home. The Argyle Commission's inquiry into girls' schools (1868) found that lack of parental ambition for their daughters was a continual drag on their progress in schooling. Teachers colluded with parents in the view that overfilling heads would cause mental collapse, hysteria or a loss of feminine softness. Most girls' schools were run half-heartedly by untrained staff and suffered from 'want of method' and vagueness. The normal pattern for girls of well-to-do parents in Scotland (as in England) was therefore light schooling, often at home, devoted to learning to read and to cultivating arts suited to feminine accomplishment, such as dancing, singing, drawing and a little conversational French. The study of Latin, Greek and commercial subjects (bookkeeping, navigation and accounting) was reserved for boys. But John Smith did not subscribe to the theory of 'mental softness' for his girls.

With no female relations to be involved in their upbringing, Agnes and Margaret's childhood was short on idle chatter and girlish frills, and long on study and exercise. Like that of most Scots of their day, it was also intensely Presbyterian.

The severities of Scots Calvinism have been set out in many reminiscences and novels. Its strict Sabbath observances were especially trying for children: starched collars, best clothes, no playing or running and only the Bible, *Foxe's Book of Martyrs* or religious tracts to be read. In the 1850s discipline reached a peak of rigour. Church was attended by most of the populace twice on a Sunday. Services consisted of spontaneous (but lengthy) prayers by the minister, metrical psalms sung without an organ (a devilish instrument) and heavily biblical sermons, usually extending over two hours. But in a life that offered most people few other vehicles for the imagination, a well-crafted Sunday sermon was welcome entertainment, and the twins were fortunate to have, as the pastor of their childhood, one of Scotland's most gifted preachers.

Sermons drawn from the stories of the Old Testament were especially exotic and stirring – Elijah's encounter with the evil Queen Jezebel, Delilah's seduction of the brutish Samson, the fiery trial of the Priests of Baal, the amorous endearments of the Song of Songs.

Egypt, the quintessential land of pagan excess, provided a particularly rich seam to be mined for dramatic incident (but of course for more exalted meanings, as well). It was in Egypt that Abraham, fearing he would be murdered by those who coveted his beautiful wife Sara, had her pretend to be his sister, only to see her taken into the pharaoh's harem. It was also into Egypt that Joseph was sold by his brothers, envious of his many-coloured coat, and where he had to resist seduction by Potiphar's wife. Most dramatic of all was the story of Moses: his call from the burning bush at Sinai; his bold words to the heartless pharaoh, 'Let my people go!'; the Nile running with blood and cursed with frogs; and the pharaoh's charioteers drowning in the Red Sea while the Israelites passed through the miraculously parted waters dry-shod. The burning bush was used by the Scottish Presbyterians as an emblem for their own confession – burning true and never to be extinguished by the treacheries of their adversaries.

Along with this religious seriousness went a tendency to dissent and rupture. Even Kilwinning, a small village of just one street some three miles to the north of Irvine, had three rival Presbyterian churches and inhabitants who would not buy eggs from a grocer who attended one that was not their own.[3]

The different churches dotted across Irvine in Agnes and Margaret's childhood provided an architectural *tableau vivant* of the struggles and divisions in Scottish religious life. Atop the hill overlooking the River Irvine stood the Presbyterian Church of Scotland, 'by law established' (the Auld Kirk) with its delicately storeyed eighteenth-century steeple and special galleries for the magistrates and the local grandee, the Earl of Eglinton.[4] Scattered across the town were its more rigorous offspring, products of splits over doctrine or church governance at one time or another. These included the Relief Church, the Secession Church, the Burgher Church, the Free Church, the United Presbyterian Church and the Reformed Presbyterian Church. There were also Methodists, Baptists and, frowned upon by everyone else, the Roman Catholic mission chapel catering to Irish labourers, from whose tin shack the pagan chords of the harmonium echoed on every Sunday.

The church of choice for John Smith was not, as might be expected for a member of the professional class, the elegant 'Auld Kirk' atop the hill, where he might have exchanged pleasantries with the Earl of Eglinton and mingled with the local magistrates, but the Burgher Church on Cotton Row. This congregation worshipped in a sober little hall, cramped and poorly ventilated. Seated on either side of the entrance were two elders who watched a brass collection plate that everyone had to pass – and was expected to pay into – on entering. A large internal staircase to a gallery made the main space even smaller.

What was lost in elegance was made up in modesty and conviction. John Smith, along with a retired India merchant and a general, was one of the few prosperous members of the congregation, the rest being weavers, small tradesmen, tenant farmers and craftsmen. At the time when Smith first attended, the minister was a former weaver, the Reverend Alexander Campbell, 'a burly form in black with great gold seals depending from an old fashioned fob, a sturdy walking stick, white hair and keen blue eyes'.[5] His lengthy sermons were filled with descriptions of the Wrath to Come. If anyone dozed off, Reverend Campbell would stop mid-sentence and, pointing to the offender, curtly ask his neighbour in the pew to 'Awaken that sleeper'. He was so strict a Sabbatarian that Sunday School had to occur on Saturday.

However, by the time the old Reverend Campbell died in 1843, the year Agnes and Margaret were born, the religious tide was turning. The Calvinistic doctrine of 'double predestination' – the teaching that some, the elect, were predestined for glory in heaven, whilst all the others, the *massa damnata* or the reprobate, were predestined for hell – was no longer wearing so well in Scottish churches.

Meanwhile evangelical preachers from England, who taught that salvation was available to all who would accept it, were attracting great numbers to 'Revival Meetings', including those held on the Irvine golf fields. In Cotton Row, church affairs had become tired and fractious and the congregation was being poached by these rival preachers. Reverend Campbell's death provided an opportunity. The church elders needed a young, energetic preacher to revive the flock, and they found him in William Bruce Robertson, remembered to this day as one of Scotland's best and most imaginative preachers. At the time, however, Robertson was twenty-three years old and untried, having only recently completed his theological studies in Germany.

He was eager to throw himself into small-town ministry. For his trial sermon he trod a careful path, balancing warnings against excursions from orthodoxy with a plea that the doctrine of election should not be interpreted 'mathematically'. He shrouded his more adventurous views in bright mists of eloquence, which pleased the elders, and he got the job.

It is almost certain that John Smith, one of the better-off and better-educated members of the congregation, had a hand in this appointment, and it was quite inevitable that the new widower and the young pastor should become good friends. William Bruce Robertson, like Smith, was proficient in literature, music, architecture and, even more unusually, travel. In a time when few toured abroad, he had already travelled extensively in Italy and France as a student. He lived first in lodgings and then in a manse that his congregation built for him, next door to the Smiths' house on the Kilwinning Road. And so Robertson and his sister Isabelle (or Jessie), who kept house for him, became almost second parents to Agnes and Margaret, often accompanying the Smith family on continental holidays. Bowling along a Parisian boulevard in a carriage, or climbing a Swiss peak in the company of intelligent and gregarious people, must have been moments of bliss to the twins, who could not only enjoy their father's company for a sustained period, but see him free of the duties and responsibilities he usually bore.

William Bruce Robertson's manner of sermon preparation was captive to his chaotic bachelor timetable – no attempts to start until Friday afternoon, after which he worked with a deepening sense of crisis through Saturday, saying nothing at meals and barely eating. His notes were fragments pinned onto successive leaves of the pulpit bible, and served as waymarks to his discourse, since written-out sermons were frowned upon as indicating a lack of spiritual spontaneity.

Though careful not to frighten his congregation, Robertson gradually introduced them to new ideas about the Bible, lacing his sermons with vivid evocations of recent archaeological finds in the

Holy Land, which he had read about in the London newspapers – the desolation of the pagan ruins of the Temple of Diana at Ephesus, bathed in moonlight and surrounded by howling jackals, contrasted with the living faith that St Paul had preached to the Ephesians.

Had the elders of the Cotton Row Burger Church known a bit more of William Bruce Robertson, they might have been wary of appointing him. His pedigree as the son of a 'right-thinking', dissenting family was impeccable. But what the cautious burghers of Irvine did not know was that, while a theology student in Edinburgh and still only in his late teens, Robertson had made friends with an altogether outré figure, who set him on his further path of studies. Thomas de Quincey, author of *Confessions of an English Opium-Eater* and erstwhile friend of Wordsworth and Coleridge, was at the time the lodger of Robertson's relation, a Mr McIndoe, in Princes Street. Robertson spent hours with this strange man, and throughout his life maintained that de Quincey had been more of an influence on him than any of his teachers.

De Quincey owed money to Robertson's relation and what had begun as a friendly extension of hospitality for a few nights had become effective imprisonment. Trying to support a wife and family living elsewhere, and constantly pursued by creditors, de Quincey wrote on matters as diverse as the English mail coach and the China situation (he took a particular interest in the Opium Wars) – anything that he could sell. At times he could not even afford paper to write on, and scribbled barefoot, wrapped in his counterpane, having pawned his stockings, shoes, coat, waistcoat and hat. McIndoe, his friend-cum-landlord, had an uncanny sense of when de Quincey was due a royalties cheque and would swoop to take his cut, charging de Quincey all the while for his miserable upkeep, so that the writer despaired of ever escaping. At the time when Robertson knew him, de Quincey scarcely left his room, in constant terror that his landlord would actualise a threat of selling, pawning or destroying the huge raft of personal papers and books from which he span out the articles for journals and newspapers that were his only means of support.

De Quincey was an unimaginable exotic for conservatively reared Robertson, and it was de Quincey's opinion that a young man of poetic sensibility and desirous of being a pastor must study in Germany. Like his friend Coleridge, de Quincey was one of the few Englishmen to keep up with German scholarship, and knew that Germany at the time was some three intellectual generations ahead of Scotland and England, especially in philosophy and the historical study of the Bible. The University of Halle-Wittenberg was most advanced and the first truly modern university, for it had renounced religious orthodoxy in favour of rationalism and free investigation. Its professors had full control over what they taught. Encouraging a young man of conservative background to go there was either a mark of cruelty or genius on de Quincey's part. But then, he was not an entirely balanced source of life's wisdom (Branwell Brontë, another of his correspondents at this time, accepted de Quincey's assurance that opium afforded good protection against consumption and that, unlike alcohol, it did not intoxicate). But in the long run his advice to the young Robertson was to prove sound.

In the city of Halle, Robertson found an old-fashioned world of decorated wooden houses, four-horse hay wagons surmounted by ornately dressed bumpkins, and troops of singing apprentices. The town's chief businesses appeared to be salt and coffins. In sharp contrast, its university was a ferment of modern thought, with Kantians, Rationalists, Hegelians, Fichteans and Pietists all striving with one another. Prominent amongst them were Hegelian pantheists who argued that the world was God's body – under their conceptual wizardry, God became everything and at the same time nothing. This 'divine', which suffused all nature and the human spirit, was quite different from the awful transcendence of God in Robertson's own inherited faith. Robertson was to recall walking in the Alps with a Hegelian student friend when they nearly met their end by avalanche. His companion flippantly remarked that their deaths would only have amounted to the merger of their individual consciousnesses with the great world-Spirit. Robertson privately felt he would rather be one of the misguided Catholic peasants they saw being led through the alpine pastures by their priest than one of these chill Hegelians. Back in Scotland, he was happy to receive 'a Call' from a small town, and subsequently refused better-paid and more prestigious pulpits else-where. He especially liked the weavers, small tenant farmers and tradesmen who made up the bulk of his congregation, writing that 'happiness is to be found in all classes; but when you ask me where it is most to be found, I would say in the lower middle classes – the better paid artisan circles'.[6]

William Bruce Robertson was not won over by radical thinkers, but neither was he afraid to keep up with them. It was almost certainly due to his influence that, even as young women, the twins read books that many pious households would have banned from the premises: the writings of Charles Darwin, for instance, and of the radical French scholar Ernst Renan, whose book presented Jesus as little more than a Galilean rustic sage. In Robertson's company they imbibed a brand of what might be called 'fearless Presbyterianism', which, because it was confident of the basics, was prepared to consider all the opposition cool-headedly. Their own view on particular providence was evident in one of their travelling maxims: 'God knows the hour of our end.' For Agnes and Margaret, this meant there was no point in worrying about a storm at sea or getting lost in the desert since, if this was the time at which God knew you would die, then you would; and if it was not, you would not. (Not all those they travelled with found this view reassuring.) Above all they took from this childhood formation the stoutly Presbyterian principle that one must *do* something worthwhile with one's life. Everyone, no matter how humble their station, had a God-given calling – it was just a question of finding out what that might be.

Few could have guessed that sleepy and undistinguished Irvine was home to one of Scotland's richest men. When the twins were thirteen years old, a distant kinsman named John Ferguson, for whom their father did legal work, left him a tremendous sum. The story of Ferguson's fortune says much about the town and the times.

Ferguson was the son of a local skipper who had died on his ship when his son was just fifteen. In his youth Ferguson and his mother were in straitened circumstances, not eased by her miserly old father who lived with them. This man – in active life a meadow farmer but with a sideline in money-lending – appears to have been universally disliked, and was described by contemporaries as 'of a narrow and contracted turn of mind' and 'penurious in his habits and peevish withal'.[7] Along with the daughter, he had five sons who, at the earliest opportunity, 'forsook the paternal roof, and one after another emigrated to America', where they showed the same love of money as their father, but considerably more skill at amassing it. With the shelter and sympathy of a merchant uncle in Boston, one son became a master carpenter, another kept a general store in New York, a third trained to be a sailor and was in charge of one of his uncle's ships and later a British East Indiaman. All the brothers devoted themselves single-heartedly to making money and, like Andrew Carnegie (another rags-to-riches Scotsman), they invested in the railroads of post-revolutionary America. Not one brother married or made a will, and when the final one died, their collective fortune came to their nephew back in Irvine.

Previous accounts have left the impression that John Ferguson was a simple trawler man, unaware that his uncles had prospered in America, and more or less startled by the American lawyers tripping over his fishing nets to tell him of his inheritance. This is inaccurate. Although only the youngest of his uncles ever revisited Irvine, they were influential – if from a distance – in the young man's life. Early on Ferguson was directed to the counting house and then used by all his uncles as a factotum. Although they corresponded frequently with one another and with their nephew back in Irvine, their letters were almost entirely commercial in content – with little enquiry after family affairs and no expression of affection. Andrew, living in Philadelphia, did not even leave his desk to visit two brothers who were dying in New York or to attend their funerals. The chief (indeed, the sole) aim in life of the brothers seems to have been to make money.[8] There is no evidence they spent any of it and, even more surprising, no indication in any of their correspondence of how it should be disposed.

When the last uncle died in 1842, Ferguson was left in sole possession of their combined fortunes.[9] Now fifty-five years old, he exchanged subordination to his uncles for subordination to his colossal fortune, whose management involved handling shares, bonds and holdings in railways and in waterworks across America, France and Scotland, and as far afield as Denmark and Russia – all of which he did from Irvine, assisted, in legal matters, by John Smith. He marked his change in status by moving from the small house by the graveyard in which he had lived with his mother to a slightly larger one in the High Street, where he lived with a cook and maid. He never married – early romantic overtures had met with rebuff and later, fearing fortune-hunters, he eschewed female society altogether. He was not, however, a recluse. For recreation he went daily for a drive with his carriage and a pair of horses and briefly perused *The Times*. On Sundays in later years, when he was too frail to get to the kirk, he allowed ministers of various churches to preach from his doorstep while he watched and listened, ear cupped, at the window. Twice a year he visited London on business.

In one important respect he showed himself to be at variance with the pointless dynamism of his uncles – he thought about where his money should go and he made a will. When drawing it up in 1855, Ferguson found he had no clear idea how much he was worth and sent for a friend (possibly Smith), who took several days to do the calculation before arriving at the sum of about £1.25 million (multiply by seventy for an estimation of what that might be worth today). Shocked and convinced that his friend had made a mistake, Ferguson sent him off 'rather moodily . . . without even thanking him for his services'.

He was known by the townsfolk to be well off and had in his lifetime made generous gifts to family members and to the poor, so the day of his funeral in 1856 found all Irvine waiting in a state of solemnised excitement for the reading of the will.

The duties paid to the government were the largest sum that had ever come from a single estate in Scotland. Half of the remaining fortune was dedicated to a trust (still in existence) to benefit local schools and religious establishments and enable capable boys to go to university. The other half was left in legacies to members of his family, all of them distant relations, for he had no near kin, and to local tradesmen. In Irvine a tailor, a baker and the family of the local blacksmith were left £20,000 apiece – enough for a family to live on very comfortably for a lifetime. John Smith, his lawyer and the son of his second cousin, was left a generous sum – something like £7 million in today's money.

   The first effect of these changed circumstances was not, from the twins' point of view, a happy one. As an Executor of Ferguson's estate, John Smith was obliged to depart immediately for the United States in order to liquidate Ferguson's huge and varied portfolio. Agnes and Margaret, now aged fourteen, were sent away to an English boarding school at Birkenhead, near Liverpool. It might have been the other side of the moon for them, away from home for the first time and separated by thousands of miles of the Atlantic from their only parent. The sole

The senior twin: Agnes Smith, aged about fourteen years

photograph we have of either twin as a girl is a studio portrait of Agnes from about this period: the soft young face peering out from under a straw hat set with roses is nonetheless the serious face of a senior twin.

During the year that their father was in America, William Bruce Robertson and Jessie were *in loco parentis*. They took the twins to the Highlands during the vacation, and Robertson wrote them humorous letters while they were at school to keep their spirits up.

Ferguson's will also made John Smith first secretary of the charity it established, so on his return from America, Smith left his legal practice in Irvine and devoted himself to running the Ferguson Bequest from its Glasgow offices. He sold the family home in Irvine and took a house called Spring Grove in Kilbarchan, a village within convenient daily reach of Glasgow on the South-Western Line. From here he could attend to the Bequest's business, which also involved travelling about Ayrshire from schoolroom to schoolroom, sitting in on lessons and examining teachers who might be eligible for grants, carrying out the mission of raising the status of teachers by improving salaries. Spring Grove might also prove a suitable place from which to launch his two daughters on the Glasgow social scene once they had come of age.

Although not a proud or, in that sense, a worldly man, Smith was realistic. His accession to wealth produced little change in the family's manner of life, but evidently he wished to protect Agnes and Margaret from some of its unwelcome effects. At that time, all of a woman's property passed to her husband on marriage, and so John Smith framed a will with complicated provisions to ensure that no fortune-hunter could use Agnes or Margaret's fortune to pay off his debts and then cast her aside.

It must also have been in consequence of their changed circumstances that Agnes and Margaret were sent to a finishing school in Knightsbridge for a year, after completing their schooling in Birkenhead. These London establishments turned out British young ladies as from a mould, accomplished in person and diction. They were taught how to engage and manage staff and servants, court etiquette, what to wear and when to wear it, and how to run an elegant home and keep a fashionable table for the entertainment of their husband's guests. The expectation was that most young ladies would marry within a year or two of leaving school. What else should they do? The universities were closed to them, as were the trades and professions. Even for rich young women – or perhaps especially for them – life's 'work' (apart from bearing children) meant the investment of time and energy, and often their own money, in their husband's projects. Early and loving marriages seem to be what Agnes and Margaret hoped for, too, at this stage, although in other respects they resisted being 'finished', at least to the extent of retaining the heavy Scottish accents that it was the aim of English finishing schools to eradicate.

But early wedded bliss was not to be. The village of Kilbarchan to which Agnes and Margaret returned at nineteen was a long way from Knightsbridge, and was thin on marriageable men. It had been home to them only in school holidays and, with the Robertsons still in Irvine, and their father travelling around Ayrshire a good deal, there was little to occupy two young ladies used to London. Agnes was later to write two lengthy novels set in this part of Scotland. *Effie Maxwell* has a rudimentary plot, which must in some ways reflect Agnes and Margaret's own circumstances at this time.[10] The eponymous heroine completes her studies, aged nineteen, at her expensive London boarding school and returns to the small Scottish town that is her home. It is an effort to fill the hours of the day: some time is spent on household errands, some directing the staff, reading to her father, practising the piano, parsing Shakespeare. It is life 'on hold' waiting for the elegant, caped, highly educated and devout young man on horseback who will sweep her off her feet and into his life.

There are other signs that all may not have been bliss in Kilbarchan. Like Agnes and Margaret, 'Effie' is rich, well educated and thoroughly ladylike, but not well connected. Her education and her money (for she, mysteriously, has come into a fortune) have in fact dislocated her, by making her more of a lady than her parentage warrants.

Snobbery, or 'pride of blood' and its subversion of the course of true love, is another main theme of Agnes's second novel, *Glenmavis*, which has a rural setting in villages and country houses not far south of Glasgow. Manufacturing and commerce are creating new fortunes and, by comparison, the rural gentry feel poor. The 'old' families no longer have the money to maintain their country houses and cannot resist the high rents offered by Glasgow merchants whose social ambitions seek a rural backdrop. The result is a restocking of the old houses with newcomers who are, for the settled gentry 'not people one would receive'. A romantic apartheid is in effect, with the sons of the old families educated into pride and contempt – all of which Agnes is at pains to denounce as inegalitarian, unpresbyterian and decidedly 'not Scottish'.

Whether through lack of opportunity or disappointment in what was on offer, both twins were still unwed in 1866 when John Smith died after a brief and unexpected illness. He had clearly benefited from Ferguson, not only by the direct legacy, but from advice about stocks, shares and land, and had built up his own fortune considerably. He left his twenty-three-year-old daughters entirely alone in the world, and very rich.

Kilbarchan had nothing to keep them. They decided to go down the Nile.

CHAPTER 3

The journey to the Nile

The depth of the twins' grief at their father's unexpected death was great, yet nothing speaks more aptly of the young ladies they had become than the course of action they took to assuage it. Their father had approved of travel, and it was the activity they most associated with happy times together. While others might feel they acted with unseemly haste, from Agnes and Margaret's point of view their father was now in a better place, and prolonged grief was for those who lacked faith in the life to come. Besides, he had brought them up to not worry too much about what other people thought. One advantage of having no relations was that there was no aunt or uncle or cousin to tell you what to do – only a twin who backed up every adventure with enthusiasm.

Most adventurously, they planned to travel without a male escort, but 'great was the consternation', wrote Agnes, at the idea of ladies on so lengthy a trip on their own. Agnes documented some of the reactions they had to their plans, and her response to them:

'Do you think they will ever come back? They are going amongst Mohammedans and barbarians', said some who knew of our intentions. But for what reason? The means of communication are now so much improved, the art of providing for a traveller's comfort is carried to such perfection, that any woman of prudence (without belonging to the class called strong-minded) can find little difficulty in arranging matters for her own convenience. And if our education does not enable us to protect ourselves from the influence of such dangerous opinion as, it is said, we shall hear in the varied society with which it may be our lot to mingle, what is education worth?[1]

It is not entirely clear whether Agnes and Margaret were simply naïve or, rather, 'knowingly innocent' in suggesting that the greatest threat to young women travelling without a male escort in the Orient was 'dangerous opinion'. Agnes would admit in a later account that when they set off from London, they really did not know if they would ever return.

How they gathered the necessary information for Eastern travel while still in mourning in a Scottish village is not entirely clear. They had travelled abroad before, but with their father in charge. They had moved from hotel to hotel, but certainly not in Arabic lands, and they had never stayed in tents. Their bible for the purpose seems to have been Murray's *Guidebook to Modern Egypt and Thebes (being a Description of Egypt including the Information Required for Travellers in that Country)*. This even listed the timetables for British steam packets to Alexandria.

The normal custom for English-speaking travellers of the day was to employ a courier, a sort of mobile travel agent who would accompany the party, act as translator and make bookings and arrangements as they went. Agnes and Margaret, though fully able to afford it, disdained such a method. They could not travel entirely unchaperoned of course, and invited one of their former schoolmistresses from London to join them. Grace Blyth, at thirty-seven, was not exactly old – just twelve years older than the twins themselves – but she had the unimpeachable merit of being 'a teacher'. She was a Scotswoman like them and, like them, a good linguist, a horsewoman and possessed of a spirit of adventure.

As for their destination, Agnes and Margaret could not very well be seen idling about in the Venetian Lido or the French Riviera so soon after their father's death. Such diversions, in any case, were not to their taste – and as they had seen most of Europe, they wanted to go further afield. If asked how it was that two young women of such sharply outlined Protestant principles, and only recently bereaved, should be travelling at all – much less going down the Nile – Agnes and

Margaret's answer would be that they were visiting the Holy Land. A visit to the Holy Land, Agnes reasoned, would silence most criticism – its scenes being 'endeared to us by so many hallowed associations'.

Uplifting though it might be, there was no doubt about it: travel in Egypt in the 1860s, while highly fashionable, was still unusual. The railways had put Europe within reach of a growing segment of the British and American middle classes, but travel in the East was reserved for the very wealthy.

Britain was going through a bout of Egyptomania. A French consortium under Ferdinand de Lesseps had been digging out the Suez Canal since 1859. The canal was due to open soon and, although few in England thought it would be successful, Egypt had for ten years rarely been out of the English newspapers. In the spring of 1862 (the year Agnes and Margaret spent at their London finishing school) the young Prince of Wales, then still a bachelor, made a highly publicised Nile cruise, covered in weekly reports by the special correspondent of the London *Times*. The year following John Smith's death saw the Khedive of Egypt, Guest of Honour at the Paris Exhibition, preside over a collection of his country's antiquities, displayed in a specially built Egyptian temple approached by an avenue of sphinxes.

But Eastern travel was not entirely safe, even for the rich and royal. Dysentery and infectious diseases regularly carried off travellers. A cholera plague had only recently devastated Alexandria, and almost as dangerous as cholera itself was the quarantine, which could confine passengers to stinking, disease-ridden ships for weeks at a stretch. All these perils were reported with relish in the English newspapers.

Murray's *Guidebook* listed three means of getting from England to Egypt. One was to sail directly to Alexandria from Southampton, and the second was to travel by railway across France to Marseilles, and then by Messageries Impériales steam packet to Suez. These two were the fastest, easiest and least expensive options. Finally one could travel by ferry, train and carriage across Europe to the Danube, by steamboat down that river to the Black Sea and then from Constantinople take a local steamer to Alexandria. The third route, having nothing particular to recommend it except circuitousness and variety, was duly chosen. After the Nile the three women planned to go on to Jerusalem.

Murray's *Guidebook* made buoyant, but sometimes alarming, reading. In between steamship timetables and guidance on the correct wine choices for the Nile (Rhine wine or a light Bordeaux), it advised that travellers would need large stocks of insect powder, magnesium wire for seeing the tombs (it burned incandescent, without damaging wall paintings with the oily smoke of torches), guns, gunpowder and a medicine chest with castor oil and laudanum. The prescription for diarrhoea was an emetic of ipecacuanha followed by quarter of a gram of opium morning and evening, and a diet of sweet white rice. On the matter of native servants, Murray's advocated strictness, but advised against the widespread practice of commencing employment with a thrashing. Kindness with authority would work better, and under no circumstances should one strike a Bedouin or 'desert Arab', since to do so might cost one's life. In the revised edition of 1843, author Sir Gardner Wilkinson added that 'when Ladies are of the party on the Nile, the boatmen should be supplied with drawers, and an order given that they never go into the water without them'.

Yet Murray's *Guidebook* also held out the promise of lively social exchange. Nile travellers were advised to bring with them a small pistol for use at dinner parties. A dinner gong was inaudible to guests on other boats, so the thoughtful Nilotic host, Murray's suggested, should fire off a 'dress-for-dinner' shot some fifteen minutes in advance of the final call.

Arriving in London, Agnes, Margaret and Grace equipped themselves with a most useful kind of trunk, 'a basket, covered with strong tarpaulin . . . at once light and impervious to rain', rubberised sheets (invaluable in tents) and a new sort of bag called the 'Gladstone', which strapped easily onto the back of a mule. They ordered side-saddles, which were shipped directly to an agent in Alexandria, and white serge riding costumes, and set off in August 1868, planning to be absent for a year. In Vienna, Grace bought a small pistol for 'firing off'.

CHAPTER 4

The boat

In December of 1868 the *Aurora*, a packet ship of the Austrian Lloyds Line, steamed out of Constantinople through the straits of the Dardanelles and into the Aegean. She was at the beginning of a ten-day journey to Egypt in which she would criss-cross the eastern Mediterranean, taking on and dropping off passengers at Smyrna, Rhodes, Cyprus, Beirut and Jaffa before her final port of call, Alexandria.

Mattresses on the third-class decks provided open-air quarters for Greek and Turkish villagers, their respective sections roped off from one another and the women separated from the men. The Turkish women sat with hennaed palms and kohl-rimmed eyes – each with her own coffee pots and quilts about her. They were making the pilgrimage to Mecca, an obligation for all Muslims at least once in a lifetime. Many of the women had never been out of their husbands' houses since marriage.

The Greek villagers were pilgrims too: Orthodox Christians who intended to celebrate Christmas at the Church of the Nativity in Bethlehem. Also on the boat were Roman Catholics shepherded by Franciscan friars, en route to Jerusalem, Bethlehem and Nazareth.

Looking down from the upper decks and the comforts of starched linen, polished silver and clinking crystal, the first-class passengers were cosmopolitan, with Germans predominating. A couple from Saxony were going to Jerusalem to see the sights. A young German who previously had worked in Cairo was returning for a visit. A Hungarian in long, black-lace national dress showed a portrait of his fiancée to those who asked. He was far gone with consumption and going to Egypt in the hope that the dry air would bring a cure. A Greek doctor escorted his frail twelve-year-old daughter, her small frame also racked with consumption. A Turkish pasha and his son were isolated from the other first-class passengers by lack of a common language.

By far the most unusual party on the boat comprised the three British travellers, although they would be quick to add that they were Scottish. They too were sailing all the way to Alexandria. Not only were they amongst the youngest in first-class, but they were, quite astonishingly, an entirely female party. These three had travelled, without male relations or couriers, by carriage, train and steamer all the way across Europe to Budapest, before sailing down the Danube into the Ottoman Empire and crossing the Black Sea to Constantinople, where they had picked up this boat. They intended to go down the Nile and then tour Palestine on horseback with their own caravan of tents and servants. They were clearly ladies of means, their trim figures sheathed in the tight-waisted, full-skirted dresses that were the fashion of the day. Misses Agnes and Margaret Smith explained that they had travelled often with their late father, from whom they had learned that one could do without a courier if one could speak the local languages – which they did, conversing readily with the other first-class passengers in German, French and Italian, the seaboard lingua franca of the eastern Mediterranean. In any case, they found it much more interesting to make their own arrangements. It brought them into contact with the people, and the 'gift of a franc', said Miss Agnes Smith, 'always supplied us with a man to carry our rugs and bags'.[1]

Travelling as unaccompanied women had also afforded them some unusual opportunities for frank exchanges with women on the way. On an eight-hour train journey in Germany they had shared a carriage with a German artist and his wife. This man became furious when Grace told him of the agitation in England over the question of giving women the vote. His wife added severely that 'such an idea never enters the mind of a German woman', but when her husband had fallen asleep she leaned across and whispered, 'You are quite right, we German women are far too much in subjection.' In Austria, a young lady from Bucharest boarded who was returning from her annual shopping trip to Paris. Madame Juanita told them that her husband did not miss her in the least since, like most Romanian marriages, hers had been arranged and her new husband played cards and drank all the time, and was too stupid to speak to her at dinner. She hated Turks and Jews, she told them. When Margaret said, 'Our Saviour was a Jew', she replied, 'A Jew is a Jew wherever he is.'

Travelling first-class did not always secure first-class comfort. In Bulgaria the rails were in such bad repair that trains were not allowed to run at night. Wind and snow blew continuously through a hole in the carriage roof where the lamp should have been. The women had only the provisions they had brought on board with them – 'a bottle of wretched wine, and a half-boiled fowl, rolled in paper', which they had to eat with their fingers. On reaching the Black Sea coast, they were whirled by chaise over rough and muddy roads to the harbour, then lifted bodily into a little boat before being rowed out to their steamer, moored on the dark sea. But travelling unaccompanied in the Ottoman Empire had posed them no particular problems. They immediately liked the Turks – veiled women and men in long coats with petticoats, with red tarbouches or turbans. The men were industrious, honest and 'most polite and attentive to strangers', and the ladies of Constantinople enjoyed shopping just as much as other women. Agnes and Margaret even warmed somewhat to veils, which they had supposed earlier to be oppressive garments, but the thin white muslin worn by the ladies of Constantinople turned out to 'set off their faces to great advantage' and preserved their delicate complexions.

With pilgrims on the decks below and consumptives above, conversation on the *Aurora* turned, perhaps inevitably, to matters of religion. The Europeans watched with interest as a Muslim man, after consulting the compass for the direction of Mecca, came up on deck to pray.

The huddle of Greeks on the deck below prompted the Dalmatian Third Officer to say that these so-called pilgrimages were just money-making schemes for the priests, whom he accounted 'very degraded'. The three young Scotswomen concurred, with Grace primly adding that one should never rely on priests for the truth, but rather study the Bible for oneself. Much to her surprise and to that of Agnes and Margaret, none of the other first-class passengers agreed. Not that they approved of priests – they distrusted both priests *and* the Bible. One of the Germans dismissed the Bible altogether as 'mere wind'. The gentleman from Saxony was in hearty accord and, when Margaret asked why then he and his wife were visiting Jerusalem, he said that it was to impress their neighbours. Even the consumptive Hungarian professed to believe in nothing at all, although, curiously, he studied the Bible daily and carried the New Testament with him in several languages. Agnes, Margaret and Grace found themselves the only passengers of quality happy to confess their belief in God. Only a French artist offered equivocal support: although an atheist and a republican, he – having observed in Italy the excesses of the rabble – was prepared to allow that religion was useful for keeping public order.

Indifference to religion, or even open disbelief, was quite common in France and Germany – simply part of the mental hygiene of a progressive outlook. But in England, and still more so in Presbyterian Scotland, atheism was almost unheard of and certainly not to be entertained lightly with near-strangers across the captain's dining table. The Napoleonic Wars had turned Britain in on itself. Atheists, especially after the French Revolution, were associated with regicide, radicalism, scruffy pamphleteers and 'the reading rooms of sedition'. Agnes and Margaret had fully expected to encounter 'dangerous opinions' on their travels in the East, but from Mohammedans and barbarians, not from educated members of the European middle classes. The Greek doctor, made reflective by his profession and the dismal outlook for his little daughter, identified the problem: the Bible, though full of good moral lessons, seemed to have little effect on those who professed its faith: 'Christians seem to me to hate most bitterly any one who does not agree with them on every point.'

The Christian pilgrims disembarked at Jaffa – little more than a 'compact pile of houses planted on a stretch of sand', its harbour ruinous. A Greek priest and a Franciscan friar, posted on either side of the gangway, supervised the process. Agnes, Margaret and Grace were rowed ashore by Arab oarsmen, across whose bent backs they stepped out onto the quay. They clambered over dirty sacks, brushed past 'dirty asses and even dirtier men', and surmounted muddy stones and open drains to the bazaars. This was their first meeting with Arabic peoples. 'How handsome all the men are!' Agnes said later to the Greek doctor. He promised her that in Egypt they would see men who looked exactly like bronze statues, but warned them that 'all who go to Egypt lose what little faith they have'.

CHAPTER 5

The perfect dragoman

Agnes, Margaret and Grace arrived in Cairo early in December 1868 and set themselves up in the fashionable Shepheard's Hotel. Travellers from northern Europe spoke of the physical shock of seeing and smelling Cairo for the first time. Amelia Edwards, who made the trip some five years later and wrote what remains one of the best Nile travel books, *A Thousand Miles up the Nile*, describes crowds that ebbed and flowed ceaselessly: 'a noisy, changing, restless, part-coloured tide, half European, half Oriental, on foot, on horseback, and in carriages'. The population was entirely mixed: Nubians, Abyssinians, Syrians, Copts, Greeks, Maltese and Italians. The general name for those who ate pork was 'Franks', and northern Europeans were 'fair-haired Franks'. 'Here are Syrian dragomans in baggy trousers and braided jackets; barefooted Egyptian fellaheen in ragged blue shirts and felt skull caps; Greeks in absurdly stiff white tunics, like walking pen-wipers; Englishmen in palm-leaf hats and knickerbockers, dangling their long legs across almost invisible donkeys; . . . blue-black Abyssinians with incredibly slender, bowed legs, like attenuated ebony balustrades . . .' and mounted Janissaries with sabres, workmen, boatmen, soldiers, traders. The merchants wore white turbans, striped Syrian silk tunics and outer robes of cashmere in 'some beautiful degraded colour . . . maize, mulberry, olive, peach, sea-green, salmon-pink . . . That these stately beings should vulgarly buy and sell, instead of reposing all their lives on luxurious divans and being waited upon by beautiful Circassians, seems altogether contrary to the eternal fitness of things.'[1]

Travellers were less appreciative of the stench and swarming insects, especially cockroaches, and of the poverty and physical disabilities. One-eyed men were common since, it was rumoured, parents maimed their own children this way in order to avoid conscription. (It was also rumoured that the pasha, to prevent these mutilations, had established a one-eyed corps.)[2]

Europeans were also shocked by the readiness of men and boys to divest themselves of all garments and swim in the Nile, while on the shore their mothers and sisters, covered from head to foot, did the laundry.

Agnes declared that she did not see much 'poetry of the east' in Cairo, particularly in 'seeing people housed like pigs, and with clothing as scanty as their bristles' and donkeys with bleeding sides. But in general, Europeans delighted in all they saw. Oblivious to the thousand years for which Egypt had been a predominantly Muslim land, they saw about them only the land of the Bible. Down any street might be found a Joseph in his many-coloured coat, or Ruth pulling her veil below kohled eyes. A stall with piles of cumin, coriander, mint and thyme gave way, in the narrow streets of the souk, to a trestle sagging with pastries, pink and golden, peppered with green pistachios and dripping with honey. Merchants, cross-legged and swathed in cashmere, sold gold and amber, necklaces of carnelian, turquoise, lapis lazuli, fine leathers, carpets and precious silks. It was a scene of gorgeous excess, made acceptable to the eyes of the beholder as a biblical tableau – there was the gold of Ophir, the topaz of Ethiopia from the Book of Job.

Visitors did not need to take the oriental life back to their accommodation. Once one crossed the broad veranda of Shepheard's Hotel, English was spoken by all the staff, English and French furniture graced every room, and ladies descended to dinner or departed for evening engagements in the latest Paris fashions. The Nile boats, too, were 'beautifully fitted up with every European luxury', from 'the last-invented portable easy chair to the latest new novel'.[3]

Although Mark Twain, who had recently stayed there, described Shepheard's as the 'second-worst' hotel in the world, by the time

Agnes, Margaret and Grace arrived it had been spruced up. Cairo was preparing for the opening of the Suez Canal, only nine months away. The khedive, Ismail Pasha, treating the nation's coffers as his own private bank, had spent a fortune rebuilding the inner city after the manner of Hausmann's Paris, creating magnificent squares and driving boulevards through the tangled streets of the old city. He built an opera house and even commissioned Verdi for an opera on an Egyptian theme, *Aida*. Celebratory balls and receptions were already being held in anticipation of this momentous event.

The great dining room of Shepheard's could seat some 200–300 travellers. Amelia Edwards found about half of them were in transit to or from India, and the others were headed down the Nile: 'invalids in search of health; artists in search of subjects; sportsmen keen upon crocodiles; statesmen out for a holiday; special correspondents alert for gossip; collectors on the scent of papyri and mummies; men of science with only scientific ends in view; and the usual surplus of idlers who travel for the mere love of travel or the satisfaction of a purposeless curiosity.'[4]

With a courtesy gun to 'fire off' and the expectation of convivial company to be found amongst other Nile travellers, all augured well for the young ladies from Scotland.

In the matter of the Suez Canal itself, the British now had a lot of catching up to do. Throughout what was by now almost twenty years of planning and digging, the British had treated the Franco-Egyptian Canal project with contempt. De Lesseps had made repeated efforts to raise money in London, only to find investors sceptical and the project ridiculed by the press. The canal could not succeed, they said – desert sands would fill it up, or its banks would crumble, or its depth would be altered by summer droughts and peculiar currents. An editorial in the London *Times* of October 1867, just two years before the canal's eventual opening, treated a recent attempt at fund-raising with disdain. The costly project would provide no return for investors for decades – maybe centuries. We are asked to open our purses, wrote the editor, if not for commercial gain, then 'for the beauty of the project'. Granted, such a canal was a sublime conception, but so would be 'a tubular bridge from Dover to Calais' or 'a company of steam balloons to the moon'. And quite apart from these mercantile concerns, such a canal would not be in Britain's strategic interest, but could become a means to cut her throat, as certain French journalists had tactlessly pointed out.

But by 1868 the British press and the government were whistling a different tune. It was now clear that the canal was soon to become a reality and, moreover, that it would transform shipping to Africa and the East. The government had some quick back-pedalling to do. Lord Napier was rushed out to Cairo, arriving at just about the same time as Agnes, Margaret and Grace, to invest Ismail Pasha with the Grand Cross of the Star of India. The Prince and Princess of Wales were to make a 'purely personal visit' in February 1869, cruising the Nile as guests of the khedive.

And *The Times* joined in. The correspondent sent to cover the royal visit now said that the English had shamefully neglected Egypt: 'all that Egypt at large sees of Europe is essentially French. The English travel – so do the Americans, but the men who get on in Egypt, who are in office, who control great public works, and who are present to the eye of the people, are not English or Americans. They are French . . .' It was only to be hoped that when the people saw 'the great respect paid to the Son of the Queen of England . . .', they would readily apprehend that a great power was here represented. Even now *The Times* could not quite admit it had misjudged the project, and contrived to blame the French for British indifference: 'if we in this country believed that the Suez Canal was a "sword to pierce the breast-plate of England," it was because the French told us so'.[5] Grumbling doubts were still voiced as to whether the canal would pay – local Mediterranean trade might go through it, but one could not expect the same of 'the vast bulk of traffic between Europe and the East'. Sailing ships would require steam tugs, not only in the canal itself, but through the Red Sea.

But Glaswegian ship-builders, more commercially adroit than the journalists of *The Times*, were already turning their attention to building the steamships necessary to take freight through the canal. Its opening would signal the gradual demise of cargo sailing ships.

Scheduled steamships had been taking paying passengers on the Nile for several decades, and Agnes, Margaret and Grace considered travelling on one, for passage was assured and cheap. But then you were constrained by timetables and could not choose, if you so desired, to linger at a particularly appealing temple or spend an extra day moored to recuperate health. The more costly alternative – hiring a private Nile sailing boat called a *dahabeeah* – made up in romance what it lacked in thrift and mechanical dependability.

Agnes and Margaret quickly overcame their scruples about the cost, especially if health might otherwise be endangered – rationalising, 'Think how much more some families expend every season on balls and theatres' – and decided to hire their own sailing boat. What finally persuaded them was the securing of an excellent dragoman.

For once, in their already long and complicated trip, they had to act against instinct and employ a courier. A dragoman, as such agents were known in the East, would hire boat, captain and crew. He would, for a fixed-term contract, supply all provisions requested, down to the sherry, library books and freshly cut flowers. He would act as guide and interpreter, for none of the three young women spoke Arabic.

They were delighted to secure an introduction to the very prince of that species, a fatherly Maltese gentleman named Mr Certezza.[6] He met them in Cairo and impressed them by driving knowledgeably about town in a carriage. 'Seldom had we seen a more handsome man . . . he might have sat for a portrait of bluff King Hal, after domestic worries had tinged that monarch's hair with silver.' He took them by the river and explained the shortcomings of steamers and the superior merits of sailing boats. His written references extolled his character, and the British Consul said they could not do better. Although the price Certezza quoted seemed extravagant, Murray's *Guidebook* advised paying well for a good dragoman. By the end of the day they had engaged him, not only for their trip on the Nile, but also for subsequent travels in Palestine.

Following advice in Murray's, a clear contract was drawn up and signed before the British Consul. Certezza undertook to hire a clean, first-class *dahabeeah*, equipped with everything but wines and spirits. He was to supply a dinghy (or *sandal*) to be at their disposal and a crew of ten sailors, a captain, a rudderman, a boy, a first-class cook and a good waiter, all of whom he was to keep in order. All expenses of travelling over the First cataract at Aswan, where the boat had to be hauled over great boulders in the river bed, were to be covered by Certezza.

As Certezza assembled the wherewithall, the twins and Grace explored the city and environs of Cairo. The changes made by a succession of modernising pashas had little visible impact on the everyday life of the ordinary people, who were still unwilling to abandon agricultural methods that had served them for three or four millennia. A land made naturally fertile by annual inundations of silt – which in addition killed the weeds – yielded so plentifully that the *fellahin*, as the Egyptian peasantry were known, needed to do little more than scatter seed, irrigate by hand-pump and wait for the crops to grow. When Mr Larkin, the British Consul in Alexandria in the 1840s, was favoured with a land grant with which he hoped to modernise agricultural technique, he found himself frustrated at every turn by the conservatism of his peasant farmers. Their method of digging a ditch was for one man to loosen the soil with a pickaxe, scrape it into a basket and then pass it to another 'stationed upon the verge', who dumped the soil out. Ten men working in this way could not, in the opinion of Mr Larkin, do the work of one skilled man with the use of a spade. When Mr Larkin himself demonstrated the efficiency of that implement, tossing the soil with one movement from ditch to side, it was to no avail. Why should the *fellahin* depart from the traditional ways? Even the offer of doubled wages had no effect on a people accustomed for millennia to expect that producing more only caused more to be taken in taxes. Why, in any case, abandon the sociable practice of working in twos, only to dig alone and work harder?

The young ladies noticed that Certezza, in the fortnight allotted to find and equip the boat, seemed to spend most of his time on the veranda of Shepheard's Hotel dressed like an emir in folds of black cloth, a turban of gold silk and a cashmere girdle, giving advice to foreign visitors. 'His face wore a smile which was meant to express the most artless sincerity; and each word as it fell from his lips seemed coated with sugar.' The British guests at Shepheard's were unanimous in their admiration. 'How we envy your dragoman!' . . . 'I would trust Certezza like a father,' said one. 'We only wish we were so fortunate.'

A *dahabeeah* is a twin-masted, barge-like sailing boat of low draught, with rooms for the passengers built on deck at the stern. The larger ones were about 100 foot long, with four to eight bedrooms, a dining room and a sitting room. Above the cabins, and reached by twin staircases, was an open-air deck shaded by a canopy and set out with rugs and divans. The kitchen was on deck nearer the prow, screened by an awning. A hold contained the luggage and supplies, and the crew slept, rolled up in blankets, on the lower deck. To find a *dahabeeah* oneself was a wearying business, which Amelia Edwards compared to choosing a house, except that they all looked the same and daily they changed their places on the river, as well as their price.

The Murray's *Guidebook* of 1845 had recommended sinking one's *dahabeeah* on the night before setting sail, to rid it of rats and other vermin, and boarding the boat the next day from the opposite bank, making sure the rats did not do the same. By the late 1860s, however, a tourist could expect a higher degree of comfort. Murray's revised edition of 1875 complained that the normal run of archaeologists, artists and invalids had been inflated by 'the rich and idle, to whom money was no object'; in consequence, the cruises had become absurdly de luxe, with dragomans competing to offer the newest accessories to pleasure: china, crystal, mirrors, bookcases, Brussels carpets and built-in cupboards. Amelia Edwards had a piano in her shipboard sitting room, and fresh flowers. The crew wore a costume still to be found on the more traditionalist Nile boatmen: loose, pale-blue cotton gowns, white turbans, bare feet and, when ladies were on board, cotton drawers. Agnes, Margaret and Grace had perfect trust in Certezza's competence to choose their boat, having already pointed out to him the sort of craft they liked.

They did not see their *dahabeeah* until 15 December, the day of departure, and it was quite unlike those Certezza had shown them two weeks earlier. Although it did have the same number of rooms (four bedrooms and a dining room), they were small, with nowhere to keep their clothes. At the stern was a poultry coop, a basket of oranges and a large heap of dry bread (which, mixed with oil and lentils, formed the staple food for the crew). The *reis*, or captain, looked in low spirits, possibly an effect of fasting for Ramadan, but Agnes had watched the look on his face while Certezza's contract was read to him at the consulate – the baffled look of a salmon being landed by a skilful angler.

Along with Murray's, the twins, like other western travellers, brought with them Herodotus's *Histories*, still a useful guide some 2,200 years after the Greek's Nile cruise. Egypt, he had observed, is the gift of the Nile. Without its water, the land would be bare sand and rock, for without the silt the river deposited annually, there would be no soil and nutrients. As it is, the Nile runs straight and constant through its green flood plain before fanning out in a delta. As for navigability, no writer of sailing fiction could have invented a broad river that runs unimpeded by rapids for hundreds of miles, its current drawing boats in one direction and the prevailing winds taking them back in the other. The ancients, unaware of the southern hemisphere's winter, were baffled as to why the Nile, unlike all other rivers, flooded in midsummer, the hottest time of the year.

As they slipped by fields of wheat, low islands with fat black cattle and the fishermen punting brightly painted boats through banks of reeds, Agnes, Margaret and Grace forgot their dismay at the state of the boat. They were rewarded soon after setting off by 'the very island' where the infant Moses was found by the pharaoh's daughter afloat in a rush basket. The sun set in fire and made the palm trees into so many black paper cut-outs on the bank. With the windows of nearby boats glistening in the sunset and the distant pyramids in bold relief, Agnes read the Book of Exodus.

Certezza followed the standard Nile practice, trimmed to his own convenience, of sailing upriver without stop while the wind was with one, and then taking in the sights at leisure as one drifted downriver on return. This sensible strategy he followed rigorously, frustrating his cabin-fevered employers, who were forced to stay on board while the treasures of antiquity passed by. At Giza the wind fell and they were obliged to moor for two days with nothing to see but a high mud wall. Certezza would not permit them to get off the ship to look at the pyramids nearby. They would visit everything in good time, he said, and kept himself busy stitching a Maltese flag to fly alongside the British one at the stern.

It was ten days before the ladies were first allowed off their boat – on Christmas Day. Certezza had decorated the salon festively with palm branches and oranges, with the unintended effect that the rats ventured from the hold on convenient green highways, running and squeaking around the twins' heads at night. When they happened upon another boat carrying their friends the Stewarts, the young ladies were made sharply aware of the superiority of that craft, equipped with every convenience in the sleeping cabins, including chiffonier and even bookcases. Arrangements were made to meet up with the Stewarts again for the New Year. Certezza promised to get a cat at the next stop.

He was full of stories, all of which redounded to his credit, and often involving European aristocracy. He had rescued an Italian count and his family from Bedouin attack in the Sinai desert, he had favoured the Prince of Wales with a drink of water; he had fought with his fists a young lord, his employer, who insulted him. He harped upon the incompetence of other, and especially Arab, dragomans. Not only the ladies' present activities, but their future plans were hemmed in by his wisdom. 'Might they go to Petra while on the Syrian stage of their travels?' No, he could not recommend it as a suitable place for young ladies. He could not be responsible for the violence of the place. No, they could not stop with the Stewarts to see the antiquities at Sioot because these, Certezza informed them, had been spoiled by the pasha's soldiers during the Abyssinian campaign. It was a fortnight before anything was done about the rats.

It was becoming clear to Agnes, Margaret and Grace that their comfort was of secondary importance. The rowing boat, by contract for their sole use, was every morning occupied by Certezza's fifteen-year-old son, Pietro, who took it to shoot birds that he and his father would then stuff on the deck, the two having a commercial sideline in taxidermy. Pietro, officially both waiter and cabin steward, was incompetent at cleaning the cabins, and the decks were not properly washed, which, given the taxidermy under way on them, was a trial and a further lure to rodents. The ladies' clothes were washed by an Arab woman who 'dipped them in the river' and, as she used no soap, returned them greyer than they had left. Certezza never quite found the time to iron them. His own shirts, they noticed, were pounded to dazzling whiteness by the sailors on board. The twins occupied their hours reading the works of Auguste Mariette, the great French excavator of antiquities.

The Nile slipped by, hedged with lush green fields that gave way to the pale sandstone ridges that channelled the river's course. On the

Felluccas

banks were geese, pelicans, ducks, cormorants, cranes and herons. Piles of freshly cut cane seemed to move of their own accord through the fields, the donkeys that bore them invisible under their burdens. Boats bore strange boxes and bundles, finely balanced loads of sugar cane, coops of fowls, and gobbling turkeys strutted about on deck. Boatmen chanted as they pulled the oars when the winds fell.

Once a contract had been signed with a dragoman for a fixed price, all the costs incurred on the journey were his, but so too were any savings. Certezza had the knack of remaining within the letter of his contract while violating its spirit utterly. Just enough of his conduct corresponded to Murray's *Guidebook* advice to seem roughly plausible. Murray's did advise that a *dahabeeah* should hasten up the Nile while the winds were good; it did not say that the travellers should rarely set foot on land. Once they had moored in the evening, the dingy was constantly in use by Certezza himself, delivering messages for one or another European aristocrat of his acquaintance on another boat.

The ladies did not benefit from his noble connections. The brisk floating social life described by Murray's was, in their case, constrained by Certezza's knowledge of the wickedness of the dragoman, or the dissolute nature of the travellers on each boat they encountered. Even the planned second meeting with the Stewarts, arranged for New Year, came to naught – they had somehow missed each other.

The sisters were well and truly snared. Accustomed to the blunt candour of small-town Scotland, Agnes and Margaret were quite unprepared for a phenomenon like Certezza, who justified himself with picturesque explanations and who, when challenged, would tearfully swear to his own integrity on the lives of his sons. But even suspecting that Certezza 'did not keep strictly to the truth', they were reluctant to journey out or make acquaintances against his approval, just in case his warnings were justified. They might as well have been in one of those harems whose listless occupants Western travellers so pitied on visits to the East. At Esneh they finally acquired two cats that were kept tied up, one in the saloon and the other in the dressing room, where they howled and struggled to escape. This 'disturbed us greatly,' said Agnes, 'but anything was better than the rats.'

Not even Certezza's florid evasions could spoil the beauty and fascination of the Nile. Herodotus had marvelled at Egypt's antiquity and believed the country to be the source of the gods, and of language itself. Everything in Egypt was the reverse of normal practice, from the Greek point of view – the women were employed in trade and the men stayed at home to weave; the men of Egypt carried burdens on their heads while the women used their shoulders. No woman held priestly office, and even the servants of the goddesses were men. In other nations priests wore their hair long, but Egyptian priests shaved their heads. The men of Egypt practised circumcision, 'while men of other nations – except those who have learned from Egypt – leave their private parts as nature made them'.[7] Egyptians, Herodotus noted, were scrupulously clean – their priests bathed twice a day in cold water, plus twice every night – and were 'religious to excess'.

The remains of this priestly kingdom lay scattered along the length of the Nile, much of it during the 1860s still half-buried in sand. In the temples nineteenth-century travellers met the snake-hipped pharaohs and their feline Great Royal Wives, kept for ever young in the wall paintings that anticipated a future life rejoined to their bodies. Here was a culture, pagan admittedly, that even Scottish Presbyterians could respect for its steady and disciplined manner of life, one whose principal value was order, or *ma'at*. Their world was so given to regulation that there was even a god for civil servants: Thoth, tutelary deity of scribes. On the walls of the tombs (not just of the pharaohs but of their high officials) were scenes of a way of life that, while not perhaps so Presbyterian, were certainly ones to which only wealthy modern Europeans could aspire – decorative gardens and artificial lakes, pleasure boats and racehorses. Their vast administrative apparatus was sufficiently meritocratic for foreigners – Nubians, Libyans and Jews – to attain rank and wealth. This was an empire with contracts, treaties, diplomats, builders and professional soldiers.

But if it was so well governed, where was it now? The whole of Egypt was a *memento mori*, a token of imperial glory grown old and, for the British – then approaching the zenith of imperial power – this brought a certain warning chill. Florence Nightingale wrote of the frustration of keeping up dinner-party conversation after a day spent examining these ruins: 'It is very hard to be all day by the deathbed of the greatest of your race, and to come home and talk about quails or London.'[8] The sands that buried the stone colossi up to their necks were emblematic for Western visitors of the sands of time that had covered this once-great civilisation from view. We know more about the life of Abraham, wrote Agnes, than of that of Rameses II.

In AD 384 the Christian emperor Theodosius decreed that all pagan temples in the Roman Empire be closed. (The last datable hieroglyphic inscription is at the Temple of Philae, carved in August of AD 394.) Both Christian Egyptians and the Muslim rulers who followed them, after the rise of Islam in the seventh century, regarded the carvings and statues as idolatrous and obscene. The looted obelisks that graced Rome's piazzas were covered with hieroglyphics no one could read. Only in 1822 did a young Frenchman, Jean-François Champollion, manage to crack the code, using the stone found by Napoleon's soldiers at Rosetta as his key. But in 1868, more than forty years later, when the twins travelled, Egyptology was still in its infancy. Auguste Mariette, then active as first Director of the Egyptian Antiquities, was one of the earliest to insist on the importance of keeping Egypt's treasures in Egypt. They were not only being spirited away by foreign governments, but pillaged by the local population itself. Mariette wrote in 1867 that 'only a few years ago, barely would they have decided on the construction of a factory, a bridge or a house before they rushed to the nearest ruins as to a quarry'. One day the twins and Grace passed Mariette's steamer, although it was uncertain if the great man was on board. He was back and forth to Paris at the time, overseeing the production of his designs for the sets and costumes of Verdi's *Aida* for which, at the Khedive's request, he had also devised the plot.

The crowning event of any Nile cruise was the passage over the First Cataract – the scree of massive boulders that blocked clear passage at Aswan. The means to overcome this obstacle were, in 1869, much the

same as described by Herodotus: ropes were attached either side of
the *dahabeeah* and teams of half-naked men hauled the vessel up
over the rocks. The young ladies were naturally looking forward to
this dramatic spectacle. But as they approached Aswan, Certezza
announced to Margaret and Grace (whom he found more pliant than
Agnes) that the boat would not pass the First Cataract unless they took
full financial responsibility should it be lost. They communicated this
to Agnes, who refused to discuss the matter, since it was the Sabbath.
The next day, armed with the contract, she pointed out to Certezza
that its terms stated they should go over the cataract and that the
responsibility was his. He seemed initially to give way, but then
claimed that the *reis* (pilot) wished to remain in Edfu for the morrow,
the last day of Ramadan, so that he could pray in a mosque. When
Agnes pointed out that Ramadan did not end 'tomorrow', Certezza
replied that for working people it lasted a shorter time. 'Very well,
Certezza, we shall do it, as we think it right to respect every one's
religion.'

When they reached Aswan, after what became two days' delay, they
found themselves eighth in a queue of boats waiting to be taken over
the massive granite boulders by teams of glistening Nubians. One
English boat was stuck on the rocks, blocking the others, and it was
very doubtful, according to a smirking Certezza, whether once it was
freed any other boats would make it up this season, for after the Nile
fell below a certain level, passage became impossible.

By way of compensation for this disappointment, the twins proposed to attend a Protestant service of worship that Agnes heard was
to be held that Sunday on board one of the boats. A horrified Certezza
tried to warn them off. It was unthinkable. He could not recommend
it. 'But a service of worship', they countered, 'what could happen?' It
was not the service, he said, but the 'talk, talk' afterwards that was the
danger. When he had worked for Lady Ford, she had been most
insistent that a lady should never receive anyone on her boat, or be
received by another even on *the pretence* of a church service.

This time they were not to be dissuaded. They listened to the
preacher with interest, but it was the 'talk, talk' afterwards that proved

most illuminating. They learned that their social isolation was well known amongst fellow travellers on the river, and that several groups had attempted to visit them, only to be told by Certezza that his young ladies were variously indisposed, asleep or were not receiving visitors that day. It was now clear how badly they were being cheated, as confirmed by their friends, the Stewarts, who arrived the very next day. The Stewarts put it to them that their New Year's rendezvous had been deliberately scuttled by Certezza. They also provided the useful information that one of Certezza's sons, a dragoman on another boat, risked forfeiting £200 if he did not get his party past the cataract, which went part of the way to explain Certezza's eagerness to delay their own passage: he wanted to give his son a head start.

But now everyone had to wait, for as soon as the stranded boat was freed from the rocks two Khedival *dahabeeahs* arrived and were given precedence. They were the advance party for the Prince and Princess of Wales, who had even now set out on their 'purely personal' Nile cruise in six blue and gold steamers, which towed behind them barges clanking with 3,000 bottles of champagne and 4,000 bottles of claret. Behind these was a posse of journalists, and then two steamers full of Thomas Cook's tourists – the very first tour of 'the eastern lands of the Bible' arranged by that teetotalling founder of mass tourism, although Thomas Cook's company strenuously denied press reports that they were running 'in full cry up the river after the Prince and Princess'.[9]

The drama for Agnes, Margaret and Grace was nearer to hand. Certezza had fed them with doubts, on the one hand, that any more boats would make it over the cataract this season and, on the other, with flowery promises that he would ensure theirs did. But the 'talk, talk' had also revealed something else: Certezza had put it about that they did not wish to go up the cataract. Already in Luxor he had told the letter-carriers that his party was going no further than Aswan (thus saving himself considerable expense). The Stewarts said they should insist.

Steeled by these reports and determined to be cheated no more, Agnes, Margaret and Grace confronted Certezza. He wept. He brought in the Stewarts' dragoman to plead for him. When Margaret accused him of intentional delay at Edfu to let his son's party get up the cataract first, he proclaimed that he would rather see his hand cut off or one of his sons brought home dead than hear her say such a thing. On their afternoon walk that day the ladies 'maintained a most profound silence, and Certezza 'looked black as the Nile mud'.

The next morning the last of the pasha's boats was drawn up over the rocks and at half-past six a team of Nubians tied ropes to either side of Certezza's craft. Their sheikh and a special pilot, the 'Reis of the Cataract', came on board and superb half-naked men surrounded the boat, swimming or darting in and out of the rapids in their own tiny craft. The Reis of the Cataract bellowed at them, they shouted back over the roar of the waters and the boat was hauled over the first rapid. The next day a thick rope was attached to the bow and a team of fifty or so Nubian men pulled the boat from the front, while others manoeuvred with ropes attached to the sides, as they attempted to haul it over a waterfall. The ladies stayed on board throughout so as not to miss anything.

When they were in the midst of the currents, with the Nile's whole force bearing down on them, the holding rope broke and the boat lurched round to one side. Their useless waiter, Pietro, pulled off his jacket to abandon ship, but the ladies stood unmoved. 'I think nothing can make *you* afraid,' cried Certezza to Grace. 'No, *nothing*,' she replied, 'I have a firm trust in Providence.' Another rope was thrown about and they crested the waterfall.

After three days of tugging and towing, the ladies found the island temple of Philae before them. Conspicuous amongst the names carved all over its ruins were those of Certezza and his sons.

They were now sailing in Nubia, the biblical 'Kingdom of Kush', and the young unmarried Nubian women wore only long girdles of twisted leather strips decorated with shells. Their bodies and hair glistened with castor oil, which made their skin 'like polished red-wood'. Agnes hoped the Princess of Wales would not be tempted by this particular fashion. They sailed on for several weeks, as far as the twin temples of Abu Simbel, built to honour Rameses II and his wife, Nefertari, at the southernmost reach of pharaonic Egypt. The ladies marvelled that these great stones had been laid one on the other during the days of Moses. Although only two weeks previously a team of 300 men had cleared the monument of sand in expectation of the eminent visitors, it was already half-covered, and would need to be cleared again before the royal party arrived. One of the great seated statues of the pharaoh, sixty-six feet high, stood mostly buried, its head peeping out of the sand 'like a bather above water'. All were covered in graffiti. At the centre of the breast of one colossus was inscribed 'Certezza'.

Once confronted, Certezza was subdued, but not broken. The crew became silent and the young ladies discovered that he had forbidden them to talk amongst themselves, suspecting – correctly – that Agnes and Margaret were beginning to understand their Arabic. Certezza was, from his point of view, 'down' financially, on account of having to take the boat over the cataract and now put other economies in place. The first ten days in Nubia he had fed them entirely on wild pigeon, shot by himself, arguing that the forthcoming royal visit had forced up vegetable prices. On donkey excursions to tombs and temples he would not let them use the elegant little saddles they had brought with them, instead charging them three pounds to use ones he provided, which were little more than scraps of brittle leather, one without a girth. Certezza had an unhappy way with donkeys: he was stout and they mostly refused to carry him, lying down in the road when he attempted to mount, so that he had to walk all the way home after his charges.

Descending the cataract, they prudently decided to observe proceedings from the shore. The Nubians who rowed them back out to their boat gave news that the Prince and Princess of Wales were already five days on the river and were consuming daily a hundred sheep, six calves and a hundred eggs. Early in the morning a few days later they passed the royal party, making its way upriver as they went down, the royal *dahabeeah* being towed by a handsome white river steamer. No one was on deck. On the kitchen steamer behind they could see a cook preparing breakfast. Certezza, with characteristic tact, fired two pistol shots. A curtain in the royal *dahabeeah* twitched and was dropped again.

Now the young ladies no longer took any notice of Certezza's warnings about 'bad reputation', but stopped where they chose. At Luxor they went to view fireworks one evening in the Temple of Karnak and defiantly took tea with some friendly Americans who had a carpet spread amongst the ruins. 'Do you know,' said one young lady whom they met, 'that we have a much more liberal table than yours, although we pay less, and your boat is an old cargo boat, that has no business to be used as a *dahabieh* at all. That is why it is so full of rats.' . . . 'Certezza says our cook gets eight pounds a month.' . . . 'Nonsense! He only gets four pounds; he's an old barber.'

Marvellous though their downstream journey was, it continued to be overshadowed by petty skirmishes with Certezza and the nagging concern that they were contractually bound to proceed on to Jerusalem with a dragoman they distrusted.

In the end they were relieved to get back to Cairo two days early. How pleasant, wrote Agnes, 'to converse without being overheard – above all the delight of being free' – that is, if they could disentangle themselves.

Certezza's intention was to transfer them immediately from the boat to the train and hurry them on for the next stint to Jerusalem, firmly under his charge. But the twins insisted on a few days at Shepheard's, where they could consider how to be rid of him. Someone suggested a severe beating, but they regretted that Certezza could not be subjected 'to such summary law', being not only Maltese, but a British citizen. They visited the British Consul before whom their contract had been drawn up, with written grounds for cancelling it. Certezza was a step ahead of them. The boat, he conceded, was not first-class, but the ladies had accepted it when they boarded. He bribed the *reis*, who – not yet having been paid – was vulnerable to manipulation, to corroborate his version of the story on other points. Not only would Certezza not allow the ladies to break the contract, but he threatened to go to the law courts, demanding compensation as well as references to protect his spotless reputation of thirty years. As his son was also called Certezza, he insisted that the family name must not be blackened.

With the consul's assistance, Agnes and Margaret got out of the contract without the humiliation of attesting to Certezza's 'character', but no doubt meeting most of his financial demands. He was, in his own way, an excellent dragoman. 'We just call them "dragons," ' said one young lady at the hotel, 'it's shorter.'

One might think that this Nile trip, during much of which they were kept virtual prisoners by Certezza, would challenge Agnes's postulation of the ease with which ladies could now travel unaccompanied, but not a bit. Their mistake was not in forgoing a male protector but, according to Agnes, disregarding their own, best travel advice: never visit a country where you do not know the language. In their case this did not mean curtail your travel, but *always* learn the language.

Free of Certezza, the trip to Jerusalem was altogether more satisfactory. They engaged an Egyptian dragoman called Armanous, whose terms were more modest than Certezza's and whose provisions more liberal. Armanous was a Coptic Christian, and they travelled by steamer from Alexandria to Jaffa with many of his relations on a pilgrimage to Jerusalem for the forthcoming Easter celebrations. They glimpsed his wife, arrayed in pink silks and shimmering with jewels as she was lowered to a small boat to be rowed ashore. After a night in a pilgrim hostel on the coast, Armanous said goodbye to his kinsfolk and set out with his clients on horseback.

Travel was more dangerous here. Armanous was armed and employed a Turkish guard, who preceded them carrying a ten-foot spear. No sooner had they left the hostel than a man on horseback made a rush at them, flourishing a club, but he turned out to be a young friar, sent to test their dragoman's mettle. Armanous passed the test by unslinging his gun.

Also in their employ was a tall Nubian cook and Armanous's brother, serving as waiter. The ladies rode side-saddle in their white riding habits. They held the reins and parasols in their left hands, keeping their right hands free for Murray's *Guidebook to Syria*. On their heads were scarves of white cambric, worn like Turkish veils beneath straw hats. It was the first time Agnes, Margaret and Grace had slept in tents.

It was March 1869 when the party rode through the coastal plain, traversing fields of high green grass along paths lined with wild flowers – poppies, marigolds, bluebells and primroses, which occasionally gave way to bogs or streams. They continued through rocky valleys whose banks bore wild roses, sweet-briar and daffodils. They ascended the mountains to the ancient and holy city of Jerusalem. They were bitterly disappointed.

In this they were no different from most British and American visitors of their day, members of the affluent middle classes and over-whelmingly Protestant. Protestants, as Agnes explained in glossing the title for her book, *Eastern Pilgrims*, believe that God may be worshipped at any spot on Earth; everywhere is hallowed, nowhere especially sacred, so they do not believe in *pilgrimage* in the sense that Catholic and Orthodox Christians do. Of the Roman Catholics who went to Jerusalem to see the grave of Christ, Agnes wrote, 'we can hardly understand what benefit they expect to derive from visiting it. Our Saviour is risen, and the distance is short indeed which separates Him from a believing soul' – wherever that soul might be. As Protestants, they had no truck with 'holy places' for their own sake, and no intention of prostrating themselves before the slab in the Church of the Holy Sepulchre, which pious tradition held Christ's dead body had lain on to be dressed for burial. Indeed, they had a horror of the icons (idolatrous), candles and reliquaries that, for more than a millennium, the faithful of the Roman Catholic and Eastern Churches had been lavishing on these lands.

Most Bible Protestants wanted – indeed actively expected – to find Jerusalem much as Jesus and his disciples had left it, or at least as portrayed in the illustrated bibles of their childhood. That was where Egypt was so deeply satisfying. In Jerusalem, Bethlehem and Nazareth, by contrast, Agnes, Margaret and Grace found that every site asso-ciated with Jesus had been long since surmounted by a church, a shrine or a chapel with gilded reliquaries containing Fragments of the True Cross or the knuckle bones of a saint. In the Church of the Holy Sepulchre alone could be found not only the Lord's tomb, but his place of crucifixion, the slab on which his body was anointed, the grave of Adam, the tomb of Melchizedek and the centre of the Earth.

The City of David in the mid-nineteenth century was a sleepy suburb of the Ottoman Empire, divided amongst Muslims, Christians and the Jews, who made up about half of its 22,000 inhabitants. Christianity in Jerusalem was even more sharply divided than the Presbyterian Church in Scotland, except that – instead of vying with one another for austerity – the Russian, Armenian, Greek, Coptic and Roman Churches outdid each other in ritual, relics and glittering robes. A recent addition were the American Protestant missionaries who, having done little but annoy Jerusalem's Jews and Muslims, were now engaged in trying to convert its indigenous Christians to the spirit of the Reformation.

In what should have been Christianity's proudest quarters, the weakening Ottoman government played the different Christian groups, together with their international protectors, off against one another in a competition for privileges – the French were the self-styled champions of the Latin Christians and the Russians of the Orthodox. In 1847 a dispute over who should have the honour of replacing a silver star that had disappeared from the Church of the Nativity in Bethlehem resulted in a brawl between Greek (Orthodox) and Latin (Roman Catholic) clergy, quickly involving their political protectors in St Petersburg and Paris. Jerusalem was a cock-pit where the slightest religious grievance could flair up into a diplomatic incident, and the disagreements regularly came to blows among the faithful.

On Easter eve, Agnes, Margaret and Grace attended the famous Ceremony of the Holy Fire in the Church of the Holy Sepulchre. During this, the first light of Easter is mysteriously quickened inside the tomb of Christ and passed from candle to candle to the assembled worshippers. Moved by curiosity rather than piety, the three women watched from a tiny gallery high up in the wall reserved for visitors, most of whom were as sceptical as they. Below pilgrims jostled for position, while discipline was maintained by Turkish soldiers and the military governor, who lashed out at squabblers, or even at overly boisterous choirs, with his *khorbash*. At two in the morning a procession that had made its way up through the city finally appeared at the door of the church, winding its way between lines of Turkish soldiers. Each pilgrim carried an unlit candle. One of the processional banners became the object of a fight for possession, until finally it was reduced to rags and order was restored with the *khorbash*. At length came the procession of priests, three abreast, with golden robes, and in the centre an ancient patriarch, supported by two other priests and bearing an unlit torch. This old man was lifted on the shoulders of the crowd and disappeared into the sepulchre. Hundreds of flailing arms holding unlit candles met him on his emergence with the miraculously lit Holy Light. As the flame passed from candle to candle, it soon bathed faces and hands amongst the ancient piers and aisles. It was 'a miracle indeed', noted a stony-faced Agnes, 'that a universal conflagration did not ensue'.

A procession of Greek, Armenian, Ethiopian and Coptic priests passed below. Flanking a Coptic priest bearing a silver cross were two others wearing robes of green and gold, with jewelled breastplates and silver crowns. The twins were amazed to recognise these as their dragoman and his brother. Armanous later explained that they were both deacons and that he hoped at some time to become a priest.

Agnes, Margaret and Grace grew weary of seeing 'the very pillar where the cock crew' and the 'actual cradle' of the infant Jesus (they saw several of these, which were explained as having been used at different stages of the Divine infancy). They were disappointed by the Garden of Gethsemane, which they seem to have supposed should have been forever preserved in the torchlit confusion of the night of the Saviour's betrayal. Instead they found a prim little park in plain daylight maintained by Italian monks, with walks lined by box and privet hedges and raised borders of marigolds and wallflowers. They were happiest riding in the valleys surrounding Jerusalem, or strolling through St Stephen's Gate – a place where they could be sure they were crossing Jesus's path.

Also to their taste was a visit to a Muslim harem. Black slaves ushered them into a room with divans, where they were introduced to the nobleman's three wives. These ladies were in gingham dresses with pearl necklaces and offered the visitors, with whom they shared no language, sherbert, coffee and a cigarette. Grace, who 'instead of taking a whiff and passing it around, kept it to herself', was enjoying this luxury when the nobleman himself entered. Through his translation one of their hostesses said that, since they did not worship pictures or kiss crosses or any such thing, she could not bear to think of Protestants under so insulting a title as 'Christians', but thought they must be Mohammedans of another sect. As they sipped their coffee and Grace finished the cigarette, they reflected that Kilbarchan, after this, would be a bit dull.

CHAPTER 6

The search for the perfect mate

Agnes and Margaret reached London in August 1869, almost exactly one year after they had left. The diversions of Kilbarchan were predictable – the small stage of provincial life, the periodic church bazaars and Sunday School teaching enlivened by the occasional visit of a celebrity guest preacher, perhaps a converted slave or Mussulman in his native dress. They decided to move to London.

London was perhaps a curious choice for two young women so ferociously attached to Scotland and their own Scots identity, but Kilbarchan had never really been home and was associated now with the sudden death of their father. Irvine was a possibility, but their greatest Irvine friend, William Bruce Robertson, having on doctor's advice largely withdrawn from pastoral duties, was now living half the year in Florence and on the French Riviera. With no near relations and few supportive friends, there was nothing to keep the twins in Ayrshire, particularly as Grace, who had returned to her teaching post, was in London.

Although Grace furnished the move's pretext, there is no doubt that Agnes and Margaret hoped to find in London a wider and more congenial circle of acquaintances, both female and male. This could still be a largely Scottish circle, albeit ex-pat, and from their home in Pembridge Square, Kensington the twins made lengthy journeys to their church of choice: Clapham Road Presbyterian.[1] Within a year Agnes had published her travel diary *Eastern Pilgrims* (1870), and Margaret had fallen in love.

It was inevitable that their paths should cross that of James Gibson.

He was a Scotsman, a kinsman of Grace's, and he too had only recently returned from Egypt, where he had witnessed the opening of the Suez Canal. More dramatically, he had on an earlier occasion travelled by camel and on horseback to Mount Sinai and Petra, where he had been briefly taken hostage by the party's own guides.

Born in 1826, Gibson was some seventeen years older than the twins. As a young man he had hoped to be a poet, but was urged by his father, a prosperous Edinburgh seed merchant, into the Church.

Few seeing Gibson preach as a young man would have had an impression of a fragile spirit: six feet tall, broad-shouldered and handsome, he had curling, light-brown hair and a good speaking voice. Agnes and Margaret had once heard him preach when they were teenagers. His theme was 'Cast thy bread upon the water and thou shalt find it after many days'. Bread found in these circumstances is seldom improved, but Agnes and Margaret understood this as an image of the impression the young preacher had made, even then, on Margaret's heart.[2]

The intervening years had not been entirely kind to James Gibson. After studies in Edinburgh and Halle, he accepted 'a call' from a congregation in Melrose. In the 1850s the heavy stress still fell upon the minister's sacred eloquence, which must at least appear to issue from spontaneous inspiration. Indeed, as Agnes pointed out in a memoir of her brother-in-law, this duty ought to have been a joyous privilege, but Gibson was a perfectionist. Preaching quickly became an ordeal, since it required two bursts of inspiration every Sunday, which his nature required him to prepare down to the last syllable, and which his congregation expected to be delivered without notes.

His sermons were famously rich in meaning and free from cant, but this came at great personal cost. Another minister who shared his quarters recalled Gibson fighting to reach his ideal of excellence in every sermon, an agony that absorbed him during the week and completely deprived him of his weekends. 'I scarcely saw him on Saturday unless at meals. He was in his study all day, he was not in bed all night. On the Sabbath morning I breakfasted alone and did not see him until we went out together to the Church.' When Gibson mounted the pulpit, there was no evidence of anything but the most complete preparation and perfect vigour.

The strain soon began to tell, and it was presently observed by his pious but critical flock at Melrose that Gibson was having recourse to jottings. A local farmer challenged him, reminding Gibson that he had delivered his trial sermon without notes. By way of analogy the farmer added that when he bought seed from Gibson's father, he expected seeds identical to those in the catalogues: Gibson the younger had promised one thing and was delivering another. Gibson's self-confidence was shattered and he suffered a period of melancholy prostration.

He began to feel weak and worry that his heart would stop beating; whether this was neurosis or true physical pathology is unclear. In any case, at thirty-three Gibson resigned his ministry and devoted himself to his own fragile health, an ample inheritance on the death of his father enabling him to do so.

In 1871 while recovering from a bout of low spirits at a hydropathic spa in Yorkshire, Gibson met Alexander Duffield, a mining engineer and world traveller who was just about to depart on a tour of some tin mines in Spain. He asked Gibson to come along, which Gibson did, and the trip changed his life. Duffield (a man of indiscriminate enthusiasms and later author of such works as *Peru of the Guano Age*) was at the time enchanted by Cervantes and set upon doing a translation of *Don Quixote*. He passed this enthusiasm on to Gibson, who remained in Spain for some months after Duffield had departed, studying Catalan literature. Such were his passions and state of mind when first he met the Smith twins.

It seems that Margaret and James Gibson were first engaged around 1872, around the time he returned from Spain, but the marriage plan was to be on and off for more than ten years, owing to the social delicacy of both parties and Gibson's recurrent illness. In 1878 Gibson was living at the Westminster Palace Hotel in London, occasionally meeting a few literary friends and playing chess. He passed his time correcting the proofs of Duffield's *Don Quixote*, struggling to perfect his own poetry and brooding over his bodily decay. In 1880 he renewed his engagement to Margaret only to fall into a deep depression that caused him to call off the marriage once again, on the grounds that his life could only be a short one, and filled with increasing pain and weakness.

Although the twins both adored James Gibson who, like many depressives, was droll and genial when well, his frailty was very much at odds with their own robust health and attitude to life. Agnes especially could not be idle while waiting on her sister's wavering suitor. Something of the fierce Scottish fuel that drove Carnegie to build railroads across America propelled Agnes's smaller engine. It had much to do with Scottish Calvinism. Calvin's demanding God, who holds each one responsible for his or her own soul and inspects each moment carefully, further requires that each human life – whether that of a weaver woman or a belted earl – be useful. For the twins, this was part of their doctrine of Providence. They took it on faith that each life was known to God and that God disliked idleness. Even if one had money, one needed a 'calling'. But this elevated work ethic had its internal contradictions, not least for ladies of their circumstances. The wealth pouring off Scotland's economy was creating a middle class whose women were not needed in the fields or at the loom. The approved feminine vocation was marriage or else tending the household of a father, brother or maiden aunt. But what was one to do if, as in the twins' case, all these needful familial appurtenances were lacking?

For a time Agnes thought she had a literary vocation. *Eastern Pilgrims* had received encouraging reviews ('a vein of novelty runs through Miss Smith's delightful volume', *The Weekly Review*), and she now turned her hand to fiction. Her lengthy novels in contemporary Scottish settings, *Effie Maxwell* and *Glenmavis*, featured beautiful, adventurous and unfailingly pious heroines. They travelled a great deal, did things that young ladies were not supposed to do and in the end married 'their soul's mates', in the teeth of snobbery and social expectation.

Agnes wrote under the influence of George Eliot, although without such talent. Still these novels, both written during the period of Gibson's extended and wavering courtship of Margaret, provide an interesting reflection of their author's contemporaneous concerns, and probably those of her twin.

It was a commonplace of the time that a girl not married, or at least engaged, by the age of twenty was unlikely to marry at all, though there is no evidence that Agnes and Margaret thought so. Their mother had been thirty-one when she married. *Effie Maxwell* and *Glenmavis*, both published when Agnes was in her thirties, would indeed read as melancholy daydreams if Agnes had given up all such hope, since the only path of female fulfilment that she projects for their heroines is loving marriage to a splendid man.

Agnes's heroines are looking for love, but the deeper anxiety threading through the novels was not that of being alone in the world, but one also faced by George Eliot's heroines: a fear that the life ahead would hold little of the epic; that hers would be a life in which a certain spiritual grandeur was 'ill-matched with meanness of opportunity'.[3] Agnes captured the sentiment in a poem entitled 'On the Shelf', in which a 'lordly goblet' addresses a delicate china cup:

'Oh, rest thee, pretty plaything!
Thou art not like myself;
Thou'rt only good to fondle,
Or stand upon the shelf.

Thou canst not hold a gallon
Of foaming ale or wine;
I'll give thee some few droppings,
To cheer that heart of thine.'

'Oh, hear me,' said the teacup,
'Oh, hear me once for all!
The shelf is dull abiding,
And fondling aye would pall.

'For work my Master made me,
I pine in languid rest;
But what you put within me,
Oh, let it be the best!'[4]

The real trouble with being 'on the shelf' was not the lack of a loving companion, but of a man whose adventures one could accompany or whose noble plans one could support. A young woman on her own, even a wealthy one, was effectively in dry dock with little access to the world or work, or even to the engaging conversation of educated men.

If marriage was one preoccupation of Agnes's novels, then money was another. Few would think of coming into unexpected wealth as a problem, but it clearly troubled Agnes. She and Margaret were not inclined to give away their inheritance in a dramatic gesture. That would not in any case fit with their Presbyterian view of Providence; so much money, acquired from so enigmatic a source, must surely be 'for' something. The question was 'what'? Her heroine, Effie Maxwell, discovers as a teenager that the somewhat run-down couple she had thought of as her parents are not, and that she is in fact an heiress. Effie overcomes this difficulty by marrying a reforming Member of Parliament, whose projects for public betterment her fortune can assist. But the wavering *littérateur* James Gibson had no such public ambitions, nor did he need money, and Agnes judged that she had not yet met her life's complement.

In the meantime they must use their God-given talents to the full and not drift into what Agnes called the 'butterfly existence' of so many women of their class – flittering about, gaily ornamented, from luncheons to teas, from dinner parties to balls with no fixity of purpose. They would carry on with Sunday School teaching, help out in the church soup kitchen and keep up with their private studies. They spent the winter of 1878 on the Riviera learning Spanish – no doubt under the influence of Gibson, who visited them there – and in 1879 threw themselves into the study of Greek.

It was this language that would prove their improbable saviour.

Agnes and Margaret had made friends with J. S. Blackie, Professor of Greek at the University of Edinburgh. This energetic champion of women's education and all things Scottish (he was a familiar figure in Edinburgh, striding to his college rooms swathed in plaid and playing an imaginary bagpipe) had a project called 'Living Greek' whose foundation was a thesis about Greek pronunciation. Blackie pointed out that Greek was taught in English schools and universities with roughly the pronunciation recommended by Erasmus in the sixteenth century. This so little resembled Greek as spoken in modern-day Athens that it might as well have been another language, with the result that an educated Englishman might learn classical Greek for ten years at school, but attain no competence in the spoken language. For his part, Blackie insisted that the best guide to pronunciation of ancient Greek was the way modern Greeks spoke their own language.

Blackie managed to weave philhellenism and Scottish patriotism together, along with some digs at the Church of England, lambasting the scholars of the University of Oxford for their insularity and arrogance in the matter of speaking Greek. 'To the majority of English scholars,' he wrote, 'Greek is still only a dead grammar and a dead dictionary . . . The contempt of living Greek, in which the typical Oxonian habitually indulges, has its origin in the stiff conservatism characteristic of the teaching profession generally, made doubly strong by its union with aristocratic and sacerdotal elements in Oxford . . .'[5]

In much of this Blackie was correct. Certainly Greek was so far removed in the English mind from the language spoken in modern Greece that each of the great public schools could pride itself on having its own slightly distinctive pronunciation: an Etonian could be distinguished from a Harrovian or a Wykehamist by slight nuances. And Dean Gaisford, of Christ Church, Oxford, recommended Greek to his pupils as follows: 'By all means pursue your study of Greek. It was the language spoken by our Lord; it places you in a position of superiority over those who do not know the language; and a knowledge of it opens the way to places of emolument and dignity.'[6]

This heady mixture of Scottish nationalism, female advocacy and linguistic aspiration intrigued Agnes and Margaret, with the result that they learned ancient Greek according to Blackie's 'Living Greek' directives, imposing on themselves the discipline of speaking only Greek to each other for days at a time.

However well taken Blackie's criticisms of Oxford snobbery may have been, scholars now believe he was quite mistaken to think modern Greek a good guide to ancient Greek pronunciation.

Nevertheless, a mistaken theory had a good effect, at least in its transformation of the lives of Agnes and Margaret Smith. They had ambitions for their Greek beyond simply reading the New Testament – they intended to put their 'Living Greek' to use by travelling in Greece itself, and Agnes planned to write about it.

Agnes's novels had not been greeted with the same warmth as had met *Eastern Pilgrims*. It seems she took a sober judgement of where her literary talents lay, and it was with the purpose of writing another travel book that she proposed an extended trip to Greece in the spring of 1883. It would be another 'Holy Land' trip, but this time in the steps of Sophocles and St Paul, rather than Moses and Jesus.

Grace Blyth was keen to accompany them, but James Gibson was very unwilling to be parted from Margaret who, after all these years of dithering, he feared he might lose. In the end he relented – or the twins insisted, it is unclear from Agnes's tactful memoir which – and the three women departed from Gravesend on a ship of the Orient Line.

CHAPTER 7

Greece

James Gibson's fears were justified. In the Bay of Biscay their ship entered a colossal storm. The *Iberia* was a screw-driven steamer and the sisters' cabins were over the noisy drive-shaft of the propellers. As the ship slowly mounted and descended 'alps of ice, each fringed with flying jets of vapoury foam', they listened intently to the slow clanking of an engine that seemed periodically to stop altogether.[1] Luggage was sliding up and down the soaked corridors, and the ship's stewards, barefooted for better grip despite the freezing temperatures, were sleepless and evidently alarmed. The *Iberia* could not be turned because of the danger of presenting a flank to the west wind and was heading slowly out into the wild Atlantic.

Agnes attempted to comfort a lady passenger by sharing her views on Providence: 'How hard it is to console others at such a moment! How one's favourite texts slip away from the tongue! I could only ask her if she did not believe that the day of our death was fixed even before we were born.' Apparently she did not.

Back in their cabin, portmanteaux, bags and a basket of medicines 'careered wildly about', but their chief anxiety was for a half-crate of claret, which Margaret tried to secure as it shot across the cabin floor with each lurch. After a long night during which, they later discovered, an almost identical steamer had foundered, the captain managed to turn the ship and, with a tail wind, headed rapidly down towards the Mediterranean.

Agnes was frankly philhellenic. In her mind, no doubt partly owing to the influence of Blackie, the Greeks' bravery and love of liberty was akin to that of the Scots. Both Greeks and Scots were, in addition, clannish, pre-eminently logical and given to theological disputes. James Gibson encouraged these associations in a string of letters from London that chased Margaret across Greece. One mapped the topography of Athens (which Gibson had visited) onto that of Edinburgh: walk 'up Lycabettus hill where you can see Edinburgh (in your mind's eye)... Right in front of you, you have the Acropolis, with its ruined columns, which represents Carlton Hill', while Piraeus represented the port of Leith. 'And if you want to see the Fifeshire hills, there they are in the Corinthian ranges!'[2]

Athens was blustery and cold, and for some days covered in snow. Agnes climbed the Areopagus and seated herself on the blustery summit with an umbrella, to read from her wind-blown Bible how St Paul had preached to the Greeks on the same spot. She wrote:

> How bold, how appropriate were the stranger's words standing on the site of a court hallowed by such awful sanctions, the proud boast of their city, before which Apollo himself once deigned to plead the cause of the suppliant Orestes. The Propylea of the Parthenon gleamed in the sunlight a few hundred yards above him and the little temple of the wingless victory stood out clear against the blue sky . . . Yet, in the presence of these almost superhuman creations of beauty, a wandering Jew had the courage to declare to a crowd of philosophic Athenians that *'God dwelleth not in temples made with hands'*. His words fell upon scornful ears; yet their echo has caused the Parthenon to crumble.

Greece interested Agnes as (politically) a young nation, and she saw it in contrast to the Ottoman Empire from which Greece had, only fifty years earlier, broken free. In Athens, Agnes and Margaret attended sessions of the Greek parliament and were suitably impressed by the democratic process. But in practical matters affecting the traveller, by comparison with the Holy Land, Greece left something to be desired, as became altogether evident when the three women began their provincial travels in early March.

Based on her earlier experience in Palestine, Agnes observed that

Ottoman dragomans were more expert than the Greeks at managing horses, tents and provisions, all of which they planned carefully in advance; they also knew 'better than the Greeks how to place a lady in her saddle'. Syria (as the whole of the littoral from what is now Turkey to Suez was known at the time) had a better supply of horses, as well as a greater and better supply of tents and dragomans, to serve the greater number of tourists. On the other hand, Syria under the Ottomans was corruptly administered and dangerous. The dragomans had to be armed, and any stranger might be an enemy. Their Greek counterpart was unarmed and was continually encountering friendly acquaintances.

The ladies had hired as their principal staff a Greek guide called Angelos, who was round and stately, and a tall, slightly cynical butler called Alexandros. They set out south, on horseback, into the Peloponnese. At the time few English tourists – and for that matter few wealthier Greeks – travelled outside of Athens. (Some Greeks told Agnes and Margaret they were waiting for railways to be built, but Agnes observed that such a lack had never prevented visitors to Switzerland before the age of steam.) The twins rode side-saddle, with mules to carry their cases and muleteers to drive them.

Angelos had advised against tents: the tendency for dogs, ducks and pigs to wander in made sleeping under canvas unpleasant and it was always possible, he said, to stay at a tavern or rent a room from a local. As the twins soon discovered, however, this was not necessarily an advance in comfort. Tents in Palestine, equipped to the traveller's specifications, could be luxurious, and one could stop for the night wherever one wanted. By contrast, hours of travel in Greece were often dictated by the distance to the nearest place of lodging. Whereas the Syrian dragomen made an initial large outlay for tents and had done with it, Angelos had to waste time every night bargaining for rooms 'and sometimes to resist extortion'. Fleas were a persistent problem, and to avoid their attentions the ladies brought with them their own small iron bedsteads, cork mattresses, bedding and quantities of flea powder, which they sprinkled about lavishly on arrival. Travelling light was not possible.

Agnes and Margaret, both very physically fit, must have made tiring travelling companions for the somewhat older Grace and their portly guide, Angelos. In Corinth they climbed up the Acropolis to the ruins of the Temple of Aphrodite, with frequent pauses for Grace and Angelos, who were continually out of breath. Margaret polished these moments by reading aloud (in Greek) those portions of the New Testament that related St Paul's doings on the plain below them. (Never mind that Grace knew no Greek and Angelos was not especially high-minded.)

Agnes and Margaret, now quite fluent in Greek, were keen to speak to native Greeks, especially since Agnes wanted her book to be embellished with such encounters. But conversations, for two Scottish ladies, were not easy to come by. A male traveller like Lord Byron might easily chat to boatmen, tavern keepers or field hands, but not so two women. Greek ladies had not yet emancipated themselves from the Turkish traditions of their former rulers. Even in Athens an unmarried woman could not visit the shops without an attendant. The twins were advised that no respectable woman would enter a grocer's shop – advice they ignored. In the countryside women were reclusive and poorly educated, and the men did not enter into conversation with passing female travellers. It seems this was the main reason why Agnes and Margaret had many of their best conversations with monks. The monasteries welcomed visitors, many of the monks were highly educated and, the twins discovered, very interested in the Bible. If the Orthodox Church was a strange new animal for Agnes and Margaret, then just as strange, to the monks, must have been the Scottish ladies with full-skirted dresses, capes and parasols, who addressed them in fluent, if strangely archaic, Greek.

The Eastern Church was in most ways the antithesis of all that Agnes and Margaret had been brought up to regard as legitimate in religion. Extravagant vestments, endless chanting and ritual were all otiose to the Protestant spirit, not to mention the unaccountable Greek fondness for what Agnes called 'dirty old pictures painted on boards' (icons).

It was Lent and fasting was strict. The twins disapproved of the practice, and thought that the women and children looked tired and sickly on it. On the other hand, Greek Orthodoxy avoided the worst elements of Roman Catholicism, the religion explicitly denounced by Calvin and Knox: there was no Pope, confessions were heard only once a year and the parish priests (if not the monks) were usually married.

They visited many monasteries and, by the time Easter arrived, the twins' views had softened – somewhat. They had come to Ithome in Messenia and were invited to the afternoon service at the monastery. Twelve monks, all in black, came chanting the *Kyrie, eleison* ('Lord, have mercy'). They disappeared into the inner sanctuary and presently returned gorgeously attired, one in cloth of gold, singing, 'Christ hath arisen, hath arisen from the dead, having trampled upon death.' An old man read from a jewel-studded Bible. At the words 'Peace be unto you', a bell was rung and each of the monks sang 'Christ is risen' in

Agnes in Greek costume

turn. Agnes thought she detected a cynical smile on the face of their butler, Alexandros, which she took to represent the modern Greek spirit protesting at centuries of ritual suffocation. But 'Protestant and Presbyterian as I am,' she wrote, 'I nevertheless felt that one precious truth was being slowly impressed on their simple hearts, and that perhaps, throughout ages of darkness and ignorance, this may have been the most efficacious means of doing so.'

Afterwards they spoke with the *hegumenos*, the superior of the monastery, both tiptoeing around doctrinal differences with stately platitudes. Agnes found that, in awkward moments of religious disagreement, an unfavourable reference to the Pope could restore harmony by turning attention to a common enemy. Indeed, the enduring legacy of this trip to Greece was Agnes and Margaret's growing and improbable liking for Greek Orthodox monks.

After nearly six months away, Margaret sent the lovesick Gibson a terse telegram indicating the tour's successful completion and her imminent return with a single French phrase: *'Tout va bien.'* He was roused to rhapsody:

> My love is in the land of Greece,
> Oh, when shall all her wanderings cease?
> She sends me flowers from hill and plain,
> From fabled well, and classic fane;
>
> She sends me letters full of charm,
> That stir my heart, and keep it warm;
> But these, her latest words and best,
> Are more to me than all the rest:
> > *Tout va bien! Tout va bien!*
>
> She is coming back across the sea
> She is coming back to home and me
> With brighter eyes and browner cheek
> With less of Scotch and more of Greek,
> . . .
>
> > *Tout va bien, tout va bien!*[3]

CHAPTER 8

The estate of marriage

A series of photographs from 1883 show a couple playing chess. The lady's chestnut hair is pulled back from her face and falls in ringlets over her shoulders. She wears a fashionable, ruched day-dress and on her left hand you can just detect a wedding band. The man is informally dressed in a wool jacket and light trousers, with a grey beard and grey hair curling to his shoulders. This is Margaret and James Young Gibson, in the photographs announcing their marriage to their friends. Margaret is forty years old and James fifty-seven.

Margaret and James Gibson, in the photograph that announced their marriage

Her trip to Greece had finally propelled Gibson into matrimony. It seems that a fellow pastor had told Gibson firmly that he must stop shilly-shallying and make his intentions clear. Gibson had not left England for some years, convinced that his health could not endure travel, but now he went to meet Agnes, Margaret and Grace in the German spa of Bad Wildbad, emboldened by a 'secret resolve' not to return a bachelor. Margaret and James were married in a quiet civil marriage by the mayor of Wildbad on 8 September 1883.

Agnes and Margaret were now to be separated for the first time in their lives, if only for the six months of the Gibsons' honeymoon – it seems there was no question of the twins ever living permanently apart. Agnes filled her time by acquiring a new language. With the help of a tutor, Mr Habib Anthony Salmoné of University College, London, she began the study of Arabic, for she already had a new adventure in mind. The newly-weds took a house with grounds called Swaynesthorpe, in Surrey, and Agnes joined them there the following spring. A number of photographs exist showing the house, with the Gibsons and Agnes in an open carriage, Margaret in riding dress seated on a large bay.

Gibson's natural hesitancy was tempered by the twins' zealous approach to life. Before his marriage he had published only a few poems translated from the Spanish, which were included in Duffield's translation of *Don Quixote*. Now, with Margaret acting as editorial assistant, he brought out his own translation of Cervantes's *Journey to Parnassus*, and in 1885 an edition of the master's tragedy, *Numantia*. All three contributed to a new Belfast-based journal, the *Presbyterian Churchman*, which along with essays on such topics as 'Why are foreign preachers preferred in America?' and 'The Road to Rome, or Sayings and Doings of Ritualism', also made room for poetry. Agnes herself contributed two early poems, 'A Drunkard's Address to his Glass' and 'Sabbath School Teacher's Hymn'. Perhaps, more important, the twins learned from Gibson during this period what was involved in producing a translation and a scholarly edition of a text.

By July 1885 Gibson had sufficiently broken free of his cautious principles to join the twins on a tour of the Norwegian fjords to see the midnight sun. The party, not content with the view from the deck, decided to climb the cliffs on one of the islands. Much to Agnes and Margaret's surprise, Gibson insisted on making the ascent, even though the latter part required the aid of a rope. He felt quite unwell on reaching the top, but after recovering walked a mile and a half over the barren moor, and to see a sun that set, only to rise again immediately. His boldness was to prove imprudent.

Gibson's health collapsed once more, preventing Margaret from sharing Agnes's plans for another trip. Agnes's sights were now set on Cyprus. Her account of their travels in Greece had been published as *Glimpses of Greek Life and Scenery* in February 1884 and the following year in a Greek translation. Less a travel book than a piece of social and political commentary based on personal encounters with those they had met, it had been well received, especially in Greece, where Agnes's approving portrayal of Greek life and progress stood in contrast to the sneering tone adopted towards the young nation by most French and English writers of the day. Doors were now open to Agnes in Greek-speaking lands, and Cyprus was one such. The island was newly under British administration, and furthermore was peppered with the Orthodox monasteries whose monks had made the twins feel so welcome on their tour of Greece. Agnes believed that a book on Cyprus might enjoy some popularity. Grace, who was still teaching in London, would accompany her, and on the way they would visit St Catherine's Monastery at Mount Sinai. The monks of St Catherine's were also Greek-speaking, and by now Agnes had a smattering of Arabic that she could use with the Bedouin of the Sinai peninsula.

In logistical terms, a journey to Cyprus via Sinai made sense enough. Ships bound for Suez departed daily from French and English ports. Cyprus was not so far from Suez, and various local steamship lines called there. Furthermore, after their unhappy experience staying in Greek taverns, Agnes and Grace were convinced of the superiority of travelling with one's own tents. Tents, and dragomans accustomed to travelling with them, could not be found in Cyprus, but could be secured in Suez or Cairo with a view to proceeding on. And if they were going to Suez anyway, then why not take the opportunity to visit St Catherine's?

But what seemed to Agnes a natural progression appeared to James Gibson to be madness and folly – at least as far as Sinai was concerned. Far from a simple excursion to be appended to a Cyprus visit like a charm on a chain, Sinai was travel of a different order. The peninsula was a wilderness that had to be traversed by camels – animals they did not know. A fall or slight infection, even a case of dysentery, could be fatal. And there were bandits. He himself had been kidnapped while travelling there. Admittedly that was twenty years earlier, but it was only four years since Professor Henry Palmer of Cambridge had been murdered at Wadi Sudr, despite being an experienced Middle Eastern traveller and fluent Arabic speaker. Admittedly Palmer, travelling alone

Professor Heny Palmer

and disguised in Arab dress, was spying for the British government and carrying £20,000 in gold, but it was still a grim precedent.

Agnes was undeterred. In January 1886 she and Grace set out equipped with all the collateral needed for ladies travelling with camels, horses, donkeys and tents, including the newest sort of trekking rug cases, waterproof and strapped, 'in W. J. Adam's latest style' and Wahrmund's Arabic dictionary.

On board the Messageries Maritimes steamer bound from Marseilles to Suez, the passengers were as polyglot as they had been on the sisters' voyage to Egypt seventeen years earlier, but nationalities and the reasons for travel had changed. Instead of a few German tourists and southern Europeans seeking warmer air for consumptive lungs, they found Chinese, Japanese, Javanese and the Burmese Ambassador to Paris.

In 1870, its first year of operation, 436,000 tons of shipping passed through the Suez Canal – most of it British. After years of lordly disdain while the canal was under construction, the British could not afford to be diffident once it had opened. The canal had halved the travel time to India, and India was the life-blood of the Empire.

At the time of its completion, controlling interest of the canal had lain with Ismail, the Khedive of Egypt, shortly followed by Britain's rival, France. The British could not allow this situation to last and would not have to wait long to alter it. By 1875 the khedive was deep in debt, owing to extravagant expenditure on the canal and its opening ceremonies, and the British Prime Minister, Benjamin Disraeli, seized the moment. Overnight, and without consulting the French or his own queen, Disraeli secured a hefty loan from Baron Rothschild and bought the khedive's controlling interest in the canal. The French, who had gone to sleep in happy confidence of having their thumb on Britain's jugular, awoke to find that their arch-rivals had checkmated them. With the khedive's debts spiralling out of control, Egypt was placed, by her foreign-administered debt commission, under dual French and British control. A few years later, in 1882, the British took advantage of a nationalist uprising to invade. The Egypt towards which Agnes and Grace now sailed was firmly under British rule.

At their Suez hotel Agnes was beset by a series of urgent telegrams from her brother-in-law, James Gibson. They must not go on to St Catherine's. It would be reckless to attempt the desert crossing. Agnes's health might be up to it, but Grace's certainly was not. Grace was, after all, his cousin, and Agnes would be taking a grievous responsibility on her head if she proceeded. Agnes was not used to being told what to do, but in the end she relented. They could at least take the opportunity to visit the Wells of Moses, some nine miles down the Red Sea coast, where the children of Israel reputedly first touched the banks of Sinai after their dry-shod crossing of the parted waters.

Agnes and Grace hired as their guide Said Mohammed, their first Muslim dragoman. He turned out to be honest and excellent in every way, and a devout man. He had a copy of the New Testament, which he read every morning along with the Koran, insisting that the differences between his faith and Christianity were slight. Said Mohammed arranged the boat and Arab crew for their excursion to 'Ain Musa – a deep-bellied boat with a big sail. When the wind needed assistance, 'two men in white and blue shirts propelled it by running along the ledge of it from bow to stern and pushing their oars against the ground, singing a rhymed chant – "He is my hope, my Lord, he is my hope, my Lord, my beloved."' 'I should like to know,' wrote Agnes, 'why it is that Moslems bring their religion, imperfect as it is, into their daily life so much more than Christians do.'[1] *Habibi* (my beloved) seemed to her a startlingly tender word, resonant of the English 'baby' and sounding like an endearment of a mother to her child. She noted a man in another boat, prostrating himself in prayer, even while contending all alone with the waters and wind.

'Ain Musa was two hours' ride from where the boat put to land, and Agnes took the opportunity to try out a camel, which she found quite pleasant, its motion easier than a donkey's or a horse's. The width of the Red Sea at this point, she thought, refuted the theory that a natural strong tide could account for the famous parting. A 'tide which could leave the bed of such a gulf uncovered, even for a few minutes, would be as miraculous as the facts narrated in the Exodus'. She tried out her Arabic on the camel drivers with limited success.

The Well of Moses proved little more than a pool of brackish water, a few palms, some walled vegetable gardens and a shed serving as coffee house for the few travellers and Bedouin who passed by, but at least Agnes had now demonstrated to herself that she could ride a camel – 'I knew I could do it!' Above all, she had laid eyes on Sinai. She saw colours known to her previously only from Eastern pictures, cliffs with purple shadows, a 'pure-sapphire sky above' and cloud shadows flitting over the distant hills before them. The boatmen rowed them back to Suez, intoning their same tender chant.

It was January, ideal for Sinai but still too cold for travelling with tents in Cyprus, and so, with a delay forced upon them, Agnes and Grace decided to decamp to Cairo and Shepheard's Hotel. Said Mohammed went with them.

Cairo was more orderly than it had been seventeen years ago – the donkey boys touting for trade had been moved from the front of Shepheard's Hotel to a side street – and it was not the French but the English who were now everywhere to be found: soldiers, statesmen, businessmen, tourists. English families and civil servants en route to India filled Cairo's better hotels, and English tourists cruised the Nile. Agnes was by now acutely aware that colonial powers were not always liked by their subject peoples. 'No visitor to Cairo,' she wrote, 'can shut his eyes to the fact that our countrymen have, as a rule, failed to earn the love either of Europeans or of natives. Some would go so far as to say that they have earned hatred, and there is no use in our altogether disguising the fact.' With the Muslims this might be religious bigotry, and with the French it was clearly envy, but might there not be some cause why people do 'not always rejoice at being under British rule?' Agnes put some of the blame down to bad manners, citing the instance of two English families who sat opposite them at the table d'hôte of Shepheard's. Over seven weeks, for three hours a day, 'these people face us, and never once said good-morning, nor acknowledged our presence by a civil bow'. Of course they had had no formal introduction, but a nod would not have been out of place, since all were in a foreign land. Instead they 'gaze on the unintroduced world with a simple stony, British stare', while others:

(these are chiefly ladies) talk to the people they do know in a loud tone, completely ignoring the presence of anyone else in the room . . . Once, in my simplicity, I thought that the mission of Great Britain was to civilise the world; that wherever her flag floated, it would be the symbol not only of all that is just, but of all that is pure and of good report. I have not yet got rid of the notion that we are, on the whole . . . a more moral and a more sensible people than – let us say our Gallic neighbours. But my two months of observation in Cairo have shaken my faith in this.

Quite as shocking as cold discourtesy was the tone of weary frivolity. The English newspapers in Cairo complained that, between picnics and lawn-tennis matches, there was scarcely time for Egypt's British occupiers to prepare for the operas and balls of the evening. And the people who got up to this sort of thing, said Agnes, 'were – the male part of them – being paid by the people at home for serious work'! She also noted that few of the ladies, though waited on hand and foot, put their idle hours to any worthwhile use, such as assisting with the mission schools or consoling invalided soldiers.

Agnes would allow herself no such idleness. With eight weeks to fill in Cairo before Cyprus became warm enough for tent travel, she devoted herself to improving her Arabic. It would be necessary were she ever to go to Mount Sinai, which – despite having capitulated this time to Gibson – she was still determined to do. Early each morning she walked with Said Mohammed in the Esbekiah Gardens for practice in conversation. During the remainder of the day she attended the American Mission School as a student, sitting amongst the little girls for their lessons in arithmetic, spelling, grammar, astronomy and Bible history and 'taking my turn in reading and answering questions, and making myself a source of much amusement to the girls'. (The less linguistically ambitious Grace stayed in the hotel.) This method of study proved very successful. In London Agnes's Arabic lessons with Mr Habib Salmoné had been only once every two or three weeks, and the native Arabic speakers she had employed for conversation practice were so afraid of offending their wealthy employer that they failed to correct her grammar or pronunciation. The little girls who were her

Cairo classmates were not so shy. 'I marvel,' said Agnes, 'that I should have been allowed to study Dr Wright's grammar and to read the Kuran carefully twice before being made aware that . . . gutturals existed.'

Said Mohammed was the first Muslim with whom Agnes had conversed at length. He was well educated and well born, his sister having married a pasha who was for many years governor of Suez. He also had many religious views that were new to Agnes. He believed the forbidden fruit in the Garden of Eden was not the apple, but wheat, and that the Lord's promise of a 'Comforter' to his disciples referred, not to the Holy Spirit, but to the Prophet. He had a particular dislike of the Copts and would not allow that they were Egyptians. When Agnes pointed out that 'Copt' comes from the Greek for 'Egyptians' (*Egyptos*) he said, 'Well, they may be Egyptians, but they are not Muslims.' Agnes and Grace scandalised him by attending the wedding of a railway clerk who was not only a Copt, but also from the lower middle classes.

In general Western travellers were uncharitable towards Eastern Christians, their attitude epitomised by an article in the *Presbyterian Churchman* from about this time. It gives the following account of the children at the Cairo mission schools, one of which Agnes attended:

> It is a striking sight to enter the spacious room . . . filled with groups in their picturesque and many-coloured dresses, of all ranks, from the rich Bey's son escorted by a slave, to the blue-shirted, barefooted boy from the streets – and all complexions, from the dark-skinned Nubian or Abysinnian, to the fair Syrian . . .
>
> The creeds represented are as various as the ranks and nationalities; about half of both sexes are Moslem, the other half comprise Copts, Greek, Syrian Maronite or Romanists, and Armenians. All these, though nominally Christian, are lamentably corrupt churches, and the ignorance of the Divine truth is almost as great as among Moslems.[2]

Agnes was not so harsh on the Copts. Whatever their ritual excesses, at least – like Presbyterians – they stood rather than knelt to say their prayers. A Coptic schoolmaster told her, 'we don't want our girls to know too much . . . We don't want to change the customs of our fathers.' Agnes replied that such a custom must come from the Muslims and not the Gospels, because, although Paul said women should keep silent in church, 'he never said they were not to learn anything'. Yet her sympathy was also growing for the Muslims, who seemed in their own way to share the Presbyterian ethos of simple devotions, dedication to scripture and an abhorrence of idols.

Said Mohammed knew no Greek, and so could not act as their fixer in Cyprus, so in mid-March Agnes and Grace sailed from Alexandria to Beirut in the hope of finding a dragoman and putting together their expedition there. It was not easy. The captain of their ship told them Cyprus was not worth seeing, as did most fellow guests at the Hôtel d'Orient in Beirut. Even the French Consul, who frequented the hotel's restaurant, opined that the island was without interest and travel on it almost impossible: they would need an Arab dragoman and Arab servants if they wanted to make their way with tents, but none of these spoke Greek, the Cypriots' only language. Furthermore, good tents were in short supply.

Agnes resolved matters by renting the tents belonging to the Hôtel d'Orient, and employing its commissionaire, George Wakil, as dragoman. George was an Arab Christian of the Maronite sect, who said their services in Arabic but owed allegiance to the Pope in Rome. He had not served as a dragoman before, but was highly thought of in Beirut, exceedingly anxious to oblige them, and a natural polyglot, speaking English, French, German, Italian, and some Greek – all learned by ear. (It was only on the last day of their trip that they would learn he could neither read nor write.) Along with George, they hired an Arab cook and waiter and one Arab muleteer. They set sail for Cyprus and, once in Larnaca, hired in addition five Cypriot muleteers, each with three mules.

Floating in the Mediterranean under the bulk of Turkey's southern coast, Cyprus had been from time immemorial the staging post of empires: Persians, Egyptians, Greeks, Romans, Venetians and latterly, for 300 years, the Ottoman Turks had governed it. Now it was the turn of the British, who, by an arcane and secretive treaty of 1878, were not *ruling* the island, but *administering* it on behalf of the Sublime Porte. The British had no real interest in Cyprus itself and no fondness for the Turkish sultan on whose behalf they worked, but who was widely understood to be incompetent and corrupt. They were, however, anxious about Russia. If the crumbling Ottoman Empire were to collapse, then imperial Russia could pick off its former territories one by one. Russia could already menace India from the north and, if she controlled Constantinople and the Bosphorus, might threaten the Suez Canal. Cyprus, it was thought, could serve as a base to patrol British interests in the eastern Mediterranean: 'In taking Cyprus the movement is not Mediterranean; it is Indian,' Disraeli frankly admitted to the House of Lords. 'We have taken a step there which we think necessary for the maintenance of our Empire and for its preservation in peace.'[3]

In 1886 Cyprus was malarial, impoverished and depopulated (fewer than 200,000 inhabitants in 1878). There were hardly any roads and no network of guest houses. It was therefore unsurprising that Agnes and Grace were amongst the first lady travellers to visit the island since Aphrodite stepped out of the waves at Paphos.

Agnes found it enchanting – especially a place like Kyrenia, with pomegranates, lemons and blooming geraniums surrounded by olive trees, wheat and bean fields. By now she had some experience of how to proceed in Greek lands and, as she went, secured letters of intro-duction to various municipal officers and church dignitaries whom they visited in their circumnavigation of the island. (Mr Maurogordato, the governor of the prison, met them in Kyrenia; Mr Jolly, of the Imperial Ottoman Bank, entertained them in Nicosia).

As an imperial traveller, Agnes veered between two perspectives: British if defending the achievements of the Empire, Scottish if criticising it as the daughter of one of England's earliest acquisitions. She was sympathetic to the Greek Cypriot desire to unite with Greece, and critical of British attempts to make English the official language of the island – all these English administrators have studied Greek, she wrote, so why don't they speak it? Agnes was the first British visitor who could speak Greek to give an account of the island.[4]

But Agnes's cheery cameos of feminine self-sufficiency could not conceal the fact that Grace was not enjoying herself. She did not speak Greek with the Cypriots they met, nor could she converse readily with their dragoman, whose English was sparse. The mule drivers had ambitious ideas about how readily a lady in full skirts and riding side-saddle could pass through streams in spate. Grace was now fifty-five, and the trip was taxing, with extremes of temperature as they moved from coastal plains to the central mountains, which rose to more than 6,000 feet and were snow-capped for much of the year. At one point she was tossed head-first over the front of her mule, which then calmly walked over her. After this she took to walking the steeper and more difficult stretches.

The villagers were even more reclusive and unlettered than those in Greece. Agnes saw a glimmer of emotion when some village women sprinkled them with rose water, which she interpreted as a gesture of welcome; though more probably it was a ritual cleansing of any evil spirits the strangers might be bringing with them.[5] For intelligent conversation, Agnes relied on local schoolteachers and Orthodox monks.

They visited many churches and monasteries. Most venerable and

The Cyprus travelling party, showing Agnes and Grace

remote of all was the Monastery of Kykkos, high in the western mountains. The ascent was narrow, with steep drops on either side. Grace did much of the final stage on foot and when the monks, after a clamorous ringing of bells to mark their arrival, asked if there was anything they needed for lunch, she was quick to request wine. This would be her last adventure with Agnes.

Agnes herself, still full of energy, asked to go to evening prayer. She still had little sympathy for Eastern worship and none whatsoever for the veneration of the miraculous painting of the Virgin, said to have been painted by St Luke himself, around which the whole life of the monastery was based. She watched as priests robed in white silk brocade moved back and forth through the church and behind the screen separating the sanctuary from the nave, incensing all the icons. It seemed to her a scene from the Middle Ages, with traditions and repetitious prayers that were 'in danger of making the Word of God of no effect' and, even worse, of deluding the votaries who flocked there on account of the supposed miraculous powers of the painting. She could only hope that the monks were as deluded as the pilgrims they received.

For all her hesitations – and as far as she was concerned, 'there is no hiding the fact' that Eastern Christians 'still persist in image or idol worship' – Agnes wrote that the Greek Church 'has life in it, for it still looks to the sacred Scriptures as an infallible guide'. The monks had been the custodians of the Scriptures for millennia. They had preserved manuscripts and texts lost to the West and only now being studied by Western scholars. Most famous of these, she knew, was the Codex Sinaiticus, which Constantin von Tischendorf had recovered from St Catherine's Monastery at Mount Sinai, which Agnes was still determined to visit.

It was June 1886 when Agnes and Grace returned to England and, once back in Swaynesthorpe, Agnes was delighted to find that her sister's husband, despite his gloomy prognostications, was well – even ebullient. The only death during her absence had been that of Lappy, a puppy that Agnes had acquired the year previously during their visit to Lapland to see the Northern Lights. Here is but a small portion of her ponderous epitaph for the dog, followed by James Gibson's amused summary:

EPITAPH by Agnes Smith

Step gently, for the soil concealeth dust
That once was quick with bounding life and joy.
'Twas but a dog's; but ah! what strength of trust,
What wealth of love did cruel death destroy!
My little Lappie, may I only be
True to my God as thou wert true to me.

EPITAPH by James Gibson

Here lieth little Lappie;
He was a happy chappie;
And he made his mistress happy
For the best part of a year;

Beneath this bed of roses,
And many fragrant posies,
He quietly reposes;
O stranger! drop a tear.[6]

Agnes could see that James Gibson was her sister's destined soulmate, but, apart from being Scottish and good-looking, he was lacking some of the virtues with which she endowed the energetic heroes of her novels. Gibson was witty, loving and intelligent, but also prey to doubts about himself and possibly about his faith – flaws that Agnes would never permit. Nonetheless, when Gibson confessed that he thought the emblem of a broken column he had once seen on an Edinburgh gravestone an apt image for himself, she turned the comparison neatly: 'He could not then perceive that the column of his life, though then apparently shattered, was only receiving the blows of an unseen chisel, blows that were not only rounding it into a form of beauty, but were preparing for it a crown of leaves whose artistic completeness would be confessed by all who saw it.'[7]

Unfortunately Gibson's lifelong hypochondria was soon to be vindicated. On a visit that the three made to Ramsgate that October he got a cold, accompanied by flutterings of the heart. He had a bad night, but none of them thought his condition dangerous. In the morning he spent some time answering letters, reading *The Times* and enjoying a few jokes. He even sent his sister-in-law out to buy him some flannel underwear – 'he gave me directions about these,' Agnes wrote, 'quite in the tone of one who expects to wear them!'[8] But Gibson had died before she returned, attended by his distraught wife.

CHAPTER 9

The Cambridge antiquarian

Agnes was later to write that in the first months after James Gibson's death she 'never left Maggie alone'. After thirteen years of courtship and only three of married life, Margaret was desolate with grief. With Swaynesthorpe an echoing loneliness about them, it was essential to make a trip somewhere, even if not very far. In January 1887 they went for two weeks to Cambridge, lodging at the Bull Hotel.

The *Presbyterian Churchman* had recently carried an article on Cambridge written by its editor. This presented the city's ancient colleges, grassy courts and famous libraries in attractive terms. The editor praised the view of the colleges from 'the backs' beyond the river. He wrote of the mulberry tree planted by John Milton, the turret that had housed Erasmus, the instruments used by Isaac Newton, the paths walked by Francis Bacon and Cromwell, and the undergraduate rooms of Alfred, Lord Tennyson. Erudition hung round every staircase and lingered in every court. Moreover, Cambridge was a place for scholars of the Bible. Brooke Westcott and Fenton Hort had only recently given the world the first truly reliable edition of the Greek New Testament, and the famous Presbyterian scholar, William Robertson Smith, had moved to the town after his expulsion, on the grounds of heresy, from a professorship in Aberdeen.[1]

Neither was the visitor to Cambridge obliged to forgo material comforts. The resident population of some 1,600 young gentlemen required (according to the *Churchman*), along with 'intellectual food', the best in eating and drinking. The town's 30,000 inhabitants included 'publishers, booksellers, butchers, bakers, upholsterers, haberdashers. &c., &c.', all gathered around the university to profit from the life of the mind. Cambridge was salubrious in every way, especially for the rich and bookish.

On the last day of their visit the twins went with a friend to see the Geological Museum. When they found it closed, their friend suggested that they go to the Parker Library of nearby Corpus Christi College. There, amongst the banks of leather-bound volumes, the Fellow Librarian, Mr Samuel Savage Lewis, appeared.

It is not to be thought that Samuel Lewis spent his days stamping out books and patrolling the stacks. Indeed, to describe his place of work as 'a library' is to risk a misleading understatement. The Parker Library is a collection of priceless medieval and Renaissance manuscripts, papers and printed books brought together initially by Matthew Parker, chaplain to Henry VIII and later Archbishop of Canterbury. As one of Henry's inner circle, Parker had been able to take advantage of the king's dissolution of the monasteries to snoop around their libraries and remove many of the choicest treasures (giving rise to the English expression 'a nosey Parker'). Something like three-quarters of the Anglo-Saxon manuscripts in existence are in the Parker Library. Also in its holdings are the St Augustine Gospels, a sixth-century manuscript believed to have been brought to England in 597 by Augustine, sent from Rome to convert the English to Christianity; and many other rarities of great interest to Agnes and Margaret.

As Samuel Lewis discoursed on the high points of the Parker collection, he and Agnes became embroiled in a heated debate on the correct pronunciation of ancient Greek. Neither party budged, but the conversation disclosed a startling range of similarities and shared interests – in Greek (ancient and modern), in travel and even in mutual friends in Eastern cities. Lewis invited them back to his rooms for nine o'clock the following morning, with the promise to seek out some illustrations for Agnes's book on Cyprus, which was about to go to press.

Few professors wish to be remembered by the derisory nicknames coined by their students, but such was the fate of Samuel 'Satan' Lewis. He occupied a warren of rooms that had been part of a monastic structure pre-dating the founding of the college. One of his windows looked not to the outside, but directly down into the chancel of St Bene't's Church. Passing this window and noticing a wedding taking place at the altar below, Lewis peered down to have a look. The bride chanced to look up and saw Lewis, 'a notoriously ugly man with a straggling black beard peering down into the gloom of the Church from above'; she cried 'Satan!' and fainted.[2] The story did the rounds of the undergraduates and the name stuck, reinforced by Lewis's dishevelled manner of dress, strange mannerisms and habit of leaving for distant parts of Europe and the Middle East as soon as the university term had ended.

Samuel Savage Lewis was in some ways the antithesis of the melancholic James Gibson. Gibson was diffident and slow-moving, quiet and withdrawn. By contrast, Lewis was an energumen of activity: librarian and keeper of manuscripts, clergyman and collector of antiquities. During vacations he had travelled as far as Russia and Turkey in search of items for his collection. 'He seemed to us,' said Agnes, recounting their first meeting, 'like someone we had read of in a book, but never expected to meet in actual life, except perhaps in some far away Greek convent, where familiarity with the records of past ages might have aroused and sharpened the intellect of some cenobitic monk.'[3]

But Samuel Lewis was not a monk and neither was he married. The twins invited him to visit them at Swaynesthorpe during the Easter holidays.

Cambridge, with or without the presence of Samuel Lewis, was an attractive prospect. The city was high-minded, but at the same time more progressive than its rival, Oxford, with growing prestige in the natural sciences. The recently deceased Charles Darwin and his disciple Thomas Huxley, both of them religious sceptics, were its tutelary deities. The editor of the *Presbyterian Churchman* had noted watchfully Huxley's distinct influence. He was constantly on the Boards of Selectors that nominated the natural-science professors and, with his secretaries, Michael Foster and Gabriel Stokes ('profanely denominated, in consequence of their Christian names, "the two archangels".'), had virtual run of the Royal Institute in London.[4]

In 1871 Cambridge had dropped its requirement that all those holding university posts be bona-fide members of the Church of England. This opened the way for religious sceptics, but also for adherents of other faiths and members of other Christian churches. Presbyterians from Scotland and Ireland were coming to Cambridge in increasing numbers, especially to study mathematics and the sciences. Their small congregation was growing, but the *Churchman* fretted about defections:

> Nowhere perhaps has Presbyterianism a more mournful record than in Cambridge. Men come up from Scotland and Ireland and England, many of them Presbyterian ministers' sons, who have been brought up on Presbyterian money and nursed by the good old Church, but for the sake of a college fellowship, before the fellowships were open to dissenters, or now for the sake of a little social advancement, they cast their Presbyterianism to the winds, and try hard to lose both their accent and their religion ... Where so many traitors to Presbyterianism are to be found, all snug, and a few famous, it will be hard work to raise the Presbyterian standard, and secure a decent muster round it.[5]

What the town needed were Protestant leaders: 'men who regard Presbyterianism as a matter of principle and not a mere matter of taste; as a system affording the requisite guarantees in doctrines and discipline against the Rome-ward and the Sceptical tendencies of our time.' And if men, then why not also some leading Presbyterian women?

As well as her manly Presbyterian heroes, Agnes had peopled her romantic fiction with villains. Among her favoured types were Anglican clergyman (vain, snobbish and condescending to women) and collectors of antiquities (interested more in the dead than the living). Samuel Lewis was both, but there the resemblance to caricature stopped. Far from being obsessed with his appearance (a tribal marking of Anglican 'ritualists', according to the *Presbyterian Churchman*), Lewis was careless to a fault. He had also been, from 1875 to 1877, a Latin lecturer to the Association for the Higher Education of Women: 'one of the first to believe in the future success of the movement, and sacrificing much of his time to it with the utmost zeal and devotion,' wrote Agnes.[6]

However fascinated he was by ancient coins, texts and treasures, no one could be more interested in life and living than Samuel Lewis. He had a particular knack of making friends and keeping them, with all kinds of people. With a few minutes to spend on a foreign railway platform, he would strike up conversation with a porter. If the porter did not share a language, Lewis would charm him into silent communication by showing him photographs of Cambridge, which he always took abroad with him.

Early setbacks had made him eager to live each moment to the fullest. While a student, the sudden failure of his eyesight had obliged him to abandon studies at Cambridge for an agricultural apprenticeship in the nearby village of Shepreth. In his cruel exile from scholarship he despaired over his future; nevertheless, he was determined to succeed as a farmer and kept diaries that listed furrows ploughed, pigs and bullocks sold, muck spread and colts broken. He went on to manage a farm in Canada, but after three years in Quebec farming sweet corn and beetroot, his father, concerned that he was selling his talents too cheap, called Lewis home. At first he tried to work as a tutor, but headaches and extreme difficulty in reading for any length of time ended that. Reluctantly he returned to farming and secured a job on the Prince Consort's model farm in Windsor – monotonous work for the most part, though sometimes he was deputed to attend foreign visitors, for which duty his competence in French, German and Italian made him ideal. His impatience was reflected in despondent diary entries, written in Greek. He had been in Windsor four years when, in 1864, an advance in surgical technique made possible an operation that restored much of his sight and even gave him, he claimed, the ability to see in the dark. So he returned to Cambridge and finally took his degree, aged thirty-six, and was in the same year elected Fellow and Lecturer in Classics at Corpus Christi College. The following year Lewis, who until recently had been unable to read properly, was made Fellow Librarian.

Samuel was forty-nine years old when he and Agnes met; she was

forty-three. Since regaining his sight he had built up an impressive
collection of antiquities, which he kept in his college rooms: coins,
engraved gemstones from ancient rings (intaglios), magical amulets
and pottery. He was delighted to show these to visitors. An American
visitor in the 1880s recalled that every surface was covered with Greek
and Roman vases, and 'on this and every side' there were piles of
manuscript papers. A door in one corner of his room led up to a gallery
some forty feet in length filled with objects from Lewis's collection. A
spiral staircase led down to 'the crypt', which contained scores of
Bronze Age fish-hooks, Greek pots and ancient oil lamps. Another
door off the gallery led to the room in which his coins – more than
7,000 – were kept in elaborately designed wooden cabinets, one of
which was in the shape of a Greek vase whose cross-sections pulled out

Samuel Savage Lewis

as circular coin trays.
Before another, designed
like a Greek temple,
'mysterious rites were
wont to be performed'
before its doors could be
opened.

Lewis astounded his
guests by making tea for
them *himself*, and by
having to hand a clothes
brush with which he
brushed their coats
where they had whited
themselves against the
walls of his narrow
plastered passages. He
kept a revolver though
he confessed he no more
expected a burglar than a
ghost of one of the
monks who had once

inhabited his quarters. On serving tea he asked them, not which tea they would prefer, but whether they would like to drink it out of Sèvres, Dresden, Berlin, Worcester or Derby china – all of which he collected.[7]

Samuel was clearly quite as taken with Agnes as she was with him, and by the time of his Easter visit to Swaynesthorpe had discovered a number of other connections between his family and hers, including the fact that his sister had briefly been at school with the sisters. He pressed tickets for a June musical concert upon the twins. By 4 August, Agnes and Samuel were engaged.

The pair were married at Swaynesthorpe on 12 December 1887, just under a year after they'd first met.

The newly-weds took up residence in Harvey Road, one of the first streets of houses built to accommodate married lecturers. It ran along the perimeter of Cambridge, with the university's cricket pitch next door and fields of cattle beyond it. Margaret, who had given up Swaynesthorpe, lived with them, as did Grace Blyth, who was now retired.

Until recently only professors and the masters of the colleges had been allowed to marry. The Fellows were mostly obliged by statute to be Anglican clergymen and to live in their colleges as single men. When a Fellow tired of that life or fell in love, he would resign his fellowship, marry and usually become the rector of one of the Anglican parishes, or 'livings', to which his college had power of appointment. But by the mid-nineteenth century the old Cambridge system was creaking, partly due to the influx of scientists. Many were not Anglican clergymen and, hoping to make their whole career in research and teaching, did not relish life as bachelors. After the university dropped its requirement of celibacy in 1860, the colleges, one by one, followed suit. According to Ada Keynes, mother of the economist John Maynard Keynes and neighbour of Agnes, Margaret and Samuel in Harvey Road, it was the need to attract scientists that moved the colleges to reform. Much of what was expected of bachelors persisted, however, especially concerning the amount of time a man would give to his college.

There were other distinguished neighbours in Harvey Road. Richard Tetley Glazebrook (later Sir Richard), a physicist at the Cavendish Laboratories, lived at number seven. Opposite the Keynes lived the newly appointed Professor of Music, the composer Charles Villiers Stanford (later Sir Charles). Mrs Keynes recalled how Professor Stanford stood at the top of his steps and raged against the hideous sounds made by the Italian organ grinder and his monkey, while the children gave him pennies to go on playing.[8] Down the road was a young couple, Francis Burkitt and his wife Persis, he an up-and-coming biblical scholar and she a great beauty: 'rather flamboyant,' recalled Mrs Keynes, with 'wonderful feathers', presumably referring to articles of dress. Around the corner on Gresham Road lived the Burkitts' great friends, Professor Robert Bensly, the Lord Almoner's Professor of Arabic, and his wife, both in their sixties.

After a honeymoon in Greece, spent à trois with Margaret, married life in Harvey Road was strictly rationed by Lewis. This was partly owing to his hearty dislike of Grace (a feeling she reciprocated); but Lewis was also obliged by the terms of his Fellowship to sleep in college five nights per week and shuttled continually between Corpus Christi and home: Harvey Road for breakfast each morning at eight o'clock, back to college by nine, returning home for lunch at half-past one, often accompanied by scholarly guests. Afternoons were devoted to correspondence on behalf of the library, dinner had to be taken in college, before Lewis retired to his rooms and wrote more letters, often in response to requests for advice or pastoral matters.

Another reason for the late hours and early starts was Lewis's difficulty in sleeping at night. Agnes discovered after their marriage that his bed in Corpus Christi had inwardly disintegrated. There was a large hole in the mattress, so that he had to sleep curled around the hole, in so far as this was possible. His college cleaner colluded in Lewis's indifference to discomfort, and so nothing had been done. Short, restless nights were part of his routine without, apparently, affecting his temperament or diminishing his energy.

At weekends Lewis considered himself obliged to act as a locum in Cambridgeshire parishes for absent clergymen. He was used to unfamiliar rectories across the countryside and preaching to unknown congregations. Agnes always went along. 'It was as well,' she later wrote, 'for our Sundays in country rectories were almost the only reminiscences of wedded life in England which I now have to look back upon, and very pleasant indeed they are.' Vacations they spent together, usually travelling, sometimes accompanied by Margaret.

Lewis liked travel just as much as Agnes. She noted that whenever they were on a train abroad, Lewis would ask the stationmaster at every stop whether there were any unusual local coins to be had. Stationmasters of the day apparently kept them on their person for just such requests. Bartering accounts for Lewis's practice of carrying his gemstones (often many of them) loose in the pockets of his greatcoat as he travelled.

He bought extensively at auction and through dealers, mostly in Paris and London, but also via British dealers settled in the Middle East, who notified him of sales and finds. His gemstones, carved to be set in rings, were sought after more for the subject matter of the carving than for their artistry – a Roman carnelian gemstone (second century AD) showing Artemis wearing a short tunic and holding a bow; a pale yellow citrine (first century AD) with Aphrodite grasping her left foot with her right hand, and so the list goes on, for dozens and dozens of gems – making up one of the finest collections of Greco-Roman intaglios in Britain.[9] At the time of his marriage Lewis was spending up to £1,000 a year on his collection. It may be wondered how a man with no family money behind him was able, within fifteen or so years of starting a collection, to spend so lavishly. The answer is that he had built up capital by trading and dealing in antiquities. He would never spend his wife's money on his pots and gems.

Lewis was among the first to take an interest in Jewish and early Christian archaeology. He collected coins from the cities of Palestine, and one of his most important pieces was a Jewish silver shekel, dated year five of the First Jewish Revolt against Rome, that is AD 70.[10]

Some of his rarest gems were Christian Roman stones, including a fourth- or fifth-century AD green jasper showing Christ bound to the cross, draped in a long tunic and flanked by standing figures and an

Alpha and Omega. Another stone of banded agate shows fishermen pulling in their nets and is inscribed IHX, for Jesus Christ.

Many of Samuel's trips with Agnes were to visit friends he had made and kept since his purblind days on the Prince's model farm – in Normandy they attended the wedding of a son of a prosperous farmer; and in Algeria they visited the owner of some vineyards. But they travelled simply for pleasure, too, visiting classical sites in Sicily, Greece and Asia Minor. Sometimes, for the sake of seeing a rare mosaic or ruin, they travelled in rough carts, over even rougher roads, and slept on straw-filled mattresses in country inns, or the spare room of the stationmaster. Locals discovering a noted authority in their midst would often bring Samuel items of antique interest for appraisal.

Travelling in Calabria, they visited Rossano in order to see a recently recovered ancient treasure: the sixth-century Codex Purpureus Rossanensis, one of the most ancient illuminated manuscripts of the Gospels, which had lain hidden in the cathedral vestry for hundreds of years, coming to light only in 1879. Arriving unannounced and without introduction, Lewis charmed the cathedral officials with photographs of Cambridge and the explanation that he was the custodian of the Gospels of St Augustine. Eventually he and Agnes were shown to the house of the archdeacon, where the manuscript was kept, insecurely, in a cardboard box in a bedroom. Lewis, worried it might easily go up in flames, started negotiations to buy it for £1,000 – whether for himself or for the Parker Library is unclear – but the plan came to naught, despite his subsequently making a late-night train journey across Calabria, alone and with £1,000 on his person. Still, he was more often successful than not, and for Agnes his efforts would be an apprenticeship in collecting.

Since few academics could afford to travel as far and often as did the Lewises, Agnes often found herself with little assignments. In Algeria she collected snails for someone making a study of them back in Cambridge. She carried them in a small unlined basket with a supply of semolina for their nourishment, with the result that her dress often had a white dusting.

But her foremost project was now her marriage. Samuel's travels became her own. She wrote the occasional article on these for the *Presbyterian Churchman*, but she did not begin any new books. She kept house, of course with a number of servants, and arranged hospitality for Samuel and his many friends and foreign visitors, some of whom were surprised to find a table where Italian and Greek could be spoken as well as French and German. Often she found herself with no more than five minutes' notice to provide lunch for the daughter of a duke or the French Ambassador.

Cambridge of the time was a carefully graded society. Gwen Raverat, a granddaughter of Charles Darwin and thus a child member of the Cambridge intellectual aristocracy, described a dinner party of the early 1890s as she remembered it:

> The regular round of formal dinner-parties was very important in Cambridge. In our house the parties were generally of twelve or fourteen people, and everybody of dinner-party status was invited strictly in turn. The guests were seated according to the Protocol, the Heads of Houses ranking by the dates of the foundations of their colleges, except that the Vice-Chancellor would come first of all. After the Masters came the Regius Professors in the order of their subjects. Divinity first; and then the other Professors according to the dates of the foundations of their chairs, and so on down all the steps of the hierarchy. It was better not to invite too many important people at the same time, or the complications became insoluble to hosts of only ordinary culture. How could they tell if Hebrew or Greek took precedence, of two professorships founded in the same year? And some of the grandees were very touchy about their rights, and their wives were even more easily offended.[11]

Neither the twins nor Samuel quite fit into the Harvey Road 'set'. Agnes and Margaret, since girlhood committed to physical fitness, surprised their neighbours by exercising on parallel bars in their back garden.[12] Mrs Keynes recalled Samuel as slightly odd, but, she believed,

'very good at his work'. In a telling phrase, she said that Samuel and
Agnes Lewis were 'outside our circle rather'.[13]

As it was, they stayed in Harvey Road for only two years, during
which time they had a new house built for them – that is, for Agnes,
Margaret and Samuel. Grace, at Samuel's insistence, could no longer
be part of the household. The twins bought her a substantial house
with gardens on the road to the nearby village of Trumpington, where
she lived, comfortably attended by servants, but conveniently distant
from their new residence.

'Castlebrae' stood near the river at the foot of Cambridge's only hill,
Castle Hill. Samuel called the place, which he partly designed, 'the hill-
side hut'. Their Presbyterian friends called it 'a lordly pleasure house'.
The less charitably inclined mocked it as aping a Master's lodge.
Certainly it was grand. A gravel sweep led from the street past a

Castlebrae

coachman's cottage to an impressive red-brick façade. Two wings flanked a central tower surmounting a porte cochère. Agnes and Margaret planted pine trees on the hill behind to remind them of Scotland.

The house was designed for scholarship and sociability: the whole ground floor could be opened up into one space for large parties. Glass-fronted cabinets in the hall displayed the best of Samuel's collection, and the large dining room had French doors that opened onto the gardens. The fireplace in the dining room was decorated with romantic scenes from the legend of King Arthur's court, with the letters A and S entwined. Agnes, Margaret and Samuel each had a separate study, and a circular stairwell in the tower accommodated exercise ropes suspended from the ceiling, on which the sisters could take daily exercise in privacy. In a roundel on the tower face Samuel placed a terracotta plaque bearing the insignia from his favourite intaglio ring – a draped female figure with the motto *Spes*, meaning Hope.

Besides Samuel's large acquaintance, the twins had friends of their own, mostly Presbyterian, for despite Agnes having married an Anglican clergyman, the twins' commitment to their denomination and its advance on the Cambridge scene remained undiminished. As early as 1888 Margaret had entered the fray, writing anonymously in reply to a piece in a local newspaper that had the temerity to describe Presbyterianism as a 'mere sect', whose members would be well advised to join the Church of England. She signed herself 'A Cambridge Presbyterian'.

Gradually, since 1871 noncomformists were gaining access to college Fellowships that were once restricted to Anglicans, and now a number of Scots and Irish Presbyterians, many of them scientists, were finding their way into university positions. When Agnes and Margaret moved to the city in 1887, this nascent community was still holding services in the Guildhall, having no church building of its own. What it lacked in bricks and mortar was made up in intellect. In its ranks (until his death in 1879) had been James Clerk Maxwell, one of the century's most distinguished physicists. And now amongst the worshippers were Sir Robert Ball, formerly Astronomer Royal of Ireland and presently Lowndean Professor of Astronomy and Geometry at Cambridge;

Professor Alexander (or Alick) Macalister, a Dubliner and the Professor of Anatomy, and Professor Donald MacAlister (no near relation), a medical doctor and Fellow of St John's College. All three of these men, and their equally intelligent wives, became close friends of Agnes and Margaret.

A jewel in the crown for Cambridge Presbyterians – if not an uncontroversial figure – was Professor William Robertson Smith. He had been five years in Cambridge as Professor of Arabic and University Librarian when the twins first arrived. Smith was near in age to Agnes and Margaret and of similar background, but in some ways he was an odd friend for two ladies of soundly orthodox views. There were those back in Scotland who would gladly have seen his head on a pike, as an all-but-convicted heretic and corrupter of the young. Robertson Smith eventually became a powerful advocate and ally for Agnes and Margaret. For this reason, and because his story says so much both of the background from which Agnes and Margaret had emerged and of the world into which they were now moving, it deserves special treatment here.

CHAPTER 10

Heresy and mortality

The year 1887 saw the start of a heresy trial that would provide front-page news in Scotland for six years. At its centre was William Robertson Smith, a young Professor of Theology in Aberdeen, and an article he wrote on 'the Bible' for that most trusted of Victorian oracles, the *Encyclopaedia Britannica*.

That a young teacher of Old Testament and oriental languages, whose class rarely exceeded six pupils, should attract such notoriety is surprising. Equally so is the fact that this man – the product of a devout upbringing in one of Scotland's most conservative denominations, and himself a faithful evangelical Christian – should in later life become midwife to James Frazer's *Golden Bough* and a decisive influence on both Émile Durkheim and Sigmund Freud.

Robertson Smith's father was a Free Church minister in the village of Keig, near Aberdeen. He supplemented his stipend by taking in three or four boarders, who were schooled with his own children at home. The atmosphere was one of high-minded and sober Presbyterian joy; in winter the pupils would run on the spot on the icy flagstones in the hall in anticipation of lessons due to begin at eight o'clock. These consisted entirely of algebra, classical languages and biblical study. Aged fourteen, William went to the University of Aberdeen, taking every prize to be had. He then went on to study for Free Church ministry at the New College in Edinburgh, during which time he made two extended study visits to Germany. At just twenty-three years old he was appointed Professor of Hebrew, Oriental Languages and Exegesis of the Old Testament at the Free Church's

College in Aberdeen. There, with a few students, he studied Arabic and comparative religion, and was persuaded to provide articles on religious topics for the Ninth Edition of the *Encyclopaedia Britannica*.

In a contentious period when divergent views on biblical truth abided in uneasy proximity, the editors wanted articles that would supply solid, uncontroversial knowledge. But what might qualify as 'uncontroversial' was fast becoming a matter of debate. For example, the contributor who wrote on 'Abraham' in Volume I included the information that Abraham's father lived at Haran until the age of 205. The editor supposed that Robertson Smith was a sensible choice for a contributor, since he understood German scholarship and had actually met many of the greatest German biblical scholars of the day. As a professor at a conservative Free Church college he would, the editor supposed, present modern German thinking in a form acceptable to the Scottish and English public – that is, conservatively. He misjudged his man.

Volume II of the *Encyclopaedia Britannica* appeared in 1875, including Robertson Smith's articles 'Angels' and 'The Bible'. The latter, a key article, was a young man's *tour de force*: clear and confident, but written in a coldly analytical tone that was startling to readers who believed the Scriptures to be divinely inspired and wholly inerrant, down to the smallest details.

Robertson Smith assumed, without explanation, that the books of the Bible should be read historically and developmentally. He denied that the Gospels were written by the Apostles (as most faithful then believed) and pointed out that the genuineness of the letter known as 'Second Peter' had been doubted even by Erasmus and Calvin. It was by no means simply a liberal tirade, and many radical scholars also suffered from the young man's searing analysis.[1] He might have evaded real trouble, but for his views on the Old Testament. Robertson Smith declared that the so-called 'Books of Moses' (Genesis, Exodus, Leviticus, Numbers and Deuteronomy) were not written by Moses, as even Jesus seemed to believe, but by many hands over perhaps a thousand years. He insisted that the religious institutions of Israel were not static, but 'the fruit of a long contest for purity of religion', and that different strands of writing in the Old Testament books indicated different sources and concerns. It followed that the Book of Deuteronomy was not, as its opening verses declared, the last words 'that Moses spoke to all Israel beyond the Jordan', conveyed to us without scribal error since his day, but reflected the later thoughts of the Prophets. Robertson Smith's readings suggested that the events in the desert surrounding Moses's receipt of the Law never actually occurred, but were inventions of later legislators – not with intent to mislead, but as a legal fiction. This contrivance, as Smith explained, 'is no deceit, but a convention which all parties understand'.[2]

Maybe all parties understood this in ancient Israel, but it was not so in Scotland of 1875. These theories were not unknown to Scottish scholars, but they certainly had not been advanced publicly. As far as most Scots were concerned, any doubts about the inspired authorship of the Bible were rumours put about by enemies of true religion.

For a time nothing happened, but in March 1876 the *Edinburgh Evening Courant* published a review of the biblical entries of the *Encyclopaedia Britannica*. This consisted of a highly critical tour of Robertson Smith's main propositions, and ended with reproach for the editors of the *Encyclopaedia*, 'a publication which will be admitted without suspicion into many a religious household and many a carefully guarded library'. The editors were warned against contributors who 'pass off rationalist speculations as ascertained facts'.[3]

With disquiet on all sides, a committee set up to look into the young professor's views produced a damning report. Principal Robert Rainy of New College, Edinburgh, and then Moderator of the Free Church, met Robertson Smith hoping to defuse the situation. Rainy's admiration for Robertson Smith's ability was overlaid with forebodings of its effect on Free Church sensibilities, especially in the Highland strongholds where the slightest aspersion upon the Bible was a damnable abomination. Had Robertson Smith been an obscure provincial minister, some quiet inebriation with heterodox notions might have been overlooked, but he was already an influential teacher. Rainy attempted to procure a retraction and had even composed a letter of apology, to which Robertson Smith only needed to append his signature.

But the young professor saw no reason to apologise for complaints that had not even been clearly formulated. For good measure he denounced Professor Charteris, who had written the damning review, as one who 'expressed himself with so little knowledge and so great an air of authority that one seemed to hear the voice of a raw preacher thrust for party ends into a Professor's chair'.[4] Accused of contradicting the Westminster Confession, the benchmark of Presbyterian orthodoxy, Robertson Smith asked his critics to point out exactly where he had done so and undertook to refute them point by point. In 1877 he was suspended on full pay and his heresy trial began.

A letter to the editor of the *Scotsman*, written by the Reverend Alex McCraw of Kilbogie in 1877, gives some idea of the conservative temper of the time. In the face of progressive scholarship, McGraw

William Robertson Smith

wrote that since the Hebrew language was not necessary to understanding Divine truth, and often led to unsound views on the authority of the Word of God, it should no longer be taught in Free Church colleges. Another letter followed, from a McGraw cousin, suggesting that logic, metaphysics, science, philosophy, Greek, French and German should similarly be expunged, for what 'are *we* poor creatures, to take upon us to say anything beyond what is written, and which all the best men that went before us believed?'[5] William Cunningham, a former Principal of New College, wrote, 'Holy Spirit not merely superintended the [biblical] writers so as to preserve them from all errors, but suggested to them the words in which the communication was to be conveyed.'[6] However, Robertson Smith was confident that he could persuade any opponent through rational argument. Photographs show him posing with a look of truculent amusement. Home schooling had given him confidence, but perhaps not tact: one reminiscence tells of him as a guest, who 'at dinner the previous evening instructed our host . . . in agriculture and the management of estates, put me right to Roman law, and convicted two other gentlemen of obvious ignorance, each upon his own subject – and all after spending the Saturday afternoon playing tennis like a demon to the discomfiture of both sexes and every age'.[7]

In good Calvinist tradition, Robertson Smith was convinced that one should stand up for what he knew to be true, and this made him a troublesome man. He launched himself into his trial with enthusiasm, seeing it as a chance to free his church from its Babylonian captivity to an unscientific reading of Scripture. Rainy decided that in these circumstances Robertson Smith must be sacrificed.

If Rainy had a low view of him, then Robertson Smith thought even less of Rainy. He wrote to a friend, 'I don't think that slimy cold blooded reptile Rainy will stop till he has got the whole Church into a hole from which it can't get out again. He must be assassinated.' Formally the charge against Robertson Smith was that of denying tenets of the Westminster Confession, the framing document of the Presbyterian Church. But his accusers encountered a difficulty: nowhere did the Confession ever actually assert that Moses had written the Pentateuch, or have much at all to say about the authorship and dating of the biblical books. At hearings Robertson Smith was surrounded by conservatives determined to be rid of him, but he also had many supporters vociferously present in the galleries. The trial provided lively copy for the Scottish newspapers over many months. Much to the annoyance of Principal Rainy, Robertson Smith was hugely productive during his suspension. He made the most of his free time and celebrity by giving lectures, aimed at clarifying his views, to audiences averaging 1,800 in Edinburgh and Glasgow.[8] A string of articles from his pen continued to appear in the *Encyclopaedia Britannica*, some of them as liable to enrage his critics as the infamous essay on 'The Bible'. He seemed to view the whole process as an opportunity to provide the Scottish nation with a challenging refresher course on the latest biblical criticism.

The heresy charge failed, but a lesser verdict was handed down, condemning Robertson Smith for 'a culpable lack of sympathy with the reasonable anxieties of the Church as regards the bearing of critical speculation on the integrity and authority of Scripture'.

Robertson Smith was dismissed from his professorship, but was re-employed almost immediately as co-editor of the *Encyclopaedia Britannica* in Edinburgh. Soon afterwards his elderly colleague died and Robertson Smith was left as sole editor. He embraced the work with characteristic vigour and was largely responsible for seeing the ninth edition into print, writing more than 200 articles himself, including 'Levites', 'Messiah', 'Sacrifice', 'Eve', and 'Animal Worship'. His new job enabled him to commission articles from leading continental scholars and to introduce their ideas to the English-speaking world. At the same time he continued to work on Semitic scholarship and made several lengthy visits to the Middle East, at times travelling incognito dressed as an Arab. In 1883, after Professor Edward Palmer was murdered at Sinai, Robertson Smith was prevailed upon to succeed him as Professor of Arabic at Cambridge.

He was a welcome addition to the small Presbyterian community in Cambridge. Although never invited to preach, he was admired by many who did not share his more radical views – Agnes and Margaret, for instance, who firmly believed in the historical truth of the Moses story.

It was through Robertson Smith that Agnes and Margaret became friends with another great Cambridge exotic, Solomon Schechter, and his wife Mathilde. Later to be revered as a builder of American Jewry, Schechter was at the time the Cambridge Reader in Rabbinics. Born in Romania and brought up in the poverty of the *shtetl*, the young Schechter so loved his studies that he ran away from home to go to school. After rabbinical training in Vienna and a stint as a tutor in Berlin, he was persuaded by Claude Montefiore, a young scion of a British banking family and one of his tutees, to move to England. There his brilliance was quickly recognised and, in 1890, Robertson Smith persuaded him to come to Cambridge, now accompanied by Mathilde, a toddler and a new baby. Robertson Smith secured for Schechter membership at his own college, Christ's, and even instructed the college cooks on kosher cuisine for him.

Schechter threw himself headlong into Cambridge life. 'Nothing,' wrote the University Librarian, Francis Jenkinson, 'could give a sufficient notion of him to a person who never saw him.'[9] A prodigious scholar who read all books of theological interest, including Christian ones, that came to the library, Schechter was able to adapt socially to his new English setting while maintaining a spirited defence of traditional Jewish piety. He could befriend almost anyone with whom he felt a common spirit. While still in Vienna, he had learned English in order to read George Eliot and French in order to read Voltaire, whom he honoured as a campaigner against religious intolerance. He told his children that Abraham Lincoln, though not exactly Jewish, had a 'Jewish spirit' in his passion for truth and his desire to keep his country united. In his rooms he kept a photograph of the founder of Presbyterianism, John Knox, another of his religious heroes who fought for what he believed was true. He was one of the few (Robertson Smith was another) to win the affection of the reclusive Cambridge anthropologist James Frazer, author of *The Golden Bough*.

The Schechters were famously generous with their hospitality, and at their home in Cambridge they welcomed Christians as well as Jews, senior professors, students and local people. Religious allegiance was no bar: Mathilde became close friends with Mary Kingsley – a young Darwinian and sceptic who would later become famous as an indomitable lady traveller and pioneer of African studies. Mrs Schechter introduced Mary to Agnes and Margaret.

All these people were in and out of one another's houses and lives: a kind of inner circle of Cambridge outsiders. Mathilde translated German poetry with Mary Kingsley. Agnes and Margaret instructed Mary on independent travel. With Alick Macalister, the sisters incubated an even more important plan.

Since the 1870s some leading figures in the English Presbyterian Church had dreamed of their own college in one of the old university towns. Cambridge, with its strong Puritan past, was naturally more attractive than Oxford, and by the 1880s increasing numbers of Scottish Presbyterians were studying or working there. The small and ill-resourced Presbyterian college in Queen Square, London, was not attracting enough students – on average only three a year – or training them to the exacting standards Presbyterians expected of their preachers. The Cambridge idea also presented an evangelical oppor-tunity, some thought, of converting Anglicans from amongst the undergraduate population. Students, including many Anglicans, already came in great numbers to hear fine Presbyterian preachers like the twins' childhood mentor, Robertson of Irvine, a frequent visitor in his earlier years, and were enchanted by the pulpit oratory. But above all other objectives many, including Agnes and Margaret, believed that the church's ministers must be educated in a bastion of Bible-text scholarship, and this meant Cambridge: Westcott and Hort had both taught there, and now Robertson Smith. By 1891, the twins and Alick Macalister were hatching a plot to buy some local farmland and offer it to the Church as the site of a college. But all this was brought to a stop.

Over Easter of 1891 Samuel and Agnes visited a clerical friend in the village of Somersham, near Oxford. It was scarcely a holiday, since Lewis preached twice on Good Friday, visited friends in Oxford on Saturday, and on Easter Sunday assisted at one early service and then preached at another. On Easter Monday he and Agnes inspected Banbury Cross and played hide and seek amongst the ruins at Kenilworth Castle. The next day, travelling home, they had a forty-minute wait for a connecting train at Oxford, but Lewis could not let forty minutes saunter by vacantly. He settled Agnes in the tea room and hastened into town on an errand, returning just in time to catch his train. He had to run across the bridge to reach the right platform just before the train pulled out. No sooner had he settled down in the compartment next to Agnes, and commented on an illustration in the Arabic newspaper she was reading, than he fell back with a sigh and was dead. They had been married just over three years.

CHAPTER II

Sinai and von Tischendorf

With the death of Samuel Lewis, Agnes had lost not only her husband, but his world. It was Samuel who enlivened luncheon at Castlebrae by arriving unannounced with foreign dignitaries and visiting archaeologists; Samuel who had the extensive network of friends in Britain and abroad; Samuel who knew how to track down a unique Roman statue or carved gemstone. To have found a satisfactory husband in middle age was noteworthy, but to have found one and then to have lost him so soon – as had both Margaret and Agnes – was a cruel fate.

Now it was Agnes's turn to be overcome with grief for a man to whom she considered herself ideally suited: all possibility of sharing in his life of scholarship vanished like a will-o'-the-wisp. Once again travel occurred to the twins as one of the few possible consolations. There was now absolutely nothing to stop them from visiting Sinai. Dangerous it might be, but there was no James Gibson barring the way, as he had in 1885. Agnes and Margaret wanted to tread for themselves the desert pathways of the Israelites on their forty-year sojourn in the desert. They wanted to set eyes on the Mountain of the Law, and view the valley floor where the assembled Israelites had met Moses bearing the Ten Commandments. Friends though they might be with William Robertson Smith, they did not share his view that the Book of Exodus was mere legend. They also wanted to see, if possible, the monastic library of St Catherine's, of whose manuscript collection they were beginning to hear marvellous things. And so they began to make plans.

From Samuel and his friends the twins now knew that, quite apart from the difficulties of the desert crossing, one could not simply launch oneself at Sinai from Suez, as Agnes and Grace had planned to do six years earlier. More precisely, one could not just arrive unannounced at St Catherine's and expect to be admitted to the monastery, let alone the closely guarded library. To visit, one needed permission from the Archbishop of Mount Sinai, who resided for the purpose of the convent's business in Cairo. Letters of introduction had to be secured. Research must be done.[1]

St Catherine's had always held out a wary welcome to scholarly visitors, but over the last thirty years it had become doubly inaccessible, not least because of the activities of Constantin von Tischendorf.

Von Tischendorf was amongst the most illustrious of the adventurer-scholars who aimed to counter growing scepticism about the reliability of the Bible. But whereas intellectuals like Robertson Smith worked by argumentation, the energetic and cocksure young German wanted to smash unbelief with physical evidence. In 1840, and already accomplished in deciphering ancient writings at the age of just twenty-five, von Tischendorf set out to examine known manuscripts of the New Testament kept in Paris, London, Florence, Venice and Turin. It quickly became evident to him that the oldest specimens (and few could be dated to before the tenth century) were products of Eastern scriptoria. Could it be, he wondered, that 'in some recess of Greek or Coptic, Syrian or Armenian monasteries, there might be some precious manuscripts slumbering for ages in dust and darkness?'[2] Spurred on by this hope, he travelled from Italy to Egypt, to the Coptic convents of the Libyan desert and finally, after four years of searching, to the Sinai desert and the heavily fortified Convent of St Catherine's, where he was lifted over its walls in a basket that the monks lowered and raised with a windlass. There he discovered what he recognised instantly to be a priceless find: a magisterial Bible, which he correctly judged to be from the mid-fourth century. It contained all the books of the Bible as known to the modern world, and its weight was such that one man alone could not carry it. It was clearly the product of a professional scriptorium of the highest order: the three scribes who had copied it in clear Greek capitals were so skilful that their hands could barely be distinguished from one another by experts.

No manuscript of the Bible was more complete or more ancient – the Codex Sinaiticus (as it came to be called) antedating most known copies by almost 600 years. One reviewer wrote, on von Tischendorf's publication of a facsimile edition, that the 'appearance of a new island would scarcely have been regarded with more interest, than its advent before the eyes of the critical world'.[3] Von Tischendorf was believed to have routed the sceptics. He was enobled by the tsar, given honorary degrees by Oxford and Cambridge, and received a personal note of thanks from the Pope. In Britain, where the blow to dangerous new 'German theology' was particularly welcome, his breathless account of his discovery ran to eight popular editions.

At first Agnes and Margaret had no designs on the library and its manuscripts, other than to view them, if they could. Then, only a couple of months after Samuel's death, Agnes read of a notable discovery. It had been believed that von Tischendorf had discovered everything worth finding at St Catherine's, but now it was reported that a Quaker scholar, Dr J. Rendel Harris, had recently unearthed there a copy of a famous text long believed to be lost.

This was the 'Apology of Aristides', a work known to posterity only because the fourth-century historian Eusebius mentioned it in his *Ecclesiastical History*. According to Eusebius, Aristides was an Athenian philosopher who had converted to Christianity, and his 'apology' was the case he made for his new religion before the Emperor Hadrian. But since Eusebius provided no extracts, and no copy of the 'Apology' had endured, one could not verify what Aristides had said, or even whether he and his 'Apology' had ever actually existed.

In 1878 Armenian monks in Venice had published what they claimed was a fragment of the hitherto lost 'Apology' in Armenian. Fragment though it was, this contained an elaborately formulated, very early presentation of Christian belief, dating perhaps from AD 120–150. Radical scholars like Ernest Renan – whose *Vie de Jésus* (1863) had presumed that such evolved Christian thought emerged only after a long period of mythical encrustation – received news of the 'Apology' with incredulity. If authentic, it would date the fully developed system of belief far earlier than critics like Renan were prepared to allow. Now Harris had found the full text in a Syriac version.

Agnes was so interested in this book that she began to study Syriac – not so difficult, she said, if one already had Hebrew and Arabic.[4] Soon she was able to puzzle out sections of Rendel Harris's text. The twins were not themselves acquainted with him, but Agnes met Mrs Harris by chance and took the opportunity to mention that she was studying Harris's text, and that she and her sister were going to Sinai soon themselves.

Rendel Harris called round at Castlebrae almost immediately. He was a lithe and gregarious man of about forty, with auburn hair and a long, full beard. In his search for manuscripts, Harris had visited not only St Catherine's but the monasteries of Patmos, Smyrna and Mount Athos. He was intrigued by the plans of these Scottish sisters, and told them what he could of the monks of Sinai. The convent was home to about thirty-five of them, mostly from the Greek islands. They lived behind high, massive walls containing courtyards, galleries, chapels and libraries of various sizes and conditions. They subsisted simply on peas, beans and lentils, Arab bread and whatever fruit and vegetables they produced in their gardens.[5]

Harris spoke warmly of the monks and of the welcome he and his American travelling companion, Frederick Bliss, had received from them. As he confirmed to Agnes and Margaret, it had facilitated matters immensely that both he and Bliss could speak modern Greek.[6]

And then Rendel Harris told them something he had not disclosed in his book. There was a dark closet off a dark chamber beneath the archbishop's rooms. This closet contained chests of Syriac manuscripts that Harris had lacked time fully to examine. He thought these might prove to be some of the earliest texts of Christianity, in the language close to the original Aramaic spoken by Jesus and his disciples. He encouraged Agnes in her study of Syriac, and planted in her mind the possibility that she, too – though only a beginner – might find something extraordinary at Sinai.

In the weeks to come, this dark cupboard was to haunt Agnes's imagination.

CHAPTER 12

The perils of Bible-hunting

Hunting for ancient manuscripts was not for the physically or the spiritually faint-hearted. Although finds like those of von Tischendorf and Rendel Harris had gone some way to reassure the faithful of the reliability of the Bible and the antiquity of their creeds, the success of these Bible-hunters, and the interest that their discoveries excited in the popular press, also had the effect of raising questions that most had never considered. What exactly is the Bible? How do we happen to have it? In what languages was it originally written? How old were its various books? The family Bible on the parlour shelf might look eternal in its rectitude, but now ordinary citizens were becoming aware that the good book had a past.

Most people assumed that the books of the Bible had simply passed down unaltered from the pens of Moses and Jeremiah in the case of the Old Testament, and Mark and John in the case of the New. But the study of ancient manuscripts revealed one fact clearly: in the long lapse of time (for some books of the Old Testament more than 2,500 years) since the texts were written, and during which they could be reproduced only by hand, there was ample opportunity for error and variation to creep in.

Out of this pandora's box of uncertainties also flew the question of how to tell which ancient copy could be trusted. The Western Church had, through the Middle Ages, relied on the Latin of the Vulgate. But in the sixteenth century Reformers called for a return to the purity of the Scriptures in the original languages – the Hebrew of the Old Testament and the Greek of the New. That was easier said than done.

A reliable Greek text of the New Testament was not simply to be plucked from the library shelf. Greek bibles were still used, of course, by the Greek-speaking Eastern Churches, and Greek manuscripts of the New Testament existed in their hundreds or thousands (no one knew how many), scattered across Europe in churches, monastic and royal libraries, colleges, private collections, even city archives. They varied in age, composition and state of repair. Most had parts missing or damaged by fire, water, mildew, theft, rats or the natural ruin of time. And even these fragmentary manuscripts contained variant readings, the result of copying errors or occasionally deliberate alterations made to suit the theological opinions of individual scribes or copy houses (scriptoria). The Book of Revelation emerged as particularly mysterious, missing entirely from many of the manuscripts. Other manuscripts lacked the epistle known as Hebrews.

Even the Codex Vaticanus, which dwelt in the Vatican, accessible only to the Pope and a few cardinals, was rumoured to have its peculiarities. It omitted the story of the woman taken in adultery from St John's Gospel ('Let any one among you who is without sin be the first to throw a stone at her'), and St Mark's Gospel ended abruptly with the frightened women at the empty tomb of Jesus meeting figures in shining raiment – and nothing else, no account of Jesus's resurrection appearances.

The very lists of the books considered to be biblical (or canonical) varied from one ancient source to another. The Protestant Reformers excluded the books of the 'Apocrypha' (which included Tobit, Judith, parts of the Book of Esther, the Wisdom of Solomon and Ecclesiasticus), because no Hebrew copies of them could be found, and Jews did not regard them as canonical.

With the invention of the printing press came the urgent need for an authoritative text, which led Erasmus to assemble a New Testament in Greek. In 1516 this became one of the very first printed bibles. But Erasmus and other scholars knew this text to be far from adequate. He had worked in haste from the only five Greek manuscripts available to him in Basel. Only one of these contained the Book of Revelation, and this with the last verses corrupt. To fill in the gap he simply translated the last verses of Revelation from his Latin Bible back into Greek. This expedient fell below his own high standards, but more pressing matters of the Reform were at hand and so the edition had to 'make do' until a better one could be established. Theodore Beza, a Swiss Reformer, revised Erasmus's text and the result became the 'Textus Receptus'. Official as that sounds – *textus receptus* is the Latin for 'the text we have got' or, more nobly, 'the text received' – the designation came rather arbitrarily when the announcement of the 1633 reprinting honoured it with it that title. This was surely one of the most successful publisher's ploys of all time. The 'Textus Receptus' would become the basis for the King James Version in English, and many other translations in European languages. By the nineteenth century it had long been simply 'The Bible' for ordinary Christians.

Erasmus had had other problems in purging corrupt emendations from the biblical texts. A classic example is the so-called 'Johannine Comma', found in the fifth chapter of the First Letter of John. The verse reads this way in the Authorised Version:

> This is he that came by water and blood, even Jesus Christ, not by water only, but by water and blood. And it is the Spirit that beareth witness, because the Spirit is truth. For there are three that bear record *in heaven, the Father, the Word, and the Holy Ghost: and these three are one. And there are three that bear witness in earth,* the Spirit, the water, and the blood: and these three agree in one. If we receive the witness of men, the witness of God is greater: for this is the witness of God which he hath testified of his Son.[1]

The words in italics were missing from all the Greek texts that Erasmus had at his disposal, and also from the best Latin Vulgate texts. Erasmus knew this was in all likelihood a pious gloss by some medieval scribe, and so in his 1516 edition he left the verses out. There was uproar at the loss of so revered a text, familiar to Christians from its settings in sung Masses and as one of the few New Testament texts that clearly expressed the doctrine of the Trinity. If, however, as these verses say, we 'receive the witness of men' but 'the witness of God is greater', then which should one follow: the old, revered – but in all likelihood corrupt – text, or the new, scientifically edited one? Just which is 'the witness of God' and which merely 'the witness of men'? When one relies on Scripture alone, then Scripture must be unimpeachable. In 1522 Erasmus had reluctantly reinserted the hallowed verses into what would become the 'Textus Receptus', where they sat, like a cocked pistol, waiting for a less pious and more critical age. Westcott and Hort's landmark Greek New Testament of 1881 was made possible by the publication of both the Codex Sinaiticus and the Codex Vaticanus in the 1860s, and by an explosion in the discovery of biblical manuscripts during the nineteenth century.

It is estimated that when von Tischendorf began his expeditions in the 1840s, there were about 1,000 known manuscripts of the New Testament and that, by the time Westcott and Hort published their *New Testament in the Original Greek* in 1881, there were some 3,000. Even so, their title was ambitious. Sinaiticus and Vaticanus, on which they relied heavily, were admirably full manuscripts, but still dated only from the fourth century AD. Now, in the 1880s, new archaeological finds in Egypt suggested to a younger generation of scholars, like Rendel Harris and the twins' former neighbour, Francis Burkitt, that even earlier witnesses to the New Testament might be found, especially if one considered very early translations into other languages, like Syriac.

Agnes's progress in Syriac was rapid. She received lessons from Mr Kennett, a young lecturer who had been a friend of Samuel's. Although some sections of the university allowed women to attend classes, there was no precedent for this in Semitic languages, so Kennett instructed her after his students had departed. Francis Burkitt also taught her the ancient Estrangelo alphabet, but, with characteristic intellectual ruggedness, Agnes did most of the work on her own, assisted by Theodor Nöldeke's German–Syriac grammar.

Meanwhile, plans for a trip to Sinai continued apace. Rendel Harris insisted that the twins learn to use a camera, first teaching them how to take photographs using his own cumbersome apparatus, and then ordering them a half-plate camera with all its appurtenances.

Photographs, he said, would be invaluable, should they actually discover anything. He even provided them with a stand suitable for balancing manuscripts on during photography. He gave them a personal letter of introduction to the monk-librarian, Father Galaktéon, whom he regarded as a personal friend.

Rendel Harris was the son of a house decorator in Plymouth, who had found his way to Cambridge by way of scholarships. He had studied mathematics before turning to the new discipline of oriental studies. While a student he had experienced 'the Second Blessing'. His secretary and biographer wrote, 'Whatever that means, it set him free in pursuit of Truth in whatever direction his vocation and guidance led.'[2] In his case it led to the Society of Friends, Quakerism – in his judgment, most nearly representing the picture of Christian life painted in the Gospels. On a first visit to new lodgings in Cambridge, Harris met the landlady's small boy and asked how old he was. 'I'm phree,' said the child. 'Praise the Lord,' said Rendel Harris, 'so am I!'[3]

After graduation he had remained for seven years Lecturer in Mathematics at his Cambridge college, Clare. In 1882, following his developing interests, he had taken a professorship in biblical study and theology at Johns Hopkins University in Baltimore, then a very new institution, only to leave it three years later due to his strong and public objections to the vivisections performed in the science laboratories. From 1886 to 1891 Harris was Professor of Biblical Languages at Haverford, a Quaker college in Pennsylvania, and it was while on study leave from Haverford that he discovered the 'Apology' of Aristides at St Catherine's. At the time when the twins met him, Harris was forty years old, shortly to take up a post at Cambridge as University Lecturer in Palaeography.

Harris was by nature optimistic and in every way encouraging to the twins: 'he radiated,' wrote Agnes, 'happiness and confirmation and it needed only a glance at his bright fact to reassure us.'[4] His bright face was an invaluable counter to uncertainties and the scepticism of some in Cambridge, and especially the wintry pessimism of Professor Robert Bensly, the university's chief expert on Syriac texts and another former neighbour in Harvey Road. He pointed out that, as women, the twins' journey would be in vain, since the monks would not allow them to enter St Catherine's.

Agnes and Margaret ignored the Cambridge nay-sayers. They reasoned that they stood apart from other travellers in their ability to speak both Arabic and modern Greek. They would be able to converse directly with both the Bedouin and the monks of St Catherine's. Furthermore, they had been welcomed by monks in Greece and, in Agnes's case, Cyprus and knew something of Orthodox ways. They were already familiar with the practicalities of travelling with dragomans, tents and pack animals. These distinctive qualifications and their own rugged good health made the sisters ideal Sinai travellers, as far as they were concerned.

As their plans became known in Cambridge, various scholarly requests came their way. The Professor of Geology asked them to find for him specimens of a peculiar stone found only on the mountain of Sinai, which gave the appearance of bearing Arabic writing. The Regius Professor of Divinity, showing considerable confidence in their Greek, asked them – should they be able to gain entrance to the library – to collate two tenth-century manuscripts of the Septuagint (the Old Testament in Greek) that resided there. To further this and other commissions the Vice-Chancellor of the University of Cambridge gave them an official letter, handwritten in Greek and magnificently stamped with the university seal, which they might show to the monks as a bona fides.

On the night before their departure the young Mr Kennett and the elderly Master of Corpus Christi, Dr Perowne, called at Castlebrae to wish the sisters well and speculate on what treasures the twins might find. What had begun as a visit was becoming an expedition with, as Agnes said, the expectation 'to make scientific profit out of it, and we could afford to laugh at the prediction that, being women, we might possibly be refused admission into a Greek convent'. They were to find that it was not women, but 'scientific scholars', whom the monks most distrusted.

CHAPTER 13

The story von Tischendorf did not tell

European scholars were frequently turned away from St Catherine's for lack of the requisite Cairo permit and, on occasion, even pelted with stones from the parapets, but the nadir of all Western visits – from the monks' point of view – was that of Constantin von Tischendorf.

In his popular account, Tischendorf described the great discovery at Sinai with selective ambiguity:

> It was at the foot of Mount Sinai, in the Convent of St Catherine, that I discovered the pearl of all my researches. In visiting the library of the monastery, in the month of May, 1844, I perceived in the middle of the great hall a large and wide basket full of old parchments; and the librarian, who was a man of information, told me that two heaps of papers like these, mouldered by time, had been already committed to the flames. What was my surprise to find amid this heap of papers a considerable number of sheets of a copy of the Old Testament in Greek, which seemed to me to be one of the most ancient that I had ever seen. The authorities of the convent allowed me to possess myself of a third of these parchments, or about forty-three sheets, all the more readily as they were destined for the fire. But I could not get them to yield up possession of the remainder. The too lively satisfaction which I had displayed had aroused their suspicions as to the value of this manuscript.[1]

Telling the monks to keep hold of the rest and to 'take religious care of all such remains which might fall in their way', von Tischendorf hastened back to Leipzig, where he swiftly published a facsimile of the forty-three sheets in his possession and released them to an astonished world. His problem was how to retrieve the rest of the text. For the next few years he was both brazenly vocal about the importance of his find, and yet highly secretive concerning its exact location, hinting only at an Eastern and monkish provenance and adding that more might be expected from the same source.

After unsuccessful attempts to secure the rest of the manuscript through an intermediary, von Tischendorf decided to return to Sinai himself – even if he could not acquire the remaining sheets, he could copy them. But once there he found the monks, from the *hegumenos* (or prior) down, could not remember what had happened to the manuscript he was asking for.[2] They were clearly wary of von Tischendorf, and what he thought of them is made plain in a letter to his fiancée during his first visit: 'I have now been in the St Catharine Monastery eight days. But oh, these monks! If I had military strength and power, I should be doing a good deed if I threw this rabble over the walls. It is sad to see how man carries his baseness and wretchedness into the lofty grandeur of this mountain world!'[3]

The question now was how to help the monks refresh their memories sufficiently to let him see the manuscript once more and, if possible, take possession of it. He would have to wait for more than a decade. But in 1856, with strategic cunning, von Tischendorf travelled to Russia and secured Alexander II's support for his researches. The tsar's ancestors had long been patrons of the convent at Mount Sinai.[4]

Von Tischendorf returned to Sinai doubly armed: with funds and an endorsement that the monks could not ignore. The Russian flag was hoisted in his honour and within a few days he discovered in a monk's study, wrapped in a red cloth, not only the sheets he had seen before in the basket, 'but also other parts of the Old Testament, the New Testament complete, and, in addition, the Epistle of Barnabas and a part of the Pastor of Hermas'.[5] He could now be certain that he held in his hands 'the most precious Biblical treasure in existence'. He suggested to the monks 'the thought of presenting the original to the Emperor of Russia'. And so it was that von Tischendorf took from them, 'under the form of a loan, the Sinaitic Bible, to carry it to St Petersburg, and there to have it copied as accurately as possible'.[6]

From the monks' point of view, the removal of the Codex Sinaiticus would come to be seen as little more than theft. Although von Tischendorf would acknowledge that he took the manuscript 'under the form of the loan', none of his subsequent actions conformed unambiguously to that understanding.

His accounts of his dealings with the monks are wondrously vague at just those points where one would want clarification. He tells us that at the time of his first visit in 1844 he 'possessed himself' of forty-three sheets of the manuscript, without any word as to the status of this possession. On completion of his facsimile edition, the sheets were deposited in the University of Leipzig library – and not, it appears, as a temporary holding. Moreover, von Tischendorf's own writings show that he stopped at nothing to get his hands on the remainder of the manuscript, while for twelve years concealing its whereabouts from the rest of the academic world.

When in 1857 he finally secured the remainder, it was seamlessly transformed into a gift to the monastery's regal benefactor. It is altogether possible that von Tischendorf presented the manuscript to the tsar as a loan, but found it absorbed as a gift. It is difficult to 'lend' something like the Codex Sinaiticus to the Imperial Tsar of all the Russias. This does not, however, explain why the first forty-three sheets remained in Leipzig. That von Tischendorf was subsequently anxious to exculpate himself is clear. Some ten years later, at his urging, the 'donation' of the manuscript was regularised by the Russian government by the presentation to the monks of 9,000 roubles and an assortment of medals.

Many elements of von Tischendorf's account failed to persuade even their first audience. To believe von Tischendorf (whose personal maxim was 'God helps those who help themselves'), we have to suppose that the monks at St Catherine's, having preserved intact for more than a thousand years a venerable manuscript, were about to burn it for tinder at just the moment von Tischendorf arrived. But fourth-century vellum smoulders rather than burns, and the monks possessed many hundreds of decrepit printed works on paper, which would have made more satisfactory fuel.[7]

But even if the monks had decided to burn, or smoulder, an ancient manuscript, why choose one that was well preserved, clear, nearly complete and written, not in an obscure language like Ethiopic, Syriac or Coptic, which none of the monks could read, but in Greek, which all of them understood?

In the 1960s documents came to light that included a receipt (dated Cairo, September 1859) in von Tischendorf's own handwriting, which says: 'I, the undersigned, Constantin von Tischendorf', attest to an ancient document 'delivered to me as a loan . . . being the property of the aforesaid monastery and containing 346 folia and a small fragment', for the purposes of copying. It concludes, 'This manuscript I promise to return, undamaged and in a state of good preservation, to the Holy Confraternity of Sinai at its earliest request.'

This is plain enough. A letter to Archbishop-Elect Cyril from an envoi in Alexandria written in October 1859 – just a few days after von Tischendorf's departure for Europe – speaks of uproar in Cairo, where von Tischendorf had spread news of his acquisition, 'either out of vanity or for some other reason'. People can talk of nothing else, the envoi Germanos wrote, and they blame the Sinai monks for losing the manuscript, 'since Tischendorf announced not that he had borrowed it, but rather that he had taken it for the definite purpose of offering it to the Emperor. Therefore people here are of the opinion that this offering has been arranged by Your Eminence in order that you might acquire the protection of the Russian Embassy there.'[8]

Admittedly Archbishop-Elect Cyril, with whom von Tischendorf was dealing, was notoriously corrupt. He had disposed of valuable items belonging to the monastery to others before von Tischendorf – and it may be that there was an understanding between them. But Cyril always insisted that he parted with the manuscript as a loan. In a summary of the affair written in Cyril's own hand sometime between 1867 and 1869 he repeats this, and notes that after being copied for printing, it was:

to be returned to the monastery as its inalienable possession. From that time until the present day the aforesaid manuscript has not been returned to the Holy Monastery. On the other hand, neither did the Community of Sinai ever contemplate nor did it deliberate in common upon any idea of offering or donating it to the Russian Imperial Government. Quite to the contrary, many (monks) were displeased even with its temporary cession, and from that time forth found the pretext for launching periodic accusations against their Archbishop [the writer], Kyr Cyril.

Cyril was later deposed and his portrait, still in the monks' possession at St Catherine's, was slashed by an outraged brother.

CHAPTER 14

Setting out for Sinai

In January of 1892, less than nine months after Samuel's death, Agnes and Margaret were in Cairo, equipped with portable water filters, a variety of medicines and photographic apparatus. Despite having managed to develop only one successful photograph of the many they had taken, they brought with them – either out of courage or, according to Agnes, temerity – 1,000 film exposures. They now had two objectives: to find a dragoman for their expedition, and to secure the requisite letter of permission from the Archbishop of Mount Sinai to visit the convent and work in its library.

They soon found a suitable dragoman, a Syrian Christian called Hanna who sported a curled black moustache and a bright-blue suit. Engineering a meeting with the Archbishop of Sinai was a more time-consuming matter. Armed with their formal referral from the Vice-Chancellor of Cambridge University and various letters of introduction, the twins were passed from hand to hand – through connections in the English Church to the Greek patriarch, from the Greek patriarch and then to the Metropolitan of Libya (also resident in Cairo), who was able, finally, to arrange for them to be conducted to the Archbishop of Sinai in his gloomy branch convent in the old part of the city.

Everything hung on their success with this elusive prelate. But, once reached, His Beatitude Archbishop Porphyrios proved to be cordiality itself – not least because he had, early in their interview, formed the impression that the twins were on a mission to convert the whole of England to the correct pronunciation of Greek. He was suitably impressed by the vice-chancellor's letter bearing the pious seal of Cambridge University – an open Bible in the centre of a cross, guarded by lions. He promised them every facility in their researches in the library, even his prayers for their protection from *khamseen*, the hot dust-filled winds off the Sahara that periodically made a Sinai crossing impossible. As was the custom, their dragoman signed his contract in front of the archbishop. Hanna then set about finding the tents, pans, provisions, a cook, a waiter and, most essential of all, the Bedouin drivers whose camels would carry all their equipment and provisions. On 28 January, Agnes and Margaret found themselves standing on the western shore of the Gulf of Suez awaiting a sailing boat that would take them to meet their laden camel caravan on the other side.

The Sinai peninsula rests between the two arms of the Red Sea: the Gulf of Suez and the Gulf of Aqaba. In the north, where the peninsula merges with Israel's Negev desert, it is a broad sand and gravel plane. Its southern third, where the convent of St Catherine's sits, is mountainous, with some peaks as high as 8,500 feet. The peninsula is hot in summer, cold in winter and dry almost all of the year – virtually devoid of vegetation except where a spring breaks through the rock to nourish a small oasis or a Bedouin garden.

The ancient Egyptians had little time for the desert, a place of exile and death. The pharaohs travelled the northern, seaboard route to what is now Israel, the ancient Via Maris, for the purposes of trade or diplomacy, to attack Hittite enemies and to bully Canaanite vassals into submission. From around 2100 BC they sent expeditions to Sinai to mine turquoise, before exhausting the supply some 600 years later, but no pharaoh lived on the Sinai peninsula, and no great monuments were erected there by any dynasty. The turquoise-miners marked their path with carvings of their boats and mules (not camels, for these were introduced to the Nile Valley only later). They chiselled on the stones of Sinai representations of the pharaoh bearing cones of the precious stone – the colour of the river and life – which had to be dug from this barren land. On the wind-swept peak at Serabit el Khadim they built a small Temple to Hathor, the cow-eared goddess of fertility. In their abandoned mines, the pioneering archaeologist Sir Flinders Petrie found some of the first instances of alphabetic writing – 'proto-Sinaitic' – where Semitic workers used Egyptian symbols phonetically to record their small contracts. They returned gladly enough from this desert outpost to the verdant Nile.

Historically, the peninsula was chiefly important as a route to some-where else: for Nabataean traders ferrying spices destined for Egypt or Rome from their blood-red capital at Petra; for Muslims crossing on their way to Mecca for the Haj; for Christian pilgrims visiting the Holy Land. These visitors carved graffiti on the soft sandstone rocks: inscriptions in Hebrew and Arabic, waymarks of the Nabataeans at cultic sites, the Greek crosses of Christian pilgrims, the Crusader crosses of the Franks. The most famous Sinai transients were Mary, Joseph and the infant Jesus, fleeing the murderous attentions of Herod. Moses – who was revered by Jews, Christians and Muslims alike – fled to this place from Egypt where he had been brought up as a prince, married his Midianite wife Zipporah, and heard the call of God from the burning bush.

The Bedouin lived in small settlements of goat-hair tents, moving between summer gardens and winter grazing, their men from time immemorial conveying pilgrims and other visitors across the peninsula on their camels. The women tended to the cooking and the children, and to the mingled herds of sheep and goats. To the nineteenth-century traveller their tents might have been as those of Abraham; the women in their embroidered dresses and coined masks might be Zipporah and her sisters; their walled gardens of pomegranates, almonds and apricots might be those of the Song of Songs, the enclosed garden of the Lord.

Apart from the Bedouin, the only other long-standing residents of the peninsula were the monks of St Catherine's, who had lived in symbiosis with the Bedouin for more than 1,300 years. Some Western travellers found it strange to encounter a Christian community so deep within a Muslim land, but the predecessors of these monks had arrived in the Sinai desert three centuries before the birth of the Prophet, and even before Constantine made Christianity the religion of the Roman Empire.

The fortified monastery to which Agnes and Margaret were now headed, and which it would take them nine days to reach, was built by the Emperor Justinian sometime around AD 557, and certainly after the death of his empress, Theodora. Justinian's court historian, Procopius, recorded the benefaction:

> In what was formerly called Arabia and is now known as 'Third Palestine', a barren land extends for a great distance, unwatered and producing neither crops nor any useful thing. A precipitous and terribly wild mountain, Sina [sic] by name, rears its height close to the Red Sea . . . On this Mt Sinai live monks whose life is a kind of careful rehearsal of death, and they enjoy without fear the solitude which is very precious to them. Since these monks had nothing to crave – for they are superior to all human desires and have no interest in possessing anything or in caring for their bodies, nor do they seek pleasure in any other thing whatever – the Emperor Justinian built them a church which he dedicated to the Mother of God, so that they might be enabled to pass their lives therein praying and holding services.[1]

Justinian found an architect for his monastery in Aila (now Eilat in southern Israel) and sent, in addition, 200 Christian families from Wallachia (now Bulgaria), and a similar number of Egyptians (also Christians), to serve and protect the monastery. When, in the seventh century, the great spiritual storm of Islam swept from Arabia across North Africa, these families became Muslims, indistinguishable in appearance from other Bedouin tribes on the peninsula. The Jabaliya (or 'mountain') Bedouin continued to work closely with the monks. They maintained an ancient weekly entitlement to the bread baked jointly by monks and Bedouin in the monastery – a tradition that continues to this day. On the feast day of St Catherine they would appear in the monastic church to attend the first part of the liturgy and a reception, for they regarded St Catherine as their special saint.

The wherewithal and basic form of a journey to St Catherine's had changed little over the centuries. Niccolò da Poggibonsi, a Franciscan friar who made his Sinai pilgrimage in the 1340s, wrote that one needed to find an Arab dragoman in Cairo who could make arrangements with the 'wild arabs' (the Bedouin) for guiding and for special camels, 'for the camels of Babylon [Cairo] cannot endure the fatigue of the journey to St Catherine's, but are for portage in the city'. The Sinai camels, Niccolò wrote, 'seemed to be made of iron, so much hardship can they support . . . if there were no camels, and this is certain, it were not possible to go to St Catherine's; and the reason is this; no animal could walk or endure such a dangerous journey, nor could it carry enough provisions to suffice for itself alone'.[2]

It pleased the twins that the oldest surviving account by a pilgrim should be of female authorship: Sylvia of Aquitaine, also known as St Egeria, had travelled to Sinai in the early 380s, 200 years before Justinian built his monastery. Egeria followed what was clearly an already well-established physical and spiritual itinerary. Indeed, all journeys to St Catherine's – including now that of Agnes and Margaret – resembled that of St Egeria, for few variations were possible.

Camels were a necessity and Hanna supplied eleven: four for riding and seven for portage. With these came eleven Bedouin drivers with a sheikh, elected from amongst themselves, in overall charge of them for the journey. The sheikh rode a camel at his own expense. As per their agreement, Hanna had also provided two heavy tents, one to serve as the bedroom and dining room for the twins, and the other as a kitchen in which the dragoman and cook were to sleep at night. As part of his office, Hanna would act as their butler at meals.

Apart from the solid objects of use – the stove, pots, pans and bedding provided by Hanna, as well as the twins' enormous camera and medicine chest – the camels had to carry water for the desert crossing and enough food for the whole expedition (forty days' stay at St Catherine's and another nine to travel back), since it was not possible to reprovision at the monastery. Crates of live chickens, turkeys and doves were strapped on the camels. 'Truly', Agnes wrote we, 'brought the flesh pots with us'.

After finding their camel caravan and after the feat of mounting, they set off across a desolate plain of sand and reached 'Ain Musa (the Well of Moses) several hours later. Their tents were pitched by the brackish well, 'where Miriam is supposed to have begun her song of triumph'. Although it was no doubt a source of joy for Miriam to have escaped the pharaoh's chariots, the prospect that now met Agnes and Margaret was not promising: 'As we gazed on the interminable succession of low, sandy ridges on our left,' wrote Agnes, 'we could not help thinking that the host of Israel had some excuse for grumbling at a leader who was taking them where no food and no water could be seen.'[3]

The first night they slept little, for the wind was so strong they thought it might blow the tent away. Rising at half-past six, they set out across apparently limitless desert over stony ground. The only vegetation was a little dry brush and the occasional lonely acacia, whose spiky thorns the camels relished as a delicacy.

Apart from Agnes's brief experiment at 'Ain Musa six years earlier, the twins had not previously ridden camels. They discovered that sitting on a camel for a few minutes was one thing, but riding the beast for hours was quite another. Camel saddles are famously lumpy, with unkindly placed horns. There are no stirrups, so the legs must dangle idly down, unless the rider is agile enough to curl one leg up and under, Bedouin-style. In any case, the sisters chose to walk a good part of the way.

The Bedouin drivers wore a single white cotton garment and a little turban, and were endlessly courteous to the twins and to one another. They loved their animals, cosseting them with morsels of grey-green vegetation that they plucked on the way. Their one luxury was a long-stemmed pipe, which they handed around in turn, lighting it with a flint. They carried swords, and the sheikh had an ancient rifle, which probably posed more danger to himself than to his target, had he had the occasion to fire it.

The caravan travelled for eight hours on the first day, with the twins either on camel or on foot. Agnes entered no complaint in her diary, other than that their attempts to read the Psalms in Hebrew while riding were frustrated by the rolling gait of the camels, which caused even large, clear Hebrew type to bob up and down.[4] Moved by the

austerity of the place and her own recent loss of Samuel, she observed
that, even though the Israelites had the 'Pillar of Cloud' to lead them,
'it must have been as hard for them to believe in its Almighty grace as
it is for us to trust in our Divine Leader when the course of this world
seems going against us. He does not always explain His purposes.'[5]

From Hanna they learned the Sinai Dragoman's Creed – 'I know
everything. You [the Bedouin] know nothing.' Hanna gave Agnes and
Margaret an entirely erroneous account of the religion of the Bedouin,
and was not above taxing their strength and that of the Bedouin to
ensure his greater profit. Despite their feeling quite unwell after their
first long day in the saddle and a second windy and sleepless night,
Hanna kept them going for ten and a half hours the following day,
pressing the most out of the Bedouin that he might gain more from his
fixed-term contract. If no better at outwitting Hanna than they had
been at foiling Certezza, Agnes and Margaret at least had sufficient
Arabic to explain to the Bedouin that this forced march in darkness was
not their idea. Sunday, at the twins' insistence, was a day of rest for all.
They paid extra for this privilege, although they found out that Hanna
did not pass the benefit on, deducting a day's wages from the Bedouin.

As they moved south the flat lands gave way to ridges of limestone
rock and white cliffs. On the fifth day they found themselves once
more by the sea, looking across the blue waters to the hazy mountains
on the African shore, before their route took them east into the rocky
defiles of the south Sinai peninsula. The wadis formed a maze that
twisted and forked through walls of wind-carved stone. Each turn
could bring a vision – a wall of rich red porphyry, or a face of black
granite – the outcome of some primal geological uproar, for the
peninsula runs along the same tectonic joint as the Great Rift Valley,
and ancient limestone seabeds have been raised up and veined with
molten rock. The same combination of soft lime and sandstone
coupled with igneous rock is the reason why, in Sinai, one could find
oases and springs of water on the face of bare rock. Without this water
the peninsula would be as desolate as the moon. The twins were told
of the rare flash floods that could run so violently through the wadis as
to sweep a camel and its rider down to the sea.

At an oasis they met a young Bedouin woman, veiled but wearing magnificent bracelets of coral and amber. Agnes and Margaret travelled, as Samuel had, equipped with little coloured photographs of Cambridge colleges as a conversation starter. The Bedouin woman could make nothing of the neat quadrangles of green turf. Married, though probably less than eighteen years old and with two children, she found it hard to grasp that these two, going about with unveiled faces, were indeed women.

Agnes could not understand the dialect of the Bedouin, but they could understand her Arabic. She explained to the sheikh, Saleem, who rode along with them that 'we had come to this country to see the way by which Neby Mousa [Moses] led the Israelites; and we consider it a figure of how God leads us along the hard path of earthly life'.[6] The sheikh politely agreed.

On the ninth day Agnes and Margaret climbed the pass of Nugb Hawa on foot, followed by the camels, and found themselves gazing at the mountain that had burned with fire. 'At length the convent

St Catherine's Monastery

appeared in view, nestling in a narrow valley, surrounded by a walled garden.'

There have been many attempts to describe St Catherine's Monastery but one of the best comes from H. V. Morton: it is, he wrote, like a child's toy cast down on the floor of a large room.[7] Although its fortifications are vast, they are dwarfed by the pink granite mountains rising sheer behind them. It is not grand in the manner of great monastic houses of the West, and deliberately so. The convent is recessive when approached by the rising path from the plain, the route taken by the twins and their caravan, its unguarded side screened by the cypresses, olives and almond trees of its garden. Its bare walls are the same colour as the cliffs around it. The image favoured by the monks and by Agnes herself, seeing the convent for the first time while the almonds were in flower, is the biblical one of a dove hiding in the cleft of the rocks.

CHAPTER 15

The treasure in the dark closet

Professor Bensly's sceptical forebodings about the twins' prospects for admittance to the convent proved groundless. The monks were expecting them and were delighted to find their new guests fluent in modern Greek. It transpired that women pilgrims had always been welcomed at Mount Sinai for the simple reason that, in the early centuries, pilgrims' lives would be endangered outside the convent's walls.

While their tents were being pitched by the well in the convent's garden, Agnes and Margaret got word that they would be received by the monastery's prior, or *hegumenos*, and by its librarian.

It was no longer necessary, as in von Tischendorf's time, for visitors to be hauled up over the convent walls in a basket – a great door now gave access to the monastic enclosure. Once inside, they were led through a warren of little courtyards, staircases and balconies, whose haphazard layout was dictated by the need to encompass two landmarks that the biblical text suggested might in fact be at some distance from each other – the well where Moses first met his wife, Zipporah, and the burning bush. At last they reached the prior's reception room for the meeting they had so long anticipated.

The monks were thin and tall, with long grizzled beards. They walked slowly towards the twins, in their rumpled and faded habits and their tall black headgear. But the prior was all kindness and the librarian, Father Galaktéon, on whose goodwill so much depended, was particularly warm, not least because they carried a letter for him from Rendel Harris. Galaktéon was delighted. Harris and his travelling

companion – Frederick Bliss, an early excavator of the walls of
Jerusalem – had stood out from other visitors in their ability to speak
modern Greek and Arabic fluently, and in their tactful manner. 'The
world is not so large after all,' said Galaktéon, 'when we can have real
friends in such distant lands.' After a quick glimpse at the outer library,
which housed the Greek books but no important manuscripts, the
twins tactfully accepted an invitation to afternoon prayers. These
lasted two hours, Agnes wrote, with 'some very fine singing, but far
too many repetitions of *Hagios o Theos* and *Kyrie Eleison*. It was the last
of their services we attended.'[1]

The following day was spent working in the library. Agnes and

Sinai monks in front of the Burning Bush

Margaret were most anxious to see the 'dark closet' of which Rendel Harris had written, but courtesies had to be observed, as the monks brought them other treasures to be examined and praised. Books and even ancient manuscripts were housed all over the convent, in the 'show' library and in the church, in the monks' cells and in scattered cupboards. When Agnes was eventually asked what she especially wished to see, she replied, 'All your oldest Syriac manuscripts, particularly those which Dr Harris had no time to examine . . .'[2] Within minutes of her 'daring speech' they were led to a dimly lit little room below the prior's quarters, off which was the dark closet. By the feeble light of their candles they could see that it contained two chests – and from one of these they removed a half-dozen or so Syriac manuscripts to be examined by the light of day.

Once in the library with this trawl before her, Agnes first looked at the manuscript in which Rendel Harris had found the 'Apology of Aristides'. It was easy to pick out, being catalogued, according to some primitive system, as No. 16. Then her eye fell on an anonymous volume: 'It had a forbidding look, for it was very dirty, and its leaves were nearly all stuck together through their having remained unturned probably since the last Syrian monk had died, centuries ago, in the Convent.' Agnes was struck that the Syriac text she was examining, a collected lives of women saints, seemed to have been written on top of something else. As she looked closer she could see two broad columns of underwriting peeping out from beneath the text and she could make out page headings, also in the Syriac language, that clearly belonged to the earlier text. 'Of Matthew', 'of Luke', it read. This was a palimpsest. Agnes had never seen one before, but their father 'had often related to us wonderful stories of how the old monks, when vellum had become scarce and paper was not yet invented, scraped away the writing from the pages of their books and wrote something else new on the top of it; and how, after the lapse of ages, the old ink was revived by the action of common air, and the old words peeped up again; and how a text of Plato had come to light in this curious way'.[3] Before his discovery of the Codex Sinaiticus, von Tischendorf had first come to public attention for deciphering a palimpsest in Paris, which had hitherto defied all previous attempts: the famous Codex Ephraemi Rescriptus (*rescriptus* indicating that the vellum had been reused). Now Agnes held her breath. Evidently the undertext was a copy of the Gospels, but could she discern any more about it?

Von Tischendorf or Rendel Harris would very likely have been able to date the manuscript she held in her hands, on the basis of its script and physical features, but Agnes was not trained in palaeography. It was thus the greatest stroke of beginner's luck that the overlying text had been signed and dated by its scribe. Agnes made out the date as '1009 years Alexander (the Great)', which meant AD 697.[4] This pointed to a very early date for the underwriting: Agnes reckoned that for the vellum to have been reused in this fashion, the undertext must date to at least 200 years before the overwriting. And if what she held was, as indeed it appeared to be, a copy of the Gospels, that would make it the earliest known Gospels in Syriac. She would have to contain her excitement, while at the same time convincing her sister and the librarian, Galaktéon, neither of whom could read Syriac, of the possible significance of this grimy codex.

They proved difficult to convince. It was such an unpromising brick of parchment – dirty and compacted. Margaret was anxious about wasting precious film exposures on what might prove to be useless lives of women saints, copies of which existed in abundance. For his part, Galaktéon was eager to show them what he considered to be a more interesting twelfth-century document, which he kept wrapping and unwrapping in a handkerchief. But Agnes was adamant. Assisted by Galaktéon, she and her sister elected to devote much of their forty-day visit, and 368 of their 1,000 nitrate negatives, to what might turn out to be either indecipherable rubbish or one of the most important manuscript finds of the century.

In the course of Agnes's life she had on many occasions blessed a Greater Providence, but never more ardently than when she stumbled across this blackened wodge of text. How fortunate that her brother-in-law had prevented her from visiting St Catherine's six years earlier. How glorious now that former disappointment! Had she and Grace not been stopped at Suez by Gibson's telegrams, they might have

The palimpsest, with Galaktéon's thumb

made the desert crossing and passed some time pleasantly enough with the monks, but as tourists – nothing more! She would not have read Rendel Harris's description of the 'dark closet' or have studied Syriac. Nor would she have had any connection to the University of Cambridge, or the interest of its scholars in directing her enquiries; and of course no signed and stamped letter of introduction from the vice-chancellor to ease her progress in Cairo. She would not have had the faintest idea about cameras or the general familiarity with antiquities and manuscripts gained simply from having been married to Samuel Lewis, the keeper of the Parker Library.

The work was not easy. A bitter wind drove the temperature in the tents to below zero at night and froze them as they worked, with ungloved hands in an unglazed room. Only brisk walks up and down the wadi could warm them up again. The leaves of the palimpsest were 'mostly all glued together . . . the least force used to separate them made them crumble'. They loosened some apart with the steam from their camp kettle. It was far from obvious exactly what the under-writing said. The text was faint, and its contents lay in random order beneath the overwriting. The twins copied the headings from every page meticulously as they photographed it. They could only hope (and it was a long hope) that the underwriting would be visible in the developed photographs – assuming, that is, they were successful in developing these photographs at all.[5] In the evenings they returned to their encampment in the monastic garden where Hanna and the cook provided them with sustaining meals.

Agnes's published diaries attest to a growing friendship between the two ladies and Father Galaktéon. He had entered monastic life when only eleven years old and had enjoyed few educational opportunities – his manners were, according to Agnes, 'entirely Oriental', that is, Arabic – but he loved his books and took every chance to learn from the scholars who visited the monastery. To Agnes and Margaret he was endlessly helpful. He brought them manuscripts; he held them open for photographing; and when Margaret's spectacles broke and she was reduced to transcribing a script with the aid of a magnifying glass, he assisted by reading the Greek aloud.

The two women had their differences with the monks, especially in matters of religious observance. The first Saturday of their visit, up very early to ascend the Mountain of Moses, Agnes and Margaret observed the monks wending their way through the gardens in procession. The sisters said 'Good morning' to those they knew and when the prior approached, Agnes thought it courteous to go out and try to shake hands. He showered her with holy water from a silver vessel he was carrying and then held up a small cross which, in Greek, he enjoined her to adore. When Agnes stepped back startled, he thrust it forward repeating, 'Adore it.' While a monk who stood behind the *hegumenos* tried to explain that 'her way is different from ours', Agnes diplomatically kissed the cross, saying at the same time, 'I adore the Saviour, who died on the cross.' Had she done otherwise, she said, the *hegumenos* 'would have thought me an atheist . . . But it was a lesson to me never again to approach a Greek ecclesiastic when walking in procession.'[6]

Lent arrived and Galaktéon was distressed to discover that the twins did not fast or, being Presbyterians, observe the season of Lent at all. For her part, Agnes thought that fasting made the monks increasingly torpid and miserable-looking, and she noted that their moments of 'occasional merriment' in the library had dried up as Galaktéon grew ever gaunter. He was inclined to be touchy, especially towards Margaret, in whom he detected some wilfulness. When he disagreed, with raised voice, to a reading that she made of a particular recurring word, Margaret, to appease him, adopted his version. But after five or six more occurrences Galaktéon suddenly changed tack, thumped the table and shouted out Margaret's word, without further explanation. However, their investigations of the manuscripts continued, as did operations with the hefty camera equipment: during their stay they would use up all of their 1,000 nitrate exposures – 368 on the palimpsest, 110 on another manuscript that Rendel Harris had asked after, and the rest on manuscripts in Arabic, Syriac and Armenian, which would bear further scrutiny back home.

★

The increasing numbers of Western travellers to the Holy Land in the nineteenth century generally did not coincide with a greater under-standing of the ways of those who dwelt there; and of all the groups that Protestant travellers encountered, those held in lowest esteem were the eastern Christians, and especially their priests and monks. Jews and Muslims might be forgiven their ways, but Christians, so it was reasoned, had the Gospels and should know better. Von Tischendorf thought it nothing short of a miracle that the ragged brethren at Sinai had actually preserved the Codex Sinaiticus intact for more than 1,600 years until he arrived to discover it. Robert Curzon described the Coptic monks who courteously assisted his pillaging of their libraries as 'men who thought it holiness to live like a beast, wickedness to be clean, superfluous to be useful in the world'. Dean Stanley, author of a popular 1881 book, *Sinai and Palestine in Connection with Their History*, did not refuse the hospitality of the monks at St Catherine's, but nonetheless wrote of their 'rat-like pony's tails' and 'the barbaric splendours of Greek ritual'.[7] There were many who condemned the monks at Sinai for not even having troubled to convert their Bedouin neighbours, the nearest of whom had originally been Christians.

Despite their visits to Greek-speaking lands and a more sympathetic attitude, Agnes and Margaret, too, found it hard to understand what would drive men to this hard life, or what spirit roused them, six times a day, to answer the call of a wooden *semantron* and spend hours in what, from a Presbyterian point of view, was empty ritual observance.[8] Agnes did not doubt that the monks were trying to follow the Gospels, but she added the following, in her published account of the trip, to the common chorus of criticism:

> During the fifteen centuries that this convent has existed, prayers have arisen from it night and day, the liturgy and the sacraments having been continually repeated. But as for being a centre of light to the population around, it might as well never have existed.
>
> This seems to me, though I am open to correction, to be the inevitable tendency of what we call 'sacramentalism,' *i.e.* attention to a

ceremonial worship which leaves neither time nor energy for the instruction of the multitude.'[9]

Agnes conceded that Margaret, who was always more open to alternative views, saw matters rather differently.

Margaret was always the more sceptical of the two, softened somewhat by life with James Gibson, whose depression and anguish appear to have issued at least in part from loss of faith. Her theory of miracles was that God would have made 'every effort' to use existing and natural forces in their execution. When Father Euthymios led them up the Mount of Moses, he was at pains to point out the spots where tradition situated biblical events – the place where the prophet Elijah was fed by ravens; the site where Moses watered his father-in-law's flock; the rock that Moses had struck to receive water ('We are here to hand on the story exactly as he received it,' he said). Margaret expressed doubt that the free-standing boulder could be the actual rock struck by Moses. It was more likely that Moses had struck 'living rock' (that is, a cliff face), for she had a theory that Moses was directed 'to tap a store of water that had been laid up in the granite by winter rain and snow'. When he heard this, Galaktéon was indignant: 'You come from Scotland. Was Moses ever there? If he was not, how are you able to come and teach us what he did?' But evidently he considered her point, for later the same evening he led them, leaning on his gold-headed staff, to a small garden of olives and almond trees watered by a trickle from the bare rock and proposed this as the true setting of the miracle. The twins thought it a shade too near the Well of Jethro, but Margaret tactfully made a watercolour and they gathered a sweet herb growing beside the spring, which they used to perfume their clothes and letters. Their doubts about the antiquity of the site only increased when they later discovered that Galaktéon had been heard to say, 'Kyria [Lady] Agnes discovered the Syriac palimpsest and I discovered the rock that Moses struck!'

As for the place where Moses received the Law, Margaret and Agnes – like most Western visitors – preferred to follow the American scholar Edward Robinson in identifying the spot. The 'Mount of Moses' venerated by the monks through the ages is not a single peak, but a cluster of peaks, the highest of which, named 'Sinai', is by tradition identified as the place where God spoke to Moses. Robinson, whose *Biblical Researches in Palestine, Mount Sinai and Arabia Petraea* (1841) also proposed where the Red Sea had been crossed and how it might have parted, concluded on biblical principles that tradition had it wrong. The peak revered by the monks cannot be seen from the valley and comes into view only once one has climbed a good way up the mountain. Robinson argued that the summit where the Law was given must have been visible to the Israelites massed on the plain below. He proposed a nearby peak that met this requirement.

St Egeria wrote that the paths of the Mount of Moses were:

> . . . ascended with infinite labour, because you do not go up them slowly and slowly like a snail, but straight up you go, as if it were a wall, and you are obliged to descend each of these mountains till you get down to the very root of that middle mountain, which is specially Sinai. And there with the help of Christ our Lord, aided by the prayers of the saints who accompanied us, I accomplished the ascent, and with great labour, for I was obliged to ascend on foot, as I could not go up in the saddle; nevertheless this labour was not felt, because the desires I had I saw fulfilled with the help of God. About the fourth hour we arrived at the summit of Sinai, that holy Mount of God where the law was given, and there is the place where the Glory of God descended on the day when the mountain smoked.[10]

Egeria had made the same observation as Robinson: that the peak known as Sinai was visible only when one was well on in the ascent. But for her and other early pilgrims, this was a parable of the spiritual life: only she who is already on the way can glimpse the goal. Agnes and Margaret, however, who did the whole climb in heavy skirts, erred in favour of more scientific speculation. They chose to ascend 'Robinson's peak' and partook of a wind-swept lunch with a wide view of the plain below. Almost as impressive to them was the fact that their guide, Father Euphemios, had brought only bread and cheese for his lunch. He told them he had spent fifteen years as a tailor in Athens before coming to follow his vocation at Sinai after his wife died. Hanna, extracting cool revenge for some unidentified slight, brought them down the mountain by the longest route so that they still had five miles to walk around its base after reaching the valley bottom, the whole excursion lasting eleven hours.

Such was their busyness that they only inspected (Agnes's word) the Church of the Transfiguration and its relics on one of the last days of their visit. This basilica is one of the greatest treasures of the Byzantine period, built and decorated by Justinian at the same time as the convent walls. From the outside it is austere and simple. The pilgrim, now as in the sixth century, passes through immense carved wooden doors from the desolation of the desert into a dark porch, beyond which lies a lamplit world of gold, rich reds and browns. Every inch of the nave is decorated, from tiled floor to coffered ceiling. The walls shimmer with icons and inscriptions, and from the ceiling are suspended golden oil lamps of all shapes and sizes, gifts through the ages, whose chains are interrupted by ostrich eggs to keep rats from running down to eat the oil. An icon screen, or iconostasis, darkly ablaze with the red and gold figures of the Virgin Mary and St John flanked by archangels, divides the nave from the apse.

To the left of the altar was the Chapel of the Burning Bush, where all were obliged to remove their shoes, as it is the spot where tradition asserts that God spoke to Moses. Nearby in a gold coffer lay the bones of St Catherine. Martyred on the wheel in Alexandria, her body was said to have been transported by angels to this refuge in the desert, and her remains were the object of special veneration to monks and pilgrims alike.

Before the seventeenth century when the iconostasis and its surmounting cross were installed, a pilgrim entering the church from the west door – dusty, tired and grateful to be alive – would have looked down the length of the nave into the face of Christ gazing down from the sixth-century mosaic that fills the eastern apse. Unlike the Ravenna mosaics with which it is contemporary, this one was never restored. Each brightly cut stone lies still at the angle established for it in the sixth century.[11] Jesus stands centrally in a blue mandorla on a gold ground, his hand raised in a gesture of blessing. On his right is Elijah, and on his left Moses. Three disciples rise up, as if from sleep, below.

The story is recounted in Luke 9. Jesus, with Peter, John and James, has ascended a mountain to pray. The disciples fall asleep and wake to see Jesus, his clothes dazzling white, speaking with Moses and Elijah. The 'Transfiguration' may at first seem a misleading reference, since the mountain in that story is not Mount Sinai but Mount Tabor in Israel. But Moses and Elijah, as those who made the Sinai apse well knew, were the two Old Testament saints to whom God spoke on Sinai – to Moses from the burning bush, and to Elijah, not in earthquake, wind and fire, but 'the still, small voice'. From here Moses was commissioned to lead the people out of Egypt, and Elijah to wean Israel away from Baal-worship.

Standard images of the Transfiguration, both Eastern and Western, show Jesus and his sleepy followers on a mountain top. The Sinai apse is novel in one regard: it shows no mountain. The pilgrim who has come through the desert and up to the convent stands already on that mountain top with the disciples, addressed by the Divine Word. All this was lost on Agnes and Margaret, as indeed on most other Western travellers of their day. Agnes did note, however, the remarkable plenitude of golden lamps. She passed quickly over the distasteful topic of relics, and of the apse mosaic said only that it was 'the richest and best-preserved' she had ever seen – adding, with Calvinist directness, 'one would rather see the rock'.

But for all their confidence in the superiority of their own forms of worship, Agnes and Margaret were touched by what they had found at Sinai. For Victorian Protestants, to hear the Word of God was to be called to proclaim, preach and convert. This meant missions, Sunday Schools and the handing out of bibles and religious tracts. For the monks to hear the Word of God was to be called to a way of perfection – prayer and thanksgiving, fasting and abstinence. The brethren, it is true, did not fan out to convert the Bedouin, but made their presence a centre of hospitality on the understanding that God brings whom He will to Sinai, and God speaks to each one as He wills.

Agnes appended the following thought to the twins' names in the visitor's book: 'There are diversities of administration, but the same Spirit.' However little she and Margaret admired the Eastern liturgy or Church, their hearts had been captured by the quiet magic of Sinai, the planted beds of beans and onions sheltered by olive trees, and the kindness of the monks. 'Who may describe the beauty of the sunsets,' wrote Agnes:

> when tall cypresses towered from the glorious masses of white almond trees against a background of bare granite cliffs, all touched with the gold of heaven; or the moonlight in that silent Wady, so clear and strong, which made the olive boughs look like fairy lace work; and the ground beneath them, strewn as it was with fallen almond blossoms, gleaming as if snow lay on it, whilst a few upward steps out of the garden revealed a panorama of lofty cliffs, where intense silence brooded; and our thoughts went forcibly back to the time when they shook and rocked at the touch of the Divine Glory.[12]

It was with a certain sadness that, on 8 March after forty days' sojourn, they said goodbye to the monks and the mountain. Still, heightened expectations brightened their eight-day trek back to Suez and the sailing to Marseilles. What would the academic confraternity make of their finds? For all their intense excitement, there was nothing they could do until they had evidence to show, and this meant developing and printing their precious rolls of film.

CHAPTER 16

The Cambridge party

The sisters were anxious for their photographic exposures all the way back, lest an over-zealous customs official open the canisters holding the undeveloped rolls of film. When they arrived back in Cambridge on 1 April 1892 they told only their close friends of their discoveries. Now it was necessary to get the films developed, printed and put to the judgement of the experts. They had 1,000 photographs: about 400 of the palimpsest, 200 of a copy of the Gospels in Arabic, 300 of other books and 100 of desert scenery. Unwilling to entrust so great a treasure to a professional photographer, the twins decided to develop their negatives themselves and set aside a special room in Castlebrae for that smelly, messy purpose.

Their work was initially delayed when Margaret developed a serious streptococcal infection, erysipelas, which could prove fatal in those days. She had cut her heel at Sinai and the wound had not been helped by being continually bumped against her camel's side during the trip back. It took her three weeks to recover, and even then their progress was slow – only about three negatives could be developed in an hour. At a friend's urgings, they sent some negatives to a professional photographer, if only to provide a standard to work from. Agnes and Margaret were appalled when these came back unusable – much fainter even than their own efforts. But by the greatest piece of luck it had transpired at some stage during photographing that Agnes had lost her place, and they had inadvertently taken duplicate shots of just those sheets of the palimpsest that had been ruined by the professional developer. Nothing was lost. It seemed to Agnes and Margaret that a

Greater Providence was guiding them. Nevertheless, when they employed a young man to make prints from their developed negatives, Agnes watched his every move with an eagle eye.

By now the summer vacation had begun and the academics were slipping away. Rendel Harris was only able to see a few of their photographs before leaving Cambridge. Agnes, who had only nine months of Syriac study behind her, and Margaret, who had none, were set on the steepest of learning curves; they were finding out all they could about the transmission of the Gospels in the very earliest Christian communities and what this might reveal about the palimpsest Agnes had found.

Syriac is the dialect of Aramaic, the native language of Jesus, which was spoken in the Euphrates valley from about the second century AD. It was this closeness to the language of Jesus and his first disciples that excited Agnes – to have the Gospels in Syriac was to have a virtual echo chamber of the lost world of first-century Galilee. For while Gospels had been written in Greek, some of the sayings directly attributed to Jesus had been kept in Aramaic, including his command to the apparently dead, twelve-year-old daughter of the synagogue official Jairus. Entering the house where she lay, 'he took her by the hand and said to her, "Talitha cum," which means "Little girl, get up!", which she did'.[1] Most poignant is Jesus's cry from the Cross where he quotes Psalm 22, not in its original Hebrew, but in Aramaic: '*Eli, Eli, lema sabachthani?*' – 'My God, my God, why have you forsaken me?'[2]

Just how early the Gospels were translated from Greek into Syriac is not entirely clear. It seems that the early Syriac-speaking Christians first relied upon a medley, or 'harmony', of the Gospels called the 'Diatessaron' – literally, 'through the four'. This was the work of Tatian, a Syrian student of philosophy in Rome who had converted to Christianity. Sometime around AD 170, either in Rome or on his way back from there, Tatian wove materials from the four Gospels together to compose a single, narrative life of Jesus – the Diatessaron – in the Syriac of his native land.

This much was known from historical records, but no one had seen a Diatessaron for more than a thousand years, probably because they had all been deliberately destroyed. Early in the fifth century, Rabbula, Bishop of Edessa (411–37), religious capital of the Syriac-speaking world, decreed that each church should have a copy of the 'Separated Gospels' and that it was these (and not the conflated Diatessaron) that should be read to the people. Very likely he feared distortion from over-reliance on Tatian's harmony. Theodoret, Bishop of Cyrrhus (423–57), went a step further and destroyed 200 copies of the Diatessaron in his insistence on the reading of the four Gospels. It was, to Rendel Harris's great regret, a highly successful purge; he had looked everywhere for Tatian's Diatessaron, but there were none to be found.

Although the Aramaic dialects subsequently declined as living languages (and are now spoken only in a few isolated villages in the Middle East), Syriac remained the language of scripture and worship for these Eastern Christians, much as Latin was retained as the language of the Western Catholic Church. Syriac bibles were still in use, printed and published like bibles in English, French or German, but until the mid-nineteenth century the only known Syriac text of the Gospels was a version called the Peshitta (meaning 'simple'), a fifth-century translation into Syriac from the original Greek.

In 1842 a British clergyman made an important discovery. Archdeacon Tattam returned from Egypt with a bunch of manuscripts from the Coptic monastery of St Mary Deipara (St Mary, the God-bearer) in Egypt's Nitrian desert, and gave them to the British Museum. From amongst a group of fragments, an assistant-keeper named William Cureton pieced together some eighty pages of a previously unknown Syriac translation of the Gospels – one that antedated that of the Peshitta.

Cureton at first thought he might even have hit upon the original of St Matthew's Gospel, which was long rumoured to have been written in Aramaic. Closer inspection, however, demonstrated that the 'Curetonian', as it came to be known, was a translation from the Greek, though a very early one.

★

Back in Cambridge and discussing her finds with Rendel Harris and Robertson Smith, Agnes soon realised that her palimpsest might hold a text to rival the Curetonian – if not better it – in both antiquity and completeness. The Curetonian was mere fragments, but what she had found – as far as she could tell – was the Gospels almost complete.

The twins needed the benediction of a great authority before they could announce their find to the world, and this meant the lean, grey eminence of Professor Robert Bensly and his brilliant young adjutant, Francis Burkitt.

The behaviour of both at this juncture seemed short of the warmth that might be expected from former neighbours in Harvey Road. It was not easy for Agnes and Margaret to engage their attention. Agnes tried to get Professor Bensly to examine the photographs in June, but he declared himself 'far too busy', even though it was the vacation. Burkitt, she says, 'did not trouble to look at the said photographs the first time I offered to show them to him, in his own garden'.[3] Perhaps this attempt seemed inopportune given the setting, but how else should Agnes and Margaret attract their attention? Their photographs were after all, to these learned men, only the travel souvenirs of two middle-aged Scottish widows, one of whom had dabbled in Syriac for a few months and the other not at all. To academics, acceptability was a matter of credentials, and the twins officially had none. They were 'almost in despair about the matter', said Agnes, before they had the happy idea of asking Mrs Burkitt to lunch, with her husband, of course, and some other distinguished guests.[4] When all but the Burkitts and Mary Kingsley had gone, Agnes steered Mr Burkitt in the direction of the grand piano, where a selection of the clearest photographs was laid out. Politeness obliged him to have a look. Agnes explained that these were of a palimpsest, whose underwriting she knew to be Syriac Gospels not later than the fifth century. Burkitt at once showed deep interest and asked whether Agnes might entrust him with a few of the images to study at home.

This was a Friday. On Saturday morning the twins received an excited note:

My dear Mrs Lewis, – Frank is in a state of the highest excitement. He
wrote down a portion of the palimpsest last night, and has been in to Dr
Bensly with it, and they have discovered it is a copy of the Cureton
Syriac. Do you know, only one copy exists! You can imagine Frank's
glee! He has just been in to tell me, and has run back to the Benslys'. I
thought you would be interested and write at once. – I am, yours
affectionately, A. PERSIS BURKITT.[5]

The next morning Francis Burkitt intercepted Margaret at the door
of the Presbyterian church; he must have gone for that purpose, since
it was not his place of worship. He showed her a letter from Bensly
urging the utmost secrecy concerning the palimpsest. It was agreed
that the next day all should meet at the Benslys' to discuss the matter
further.

Burkitt and Bensly's attitude to Agnes's find had turned overnight
from indifference to frantic excitement, undershot with fear that other
scholars might get to the manuscript first. Professor Bensly, at sixty-
two, was not a robust man, but he had been at work on an edition of
the Curetonian Syriac Gospels for many years and its publication was
already announced.[6] He had to find out whether this was a rival to the
Curetonian, perhaps even a pre-emptive one. The twins' grainy
photographs launched him into what his friends regarded as a rather
venturesome enterprise. It was agreed that, since the palimpsest could
be copied accurately only from the original at Sinai and not from
photographs, a scholarly expedition must be planned for the soonest
opportunity: the coming January. Any suggestion that the twins might
stay behind was, as Agnes put it, 'quite out of the question'. The
palimpsest was her discovery, and it was she and Margaret who were
the friends of the monks. At their urging, Rendel Harris was to be
invited too. Harris had only recently returned to Cambridge as
Lecturer in Palaeography, after a few years working in the United
States, and did not consider himself a Syriac scholar of the order of the
other two men, but Agnes and Margaret valued his friendship, as well
as his experience in working with manuscripts.

Although the twins had travelled independently all over Europe and the Middle East, and even across Sinai without the protection of a European male, it was unacceptable for three English men to form a travelling party with two Scottish ladies not their wives, even if the ladies were widows in respectable middle age. The improbable solution was that Bensly and Burkitt should bring their wives, who both agreed with alacrity to the plan.

They would make an eccentric travelling party. Bensly had met his devoted and aristocratic wife, Agnes, eldest daughter of a German baron, when both were young and he was a student in Germany. Now Mrs Bensly was in her late fifties with failing eyesight: a photograph of the party en route shows her to be a small, trim woman with grey hair swept up, and very thick spectacles. In her memoir of the trip she recorded that in the early days of their marriage they had dreamed of travel in Eastern lands – 'we bought maps and guide books, we saluted each other with Bedouin phrases and gestures' – but for thirty years the education of children, the demands of Bensly's work, lack of money and the illness of a son had intervened. In fact, apart from occasional visits to European libraries, Bensly had rarely left Cambridge since returning from his studies in Germany. He had visited Arabic-speaking lands only twice, and neither time with academic purpose. He and Mrs Bensly had taken their ailing son to Algeria, hoping the climate would cure him (alas, the boy would die there), and in 1892 they had made a Thomas Cook's pleasure cruise down the Nile for the sake of Bensly's own lungs. Now Professor and Mrs Bensly were to have their hour in the Song of Songs.

The Burkitts, by contrast, were a golden young couple. At thirty-three, Francis Burkitt already had a reputation as a brilliant Orientalist. The scion of a tin-can fortune, he had initially studied mathematics at Cambridge, but had taken up oriental languages, especially Syriac, under the influence of Professor Robertson Smith. His young wife, Amy (known to all by her middle name, 'Persis'), was a great beauty – she of the 'wonderful feathers', in the words of Mrs Keynes.[7] Delicate health and doctors' advice notwithstanding, she wanted to be part of so bold a venture. Their young son would stay behind with his nanny.

Professor Bensly swore all to the strictest secrecy about the palimpsest.

Having already accepted an invitation from Professor Robertson Smith, Agnes was to be allowed to present a paper to the forthcoming International Congress of Orientalists in London – but she was to make no mention of the palimpsest; nor could she talk about it in her hotel or to anyone she met. She accepted these strictures gladly for the sake of the great work that lay before them. But the twins also heeded the advice of Robertson Smith, a man familiar with the intrigues of the academy, and well aware that high-minded scholars were not above low-minded tactics, especially where precious manuscripts were concerned. Though friends to all the parties (indeed, he had inspired Francis Burkitt to study oriental languages), Robertson Smith recommended that Agnes put a notice in *The Athenaeum*, alerting the world to an important new find and staking a claim. There were two difficulties; first, the notice had to be credible without giving anything away as to the location of the manuscript, lest other scholars dash off to Sinai before them to examine it; second, Agnes was, to the editors of *The Athenaeum*, a complete unknown. The solution was that Rendel Harris send the notice in his name. So it was that on 6 August 1892, the following notice appeared in the journal's 'Literary Gossip' section:

> WE ARE asked by Mr Rendel Harris to announce the discovery of a new text of the old Syriac version of the Gospels (Curetonian Syriac). A copy of the text has already been made, and is under the examination of well-known English editors.

Agnes and Margaret were elated at the idea of returning to Sinai so soon, and in such august company. A note from Agnes to Persis Burkitt bustles with expectant planning. She had been to London, where she and Margaret sat up until the small hours listening to the tales of a real Chaldee Christian (perhaps an Iraqi), who was indignant that his mother tongue should be called 'Syriac'. She had found a water filter that would do for four people. She had visited Mr Scott, Keeper of Manuscripts at the British Museum, and he had demonstrated a chemical reagent that could be used to darken the faint underscript – 'Mr Scott has told me where to get the stuff. Its only drawback is that it has a horrid smell.' She finished by enclosing some dress patterns to be made up by a local Cambridge provisioner, Eaden Lilley, as suitable desert attire for ladies.

Agnes divided some 350 photographs among the three men for them to work on, corresponding to the sections they would work on at Sinai. While Agnes devoted her time to the study of the Syriac of the palimpsest, Margaret – at Robertson Smith's suggestion – worked towards the publication of an important Arabic find. She was more than aware of her limitations in this effort, but Robertson Smith assisted and used his influence as a Syndic, or board member, of the Cambridge University Press to secure her a contract.[8]

Amid all this, their other schemes did not suffer. The twins and Alick Macalister, who was a Fellow of St John's, had conceived an interest in some of that college's farmlands not far from Castlebrae. By the end of 1892 Agnes and Margaret proposed to buy this land, at a cost of £4,500, and offer it to the Presbyterian Synod as a site for a theological college; as a further inducement to the wavering Synod, another £5,000 was to be paid immediately towards a building and £15,000 more on their death. The Synod was divided.[9] Those favouring 'the Cambridge plan' wanted to raise the tone – social as well as intellectual – of the English Presbyterian clergy so that they might live 'on a level socially and economically with the rectors and deans of the English establishment'. A house in Cambridge would attract a better sort of student (that is, from the wealthier classes), and might even prove a beacon for Anglican fugitives wishing to escape the ritualism and popery that were alleged to be disintegrating that communion. The site in Cambridge, near the ancient colleges, seemed to its advocates a 'providential gift' at a time when the London college was financially hard-pressed.

Those opposed to the move argued that the clamour of London was 'real life' while Cambridge in the 1890s was a somnolent, medieval university town. They feared the 'relaxing' (that is, enervating) air close to a slow-moving river. To say the site was 'near to the colleges' was an exaggeration – it was near to the back entrance to St John's College, but nearer yet to Cambridge gaol, three noisy schools and the slum housing of Bandyleg Walk. It was, in fact, in the middle of the highest concentration of taverns in Cambridge. There was a further risk of corrupting the Presbyterian inheritance: Cambridge might be less infected by ritualism than Oxford, but it contained the same virus. Students exposed to the specious charms of Anglicanism at an impressionable age might end up aping genteel Anglican curates – presentable and mellifluous essayists, rather than fiery preachers of the Word. What if, instead of sheltering refugees from popery, the Presbyterian college found its own students (especially the socially ambitious or those far from home) attracted to ritualism? The proffered gift of the site was, its opponents argued, 'a gift which blindeth the eyes of the wise'.[10] It was decided that a deputation of the Synod should come to Cambridge the following April to see the land and discuss the plans with the twins and Alick Macalister.

Meanwhile, plans for Sinai continued apace, though the Benslys and Burkitts were reluctant recipients of Agnes and Margaret's travel advice. The Benslys, timidly, wanted all arrangements to be made by Thomas Cook's, including the provision of a dragoman. The twins thought Cook's terms absurdly expensive and inflexible. Emboldened by the counsel she had received from one of the monks, Margaret went so far as to suggest that no dragoman was necessary at all: the Bedouin were the real guides in Sinai; they understood camels and could get on with the brethren at the convent. The wild liberty of this proposal so alarmed the Burkitts and Benslys that they agreed to let the twins, who were to precede them to Cairo, make the initial selection of a dragoman, subject to the others' subsequent approval.

For all the planning it was, rather unfortunately, never made entirely clear whose expedition this really was. All parties appear to have paid their own way, which made for democratic esprit but not, perhaps, unity of vision. Agnes and Mrs Bensly, in their respective memoirs of the trip, provide divergent understandings of who it was that initiated the expedition and who had merely volunteered to go along: and herein lay a fatal fault line.[11]

CHAPTER 17

The disjoint expedition

The expedition proceeded in this slightly disjointed manner. While the twins travelled to Egypt the most direct way – by steamer from Marseilles – the Benslys chose to go via Italy, sailing for Egypt from Brindisi; meanwhile the Burkitts paused for some days on the French Riviera. Arriving in Cairo in advance of the others, Agnes and Margaret took rooms in the Hôtel d'Angleterre (Shepheard's now being, to their minds, absurdly touristic), and secured the notional agreement of a highly recommended dragoman called Ahmed abd-er Raheem. They then set about preparing the ground with Archbishop Porphyrios, now resident in a new, more splendid building.

The blessing of the Archbishop of Sinai was essential for the success of the enterprise and the twins had no reason to doubt he would grant it, but they felt burdened by the secrecy to which Bensly had sworn them – 'this secrecy from one who had befriended us,' wrote Agnes, 'was quite against my judgment'. Their meeting took place on 11 January 1893, the twins' fiftieth birthday, and proved auspicious. Agnes and Margaret had read a recent essay by Pericles Gregoriades, Professor in the Theological School of the Holy Sepulchre, who singled out two urgent needs for the convent of St Catherine's: first, a systematic catalogue of its manuscripts to prevent anything else from going missing; and second, a new library. So the twins came with a proposal for a public subscription to fund the structure. Porphyrios was enthusiastic and showed them plans for the library he had already commissioned, detailed down to the number of camel-loads of sandstone from a quarry fourteen days' away. Margaret 'improved the occasion' by proposing that she catalogue the Arabic manuscripts in the convent and volunteering Agnes – without having asked her in advance – to do the same for the Syriac. She produced a wad of gummed labels brought from England for the purpose. His Eminence was surprised and somewhat amused: he politely wondered if it was not too much work, but agreed, with the proviso that copies of the catalogues, written out in Greek, be left at the convent. He wrote to his monks requiring them to assist the ladies in every way.

The Benslys were next to arrive and they settled into Shepheard's. They had been delegated by the Burkitts, who were still in France, to approve the choice of dragoman, but Professor Bensly's first act was to scare off Ahmed, the man so carefully selected by Agnes and Margaret, by incautiously reading aloud to him a passage from Baedeker's guidebook to Palestine on the adequate provisioning of claret. Ahmed withdrew, most likely for fear of incurring extra costs when the terms of his contract were already agreed. Since Professor Bensly's response to the chaos he had produced was to become immediately engrossed in the study of a manuscript in the Ghizeh Museum, the task of selecting a replacement fell to his wife.

Mrs Bensly had no shortage of applicants. They were not allowed to enter Shepheard's itself, but the moment she appeared on the hotel terrace she was besieged. If she sat down, they took the next chair; if she strolled, they walked next to her. All had letters of recommendations, which they kept up their sleeves and would spread out on tables or, if Mrs Bensly was out walking, on the street before her. Everyone seemed to be named 'Mohammed', and she began to suspect that one Mohammed would lend his letters of recommendation to another Mohammed in need. She rapidly agreed with the twins that it would be better to persuade Ahmed to return, which he did, but not before having negotiated improved terms.

Agnes and Margaret brought the Benslys to meet the archbishop so that, as was standard practice, he could witness their contracts with both Ahmed and the Bedouin sheikh who would be in charge of the camel drivers. The twins translated into modern Greek throughout. They introduced Professor Bensly as a figure of the greatest scholarly eminence, while Mrs Bensly looked on approvingly. To add lustre to the occasion Bensly had brought with him a specimen copy of the recently discovered 'Gospel' of St Peter, a text that had never been canonical, but which had excited a good deal of interest in the 1890s. The archbishop, glancing at it distantly, remarked that the four Gospels were enough for him, but graciously accepted as a gift the copy that Bensly had merely meant to show him. Finally His Eminence offered them coffee and sweetmeats, and instructed his secretary to draft letters of permission.

The Burkitts soon arrived and joined the Benslys at Shepheard's. As their contracted dragoman, Ahmed was now able to come and go freely at their hotels, consulting the party on all matters relating to their comfort and acting as their guide to Cairo. He took them to his home, a roomy house with stables outside the town, and introduced them to his plump and pretty young wife (number two), adorned with rubies, velvet and silk and hung with gold bangles. They met his young son, a Sudanese slave whom he had found being ill treated and had adopted, and who would accompany them on the journey.

At last all was ready. The camels and stores set out in advance for Suez and, after three days' final stocking up on such last-minute items as spectacles with blue glass lenses (the precursors of modern sunglasses) and cork helmets with puggarees, the Cambridge party followed by train. They left a letter to the London *Times* with a British associate in Cairo, who was under clear instructions to post it once they were under way. In phrasing approved by all, it announced the astonishing find of the palimpsest and the composition of the group who now set out to work upon it. The time for secrecy was over, and the whole party anticipated the astonishment and acclaim of *Times* readers back home.

Rendel Harris met them at Suez, having hesitated about whether to join the party until the last moment, and on 30 January 1893 the whole expedition, travelling united for the first time, sailed by felucca down the Red Sea to 'Ain Musa to await their camels and drivers. They sat waiting on the wooden benches until nightfall when, at last, their caravan appeared, the weird and fantastic shapes of the laden camels bathed in the silver sheen of a full moon. There was a commotion of snorting camels, shouting, clanking tent poles and flapping ropes, followed presently by a gong as the waiter bowed them into the dining tent. On a floor covered with matting stood a table with a snow-white cloth, a large bunch of flowers, candles, bowls of oranges and pomegranates and two glass flagons of pure water. Excellent soup, meat, pudding and freshly ground coffee followed – Ahmed had passed his first test.

The Benslys had dreaded the prospect of riding camels. They had even experimented in Cairo with a litter suspended between two of them by poles and chains. This was a dismal failure, for although the camels were elaborately decorated, the comfort of the travellers was sadly forgotten in a Noah's Ark-like box without cushions. The passenger, sitting on dusty boards, was too low to look out, half-choked by the blowing sand and strangely seasick.

But, once in Sinai, the Benslys found they liked riding camels. Agnes pointed out that the creatures' aversion to getting up and down, and to any other rapid or taxing movement, made them reluctant to buck or bolt, and riding them was as safe as sitting on a boulder. 'A camel,' she wrote, 'becomes an intensely interesting being when he is carrying you . . . You regard the elastic spring in his spongy foot, the not ungraceful movements of his long massive neck, with as much interest as you are wont to bestow on the telegraphic column of your newspaper at home, and all his humours become as important as the last piece of gossip in your visiting circle.'[1] In time Mrs Bensly even forgave them their hissing snarl, allowing that 'it is the only voice vouchsafed to these animals, and by no means always a sign of anger; they use it when meeting their friends, and when calling to their young', and in any case it 'is much softened by distance'.[2]

Every photograph of Ahmed shows him with a cigarette: running a first-class, mobile hotel in the midst of a wilderness was a taxing experience. He was an honest and competent dragoman, but had little direct experience of the Sinai, or of the Bedouin. Agnes observed that at first he ordered them about with the 'overbearing manner which a Mohammedan Egyptian is accustomed to use . . . to inferiors. The

Ahmed, the dragoman

Bedouin would not stand this.' On the second night they refused to help pitch the tents, a crisis only resolved when Ahmed became more deferential, adding 'please do me a favour' before every order. Agnes thought this took politeness too far. She observed that another dragoman, when he lost his temper with the Bedouin, bestowed 'a savage kick on his own canteen. I do not quite see the utility of this proceeding . . . but it has one advantage, for the canteen harbours no grudge against him.'

Ahmed's only other shortcoming was that he had failed to bring enough fresh, or even tinned, vegetables, with the consequence that the group dined almost entirely on soup and meat, followed by plum puddings – fare he thought suitable for Europeans. This was hard on everybody's digestion, but especially for Rendel Harris, who was a vegetarian. Agnes had experienced something similar with hotel-keepers in Jerusalem. Vegetables were cheap, so it was assumed they 'are therefore not good enough for European gentry, and you grind the

most stringy of meat, trying to like it, whilst a few doors off, magnificent cauliflower and asparagus lie in the shops as if under a ban.'

Mrs Bensly thought their thirty camels with drivers excessive for
seven travellers until she saw what must be carried: casks of sweet
water from the Ataka mountains, flour barrels, sacks of charcoal, a
cooking stove, crates of fowl (more than 200 turkeys, chickens and
pigeons, with water skins and grain sacks set aside for them), chests of
beans, lentils and rice, five tents, folding bedsteads, trestle tables,
chairs, mattresses and blankets, baskets of oranges, dates and dried
apricots. All had to be loaded onto the back of growling camels, each
of whose owners protested if his beast's load seemed heavier than the
next one's. A huge camera with its heavy box, belonging to Rendel
Harris, caused daily disputes amongst the camel drivers and, in the
end, turned out to have been broken all along. The best photographs
of the trip across were taken with Mrs Bensly's Kodak, which she kept
lightly slung over her pommel.

Each British traveller was seated on large saddle-cushions and
carried his or her own luggage, that of the driver (which comprised
only a blanket and water bottle) and a private store of bread, dates and
beans for the camel. Ahmed himself carried a quantity of tobacco to
dole out, to enhance the general good humour. The Bedouin walked
the whole way, normally barefoot, but on rocky ground wearing
wooden sandals held on with leather thongs.

To the camels, all the British were equal, but each proceeded into
the desert with a different estimation of their own self-importance:
Professor Bensly confident in his scholarly pre-eminence, Mrs Bensly
proudly the wife of the professor; Agnes as discoverer of the palimpsest
and experienced Eastern traveller. Yet it was Persis Burkitt, as graceful
socially as she was fine-looking, who emerged as the darling. It must
have been galling for Agnes especially, glowing with pride in her (as yet
unannounced) discovery, that in Cairo or Suez, whether at diplomatic
introductions or hotel soirées, Persis effortlessly became the centre of
attention. A studio photo of the day shows Persis, at thirty-three years
of age, to be a perfect belle époque beauty: full brown hair swept up
into a loose chignon, a lovely face framed by quantities of Brussels lace

and a Bedouin silver necklace. Even now, in the desert amongst the Bedouin, which Agnes might reasonably claim as her own domain of expertise, Persis proved a natural – surprising them all, herself included, with an impressive command of colloquial Arabic.

As a young child she had lived for several years in a Lebanese village, where her mother had retreated for reasons of health. Persis and her sisters played freely with the village children, speaking Arabic, which she thought she had forgotten; Agnes's few attempts to run through some verbs with her while they were still in Cambridge had been a failure. Now, overhearing the camel drivers speak amongst themselves in unvarnished terms about their new clients, her Arabic returned. And it was of the most useful sort. While in Lebanon her mother had spent

Persis Burkitt, aged thirty–three, in an oriental necklace

her evenings riding through the countryside distributing Bible Society New Testaments to the villagers, with her children carried in panniers slung over the backs of donkeys. As a result Persis had acquired not just colloquial Arabic, but the salty vocabulary favoured by donkey drivers and, it now appeared, camel drivers. She upbraided the Bedouin in their own colourful dialect and was from that moment their firm favourite.[3] They called her 'Princess'.

Persis's greatest admirer was the youngest of the drivers. Just twelve years old, he was the eldest son of a sheikh recently deceased, and so was now a sheikh himself. Though young and poor, he was responsible for his mother and had to work. Mrs Bensly noted that the older men were kind to him, letting him lie close to the fire during the nights, which were still bitterly cold, and covering him with their blankets. It was on his camel that Persis rode and he poured out his heart to her. On one occasion Mrs Bensly saw him kiss the leather of her boot, the only part of her dress he could reach while she sat in the saddle.

On the third day the veneer of civility amongst the men cracked. It was Rendel Harris's custom to set out walking immediately after breakfast, sometimes in the company of Agnes and Margaret, but on this occasion alone. He got lost, only for ten minutes, but when he caught up with the party he was in disgrace with Bensly and Burkitt. They seemed to have agreed, according to a letter from Harris to his wife Helen, that Professor Bensly 'should read me a lecture, which he did in a towering passion . . . I don't think I have been so pitched into for twenty years.'[4] Harris's apologies were reluctantly accepted, but the incident served to convince him of what he had already suspected – the other two men did not want him on the trip at all.

The rest of the day passed in aggrieved silence, softened for Harris by the commiserations of the twins and the beauties of riding amidst a primrose sunset along a perfectly calm Red Sea. Mrs Gibson and Mrs Lewis, Harris wrote to his wife 'would amuse thee: they have hemmed me some handkerchiefs & helped me to make my bed'.[5]

At the insistence of Agnes and Margaret, Sunday was observed by everyone, except the cook, as a day of rest. The tents were organised in a circle at the foot of a hill and a Union Jack was hoisted above the dining tent. Cushions and rugs were put outside in the shade, and prayers read in English and Arabic. After an elegantly set-out lunch, Ahmed invited the party to afternoon tea – not part of his contract, but as a nod to British custom.

In the afternoon the cook showed off his kitchen: copper pans hanging on portable handles, which telescoped into one another; an ingenious oven that folded up into a tiny box and on which he prepared three meals a day for twelve people – the Bedouin looked after themselves. The travellers admired his tiny pans of charcoal sunk into the sand, which could keep a kettle on the boil for hours. He even had equipment for roasting and grinding coffee, although the Bedouin achieved the same effect on a fire fed by camel dung, grinding their beans between two stones. In the evening they had a festive dinner: pea soup, roast turkey, pigeon pie with sauce and compotes, plum pudding, tarts and jellies, and fresh fruits for dessert. Agnes rounded things off by reading the seventeenth chapter of Exodus for an account of a more austere crossing.

★

The desert rest; the Cambridge party and Ahmed, en route

Although no wires were in place, the monks knew all that was afoot on the peninsula by 'Bedouin telegraph', and that a party of scholars was soon to appear with permission to study. They did not know who comprised it. When, ten days after leaving Suez, the Cambridge visitors arrived, walking on ahead of their camel caravan, Father Galaktéon's delight at seeing Rendel Harris (whom he had liked) and the twins (whom he adored) knew no bounds.

Galatktéon was now abbot. Welcoming them all, he paid special attention to Agnes, patting her affectionately and dancing around her like a schoolboy. Insisting that she sit by his side, his arm around her shoulders, they enjoyed a lively conversation punctuated by loud bursts of laughter. He plied her with questions about their former cook at Castlebrae, whose plans for marriage had been described to him during the long hours of photographing the previous year. He chided Rendel Harris for not bringing Mrs Harris.

Through all this the Benslys and the Burkitts stood by bemused, unable to follow the rapid, spoken Greek. Mrs Bensly was not certain this unexpected familiarity from the 'highest dignitary of the Holy Catholic Church in this wide Muhammedan district' was at all seemly, but at least, she wrote in her memoir, the abbot's excessive friendliness augured well for his willingness to let them see the manuscript they had travelled all this way to study. They were served quince jam from a beautiful glass bowl, with a silver spoon for each guest; shown the garden where their tents would be set up, once their baggage camels arrived; and then deposited in the abbot's reception room with the promise that he would shortly be there to give them a first tour of the library.

They had some time to wait before 'hasty steps, a fall, a cry' announced the arrival of Galaktéon, who appeared before them with 'a bleeding face and dishevelled hair'. He had slipped on the stairs, but nonetheless insisted on taking them to the library without delay. As they were leaving from this first inspection, Galaktéon took Agnes aside and told her that he would be guided by her advice in everything, 'and that as four of the party were as yet strangers to him' he would prefer that all requests for books, etc., should come to him through her. After that, since he and his brethren must turn once again to their prayers, the Cambridge visitors were politely taken outside the monastic walls to the monastic gardens. The sun had disappeared behind the wall of mountains before the travellers, huddled against the cold awaiting their caravan, were heartened by the growls of kneeling camels, the clatter of tent poles and then, soon afterwards, cups of thick, sweet Arab coffee.

The next day the men had their first close look at the palimpsest. It was smaller than they had expected from the photographs – its pages only eight and five-eighths by six and a quarter inches – and the whole bound within boards. The yellowish-red underwriting of the Gospel was easily distinguished from the clear, black letters of the lives of women saints that overlay it, but this underwriting, if readily distinguishable, was not easily deciphered – in fact, almost illegible in many places. Rendel Harris, the palaeographer, declared the palimpsest not overwhelmingly difficult; he had seen worse. Nevertheless, the task that lay before them would require immense skill, labour and united effort.

The transcription of even a well-preserved manuscript is more than a mechanical matter. It involves the sort of educated guess that is only possible for someone steeped in the language and comparable ancient texts. Even the ambitious Agnes, who at one stage hoped to help in the copying, had to cede this task wholly to Bensly, Burkitt and Harris.

Before journeying to Sinai, Agnes had already given the photographs of the first 100 or so pages of the palimpsest to Rendel Harris, a similar amount to Burkitt and the final eighty-four to the slower and more meticulous Professor Bensly. This division determined the section of the manuscript that each would work upon. Since the palimpsest was a tiny book and bound, only one reader at a time could work on it. Professor Bensly went first and, finding the light in the transcription room very poor, pushed the rickety table out onto the gallery outside. There each transcriber sat in turn, an icy wind fluttering the pages on which they wrote, and chilling him to the bone. At 'eleven', according to the monks (five o'clock in the afternoon according to the Cambridge party), work was cut short when a monk informed them that it was time to stop and lock up the convent for the night.

So the transcription continued, day after day, constrained by the limited daylight hours, the timetable of the monks and the cold. It was not helped by increasing tension within the party. Rendel Harris posted regular letters to his wife Helen, by means of passing camel caravans and groups of Russian pilgrims, which document an atmosphere of growing bitterness and distrust.

Ten days into their stay there had been another 'blazing row'. Professor Bensly immediately on their arrival had seized upon the volume in which Rendel Harris, several years before, had discovered the 'Apology of Aristides'. Bensly's plan, apparently (although it was not one he had shared with Agnes, Margaret or Rendel Harris), was to do an edition of several other Syriac tracts bound in the same volume, and he was now outraged to learn from Agnes not only that she had already photographed half of them on her previous trip, but that Harris had them ready for the press. 'There was a great outburst,' wrote Rendel Harris. 'I offered to give all my transcripts to Bensly, but this would mean the desertion of my lady friends, who had had as much to bear as myself, if not more. I am ashamed to write such unpleasant letters from my paradise.'[6]

Already longing to be anywhere but in the presence of Burkitt and Bensly, Harris found the work painfully slow, but did not see how it could get on any faster, 'unless by some unexpected chance, the authorities should give us the loan of the MS. I wish they would but see not the slightest prospect.' In forty days the camels and Bedouin drivers who had brought them would reappear to take them back, whether or not the transcription was finished. The monks are increasingly kind, wrote Harris, 'especially to Mrs Lewis and myself': 'I am certain our other friends [Bensly and Burkitt] would have done nothing without us. As it is they are regarded (by the monks) with much suspicion. But they have given us to understand that they consider themselves in no wise indebted to us, & that they could have got on very well without our assistance. So thee can see how we stand. Meanwhile the two Scotch ladies & I get on very well.'[7]

There was then a breakthrough. As a sign of special favour to Agnes, Galaktéon granted permission for the manuscript to stay in their camp, provided that Agnes alone should guard it in her tent by night. This made for a great improvement in their working conditions. As soon as the sun was up, one of trestle tables (otherwise serving as Mrs Bensly's washstand) was set outside and transformed into a rickety desk at which the men could work in turn on the manuscript. Agnes asked for a more substantial work surface and a large and steady table was brought down from the monastery on the shoulders of four monks, but Ahmed immediately impounded it 'ostensibly for the purpose of ironing shirts, but really for that of washing dishes'.[8] Professor Bensly took the first shift each day at the washstand, bundled in greatcoat, comforter and Homburg hat – and wearing woollen gloves on the February mornings. It remained bitterly cold, and once they woke to find ice on their washbasins. Ahmed's young Sudanese son – who had never before seen ice – took a circular piece and danced it about in front of him like a mirror.

The men were now able to work on the manuscript in continuous

Professor Bensly taking his turn with the palimpsest

shifts, with the camp's chickens and ducks, freed from their travelling cases, pecking about at their feet. Breakfast, lunch and coffee were brought to the worker at his washstand, and silence observed in his vicinity. A monastic assistant was on hand to sharpen pencils, pass bibles and dictionaries, and hold down pages should the wind get too high. The monks would stop and look on their way to and from the garden, sometimes bringing gifts of dried apricots and date wine. In this way the men worked steadily through the nine or ten hours of daylight, until the sun descended and the mountains threw the valley into shadow.

The camp began to assume a settled and orderly appearance. The tents were evenly arranged around an open space that was scrupulously swept by Ahmed's son each day. Bibles, dictionaries and grammars were neatly stacked and clothes hung on pegs, and the monks even provided a few rush-bottomed chairs.

Agnes and Margaret were getting on with their promised catalogues of the convent's Arabic and Syriac manuscripts, which lay dispersed about the compound. Most of the Greek manuscripts were in the upper 'show' library next to the archbishop's reception room, but those needed for the liturgy were in the church, and others were in the monks' cells, reading rooms, cupboards and closets. The twins worked in the archbishop's room, which, despite its grand title, Agnes described as 'a small place with no glass to its three windows, with several ill-fitting doors leading into tiny rooms, where numbers of vellum MSS are stored in wooden chests, but into which only the very favoured of our party are allowed to peep'.[9] Each day the monks would bring a new set of volumes to be assessed.

A rough catalogue existed, which gave numbers to the Syriac and Arabic manuscripts, but these were stored haphazardly in closets, boxes and open baskets without regard to the numbering system. The sub-librarian, Father Euthymios, often had to search several days to find a manuscript so that the twins could count its pages, note its contents and write the short catalogue note in Greek, as demanded by the archbishop. Rendel Harris, when not taking his turn at the palimpsest, would read out to Agnes the titles of the treatises contained in any particular Syriac volume – of which there was usually more than one – and she would copy the titles down in English, translating her comments into Greek in the evenings in the solitude of her tent. Agnes said that listing titles was a relatively light matter, the greatest labour of cataloguing manuscripts being 'purely mechanical, it consists of measuring and of counting pages'. Whoever had numbered the manuscripts previously had done so in order of state of preservation, so that, after the first fifty examples, the rest 'ran to seed' in damage and incompleteness, making it tedious and difficult to count and describe them.

Margaret, cataloguing the Arabic manuscripts, had almost three times the number of volumes that Agnes had. Most of the Arabic manuscripts had lost not only their title pages, but their last leaves,

A page from the catalogue of Arabic manuscripts which
Margaret did for the monks, Arabic into Greek

probably to Western trophy-hunters, so it was difficult to find dates. 'One is ashamed to think,' Margaret was to write in her introduction to the published catalogue, 'that some scholar in former years must have abused the hospitality of the monks, and that a choice collection of title-pages may be found in some European library.' Some – fortunately not many – of the manuscripts had been 'inwardly digested' by little rodents more innocent than scholars'.[10] Persis Burkitt helped by transcribing an Arabic text, and even the seriously shortsighted Mrs Bensly, along with the monks, helped with the 'irksome duty' of counting pages. The twins took photographs to assist them with the eventual editorial work back in Britain.

This seemingly innocent work undertaken by Agnes and Margaret on behalf of the archbishop and monks proved another flashpoint. It was now entirely evident that Bensly and Burkitt resented Harris's presence and considered Agnes and Margaret upstarts – in which judgement their wives concurred. Mrs Bensly, normally gentleness itself, tore a strip off Agnes for having in her tent (and showing to Rendel Harris) a manuscript not previously examined by her husband.

Like many of the most heated disputes, this one was fed by indignation felt on behalf of another – in this case the Burkitts weighing in on behalf of the aggrieved Professor Bensly. Briefly and sympathetically their position was this: Professor Bensly was the greatest Syriac scholar in the land, and the glory of the new Syriac palimpsest and any important new finds should, by right, be his. Harris was not a Syriac specialist, but someone who had the good fortune to discover the Syriac 'Apology of Aristides' on a previous Sinai expedition, and was now trying, opportunistically, to horn in on the discoveries on this one.[11] Harris's every action was cast in a malign light. The note published in *The Athenaeum* under his name, announcing in vague terms the find of ancient Syriac Gospels – a note that Harris had only sent at the request of Agnes – was taken as evidence of his ambitions. Now Burkitt and Bensly regarded his assistance in cataloguing as a scheme to be the first to find anything new.

On 23 February Rendel Harris walked for an hour or so down the Wadi esh-Sheikh to intercept a caravan that was said to have some letters. He was rewarded by one from Helen, written only ten days earlier. In a note sent by return he wrote of the incident between Agnes and Mrs Bensly, adding: 'they are carrying this theory of Bensly's priority ad absurdum. However, when I heard what was the matter, I followed Mrs Lewis's suggestion & gave him the book . . .'[12]

To placate enraged honour, an agreement was reached whereby, before Agnes, Margaret and Harris even touched any new batch of manuscripts brought to them for cataloguing, Professor Bensly and Mr Burkitt would inspect them, so that no one should have the advantage of a new discovery.

This atmosphere of increasing suspicion and resentment, which was concealed from their hosts for the sake of decorum, was at odds with the peaceful, self-reliant world of the monks and Jabaliya Bedouin, which carried on around them. Men fetched water from the garden's great covered cistern, with steps that descended into it, while children with 'beautiful wondering eyes' flitted around in search of baksheesh.

Mrs Bensly, having least to do with the manuscripts, had the most time to observe the monks. Her notes, published as *Our Journey to Sinai*, are like those of a naturalist observing a new species. The monks, it is true, did not spend much time in scholarship, but they had little time to give: eight hours a day were devoted to prayers, slightly less to sleep and in the remainder they were their own masons, carpenters, shoe-makers, tailors and gardeners. They were, she observed, docile, gentle and industrious – and in every way respectful and kind to their visitors. One day she and Professor Bensly watched an old monk pruning the vines on the terrace below, observing 'how deftly he used his scissors, when he suddenly dropped them, and ran away as fast as his old legs would carry him. We were afraid of having offended him, but he soon returned with a basket of beautiful raisins, which he presented to us as the fruit of these his own particular vines.'[13]

But it was the steward, Nicodemus, who elicited her special praise, perhaps because he spoke French as fluently as she did and so they were able to converse. As *economos*, or steward, he was responsible for the visitors, as well as for the day-to-day material needs of the convent. Father Nicodemus emerges from Mrs Bensly's account as the

Renaissance man of monastic life: handsome and intelligent, fluent in several European languages and a writer of scholarly articles. He attended to repairs on the church and oversaw a new plantation of fruit trees. One day might find him clearing and deepening the channels that brought fresh water to the convent cisterns; the next he might be away for a journey to Suez or Tor, another small Red Sea port, to fetch flour, fuel or cloth by camel.

Mrs Bensly also had time to teach a Bedouin woman to knit. They did not share a language, and the strings of coins that veiled the woman's face made it difficult for Mrs Bensly to read her expressions. She might have succeeded, but for the active interest of the men and boys who gathered whenever they saw the two women at work. As soon as they appeared, the woman hid her face in her cloak and the lesson was over. However, the men and boys themselves proved keen and quick pupils. Mrs Bensly had to draw a semicircle in the sand in front of her lest they crowd too close, but in this way passed many happy hours until her wool was gone.

The Bedouin who had brought them to Sinai had dispersed to their own camps, with an arrangement to return with the camels when the party was ready to depart, but one day the boy sheikh, Ayeed, appeared, having walked eight hours across the desert. He had remembered how Persis Burkitt enjoyed goat's milk at one of the evening camps and, unaware that the travellers had now purchased their own milk ewe, was bearing a bottle from his mother's flock, stoppered with a twisted rag. He insisted on returning the next day, for his mother would miss him. Persis gave him an English shawl, but the Bedouin would report that this had attracted the 'evil eye', for shortly afterwards his camel died and he was unable to join the party for its return to Suez. The Bedouin women who came, on certain days, to receive their gift of bread from the convent carefully covered the faces of their babies for fear of the same curse or, as Mrs Bensly said, lest the British party 'should injure them by coveting their beauty'.

Little by little the composition of the palimpsest was revealing its secrets. They discovered that the upper texts concerning female saints had been copied out and signed by John, the Recluse of Beth Mari – a monastery in the district of Antioch. This martyrology was, according to Agnes, 'of a very racy nature'. Along with the lives – and, even more importantly, the deaths – of the Blessed Lady Thecla, disciple of Paul, the Blessed Apostle, and of the Blessed Eugenia, St Irene and St Barbara, they included the 'virtuous acts' of 'Pelagia, the harlot of Antioch, a city of Syria' and the 'martyrdom of Theodota, the Harlot'. Such writings were not to be found in the lending collection of St Columba's Presbyterian church, and Agnes concluded that they threw 'a curious light on the monastic life at its prime. They have apparently been well read, perhaps by generations of Sinai monks, if we may judge from the thumb-stained margins.'[14]

It was now possible to make out how John, the Recluse, had pulled apart a discarded copy of the Gospels in Syriac, scrubbed out the writing on it and reused it for the text he was copying; 142 of 182 leaves of vellum that made up his 'Lives of the Saints' were from the Gospel manuscript.[15] To John's eye, the original text on the vellum he scraped had been totally erased. Only the passage of time had brought it forward again.[16] Once he had run out of the sheets of the Syriac Gospels, the sainted Recluse gathered sheets from elsewhere: some from a Greek copy of the Gospel of St John, others from a Syriac volume of the Apocrypha, all presumably derelict copies or fragments which could be sacrificed for the completion of his copy of the martyrology. As a result, each turning of the page that brought the transcriber the next helping of the libidinous lives of the female saints also brought him at random into a ghostly section of the Gospels – pages one and two of the 'Lives' being written, for instance, on Matthew 15, whiles pages three and four lay on Luke 8. Each page had to be puzzled out afresh, and some were so faded that the writing, according to Agnes, 'could only be discerned by letting the noon-day sunlight shine through it', revealing the scratches of the stylus. As Margaret observed, 'There is nothing that does not leave its mark in this serious world of ours.'[17]

Progress continued at a snail's pace, and Agnes's thoughts turned to the chemical reagent she had bought on the advice of the British Museum. Professor Bensly disapproved of such things – a manuscript

in Paris had recently been ruined by use of a reagent. Even Rendel
Harris counselled delay. But their fears, Agnes reckoned, applied to
earlier reagents, whereas hers was the latest innovation. She waited for
her moment. Eventually, when she had in her hands a manuscript of
secondary importance whose ink had faded from brownish-black to an
almost invisible yellow, she explained to Galaktéon that she 'had a
preparation which could restore it to its pristine beauty and which was
approved by the authorities of the British Museum', but that she must
use it out of doors and after lunch, for otherwise its appalling smell of
rotten eggs would make her retch.

Seated at her little table and beneath a shady tree, she opened her
bottle for the experiment.

> I was not a little nervous, for though I was accustomed to the handling
> of water-colour brushes, I neither knew how this stuff or how the
> ancient ink of the manuscript would behave on close acquaintance with
> each other. To see Mr Scott do it and to do it myself were entirely
> different things. Moreover three learned and critical representatives of
> Cambridge University were behind me and a group of curious Orientals
> in front. So with apparent boldness, but not a little misgiving, I dipped a
> large brush in my bottle and passed it lightly but rapidly over the vellum
> leaf.

The results were instant and almost miraculous: 'up came the old
script in a rich dark olive green hue . . .' The Arabs shouted with
delight and the cook came running with a spoon in his hand to see
what was the matter. On looking round at the more critical
spectators, she found nothing but expressions of delight – Rendel
Harris was 'quite unconsciously to himself, pirouetting round one of
the tents in the fullness of his joy'. Only Professor Bensly remained
unconvinced. 'How long will it last?' he asked. Agnes explained that
it was meant to last a century. 'It has not been tried for a century,'
came the reply.[18]

Galaktéon showed a true librarian's instincts in insisting that,
wherever Agnes wanted to treat a whole page with reagent, she leave

Agnes with the reagent

at least two lines untouched to show what the original had been. Eventually even Bensly, whose extreme meticulousness meant that he was falling behind, gave in and started calling for the 'delicious scent'.

As much as one-sixth of the words were deciphered in this way. These included important colophons: texts addressed to the reader, which were added by the scribe at the end of the Gospels of Mark, Luke and John. Perhaps because of having been written in different ink, the colophons had become invisible and 'the spaces between one end of one Gospel and the beginning of another were pronounced to be blank', but a touch of Agnes's brush brought them up in a rich brown colour.[19]

The final and most important colophon included a request that the reader pray for the scribe:

> Here ends the Gospel of the Mepharreshe, the four books: glory to God and to His Christ and to His Holy Spirit. Let every one that reads and hears and observes and does, pray for the sinner that wrote it, that God may have mercy on him, and remit his sins in both worlds. Amen and Amen.

Cureton had found the word 'Mepharreshe' (meaning 'separate') in a colophon of his codex, but had been uncertain of its reference. He thought it might refer to the Gospel of Matthew as being 'separate' or distinct from the rest of the work. Now the Sinai Palimpsest confirmed that it was not Matthew, but all four Gospels that were referred to as 'the Separate ones', probably to distinguish them from Tatian's harmony of the Gospels, the Diatessaron.

'Slowly but steadily,' wrote Mrs Bensly, 'letter upon letter and line upon line, by the help of sharp glasses and chemical agents, the long-lost Gospels were brought to light. There were, indeed, day by day, new doubts and new difficulties: lost pages, long gaps, unknown words, and shapeless letters. There were aching eyes also, and burning brows; but, on the whole, the work prospered beyond expectation.'[20]

What were they finding? It was not an entirely 'new' Gospel, but the familiar ones – Mathew, Mark, Luke and John – in a different and earlier translation than that of the Peshitta, the Syriac version known to posterity. At issue, then, was not simply the age of this particular book and its sheets of vellum, but, more importantly, the date and provenance of the translation it bore. At the time of the Cambridge expedition many questions of dating were unclear, and some are still debated. From the handwriting, the manuscript as a physical object could, fairly confidently, be attributed to the late fourth century. This put it as early as the Curetonian. It would eventually prove to pre-date that manuscript. But further to this the particular translation it bore was, it was agreed, of a much earlier date. Specialists like Bensly and Burkitt could confirm from linguistic variations what Agnes could only guess: that this translation was, like that of the Curetonian that it closely resembled, dated from the late second century. This put it very near the fountainhead of early Christianity.

The monks represented a different world from that of the Bible scholars, even those as sympathetic as Rendel Harris. Agnes was called upon one day to mediate between Rendel Harris and Galaktéon, who was bearing a cloth of crimson velvet within which was one of white silk, and within that a magnificent illuminated manuscript: 'Kyria Agnes,' he exclaimed, 'tell me what I can do to satisfy this naughty man! He asked me to show him the finest manuscript we possess, and I have brought him this, the very Gospel we read in the church and still he is not contented!' The book he carried was a gorgeously illuminated work of art from the twelfth century, but Rendel Harris would have preferred more unlovely, grubby sheaves, if only the text they carried was from the dawn of faith and previously unknown. Above all he hoped that somewhere in the convent they might find a copy of Tatian's Diatessaron.

But as the cataloguing progressed, it was not new finds, but rather disturbing new losses, that were discovered. Rendel Harris noted that a beautiful sixth-century Syriac manuscript of Maccabees that he had photographed in 1889 was nowhere to be found, spirited away perhaps by a disgruntled monk or a light-fingered visiting scholar.

As Lent approached and the monks prepared for a rigorous fast, the Cambridge party invited Father Galaktéon and Father Nicodemus to dinner. Ahmed insisted on killing his fattest turkey, and Mrs Bensly noted disdainfully that Galaktéon 'fairly shrieked with delight when that goodly dish appeared upon the board, clapping his hands and smacking his lips until better employed with the portion on his plate', while the suave Nicodemus looked on indulgently as one might smile at a frolicsome child. Agnes later corrected Mrs Bensly's misunderstanding, which she credited to that lady's poor eyesight and ignorance of modern Greek. Galaktéon refused to touch the turkey at all; he did not eat meat. His amusement arose from teasing Rendel Harris, also a vegetarian, by planting a large turkey leg on his plate. As this was the only time Agnes ever ate with the monks, she could not be sure how strictly vegetarian they were, but she concluded anyway, 'I confess the point is of little importance as I am disposed to follow St Paul in thinking that the Kingdom of God is something else than eating and drinking!'

In some ways Mrs Bensly had a greater understanding than Agnes of the way in which the monks perceived the Kingdom of God. True, she thought the informality and impulsive warmth of Galaktéon, which so delighted Agnes and Margaret, quite unsuitable for a priest and a man of rank in the convent community. On the other hand, perhaps because of her observation of the monks at work, Mrs Bensly had more sympathy for their life of prayer. She was taken on a tour of the church with its marble and gilding, its glowing iconostasis and dripping tiers of golden lamps, but found the overall effect more solemn than gaudy – and noted the sharp contrast to the bareness of the monks' own

Inside the walls of St Catherine's

quarters. She did not sneer at the relics of St Catherine in the silver
sarcophagus given by the Empress Catherine of Russia. She even took
off her shoes to enter the most holy Chapel of the Burning Bush.
(Rendel Harris admitted to often doing likewise, for reasons of awe.)
On the whole, the beauty and calm of the old church was only marred
for Mrs Bensly 'by the grotesque old pictures, chiefly of apostles and
martyrs, that abound on its walls' (that is, the icons); but, she added,
bemused, the monks seemed to admire their church 'all the more for
these pious additions'.[21]

'Admiration' does not express the place held by icons in the Eastern
Church. In Orthodox thought, the icon is not simply a picture, but an
emblem of the Incarnation: just as the icon is simultaneously an image
and a physical artefact – wood and pigment – so Christ was at the same
time Word and flesh, God and man. The icons of saints are honoured
because the holy men and women whose images they bear shared the

life of the true image of God: Christ. The monks at Sinai did not just honour but venerated their icons, regarding them almost as members of their community at prayer. For related reasons they also reverenced the physical form of their bibles and religious manuscripts, as well as the contents. For the Western visitors, the idea of processing with a Bible whose covers were studded with jewels and whose pages were illumined with gold, of incensing it and bowing before it was abhorrent. But to the monks, the Bible processed in church and embellished with leaf of gold was, metonymically, the Word Incarnate present to their community.

For Burkitt, Bensly and Rendel Harris, a book was above all its contents. The physical aspects of the writing – whether on vellum or papyrus, in codex or scroll, in uncial or minuscule – while interesting features, were important only in so far as they helped to date and place the manuscript. For the contents, a good printed facsimile could serve just as well as the original. But prior to the invention of printing, the reproduction of a book was a costly, lengthy and – for the monastic scribes – a devotional matter. Despite tired and frozen fingers, which copyists sometimes documented in marginalia, the literal *traditio*, (passing on) of the holy words, line by line, chapter by chapter, was a pious exercise in itself. For those who first wrote and read the manuscripts at Sinai, the formed strokes of ink that made up the words of the Gospels in a handwritten manuscript, the words laid laboriously letter by well-formed letter on sheets of precious vellum, or the paints laid on wooden boards that were the images of saints, were emblematic of a God who indwelt the physical world as man.

The new breed of scientifically trained Bible scholar who visited them in the nineteenth century thus presented challenges to the Sinai monks quite unlike those posed by the Christian pilgrims, the Muslims, the Jews or even the occasional aristocratic shooting party that passed their way. These scholarly Westerners wanted to see the books – but not to venerate them. A book for the monks was the physical trace of some long-departed brother or sister in the faith, who had executed it letter by letter, prayer by prayer. Was this to be handed over to men whose only concern was with comparative philology? For their part, the scholars often had difficulty understanding why the monks should sit so protectively on their hoard, and why their own scholarly interrogations had to cease at regular intervals while the monks said their prayers or retired early to their beds before rising, before dawn, once again to pray.

CHAPTER 18

The final falling-out

As the days lengthened and grew warmer, the visitors took more extensive walks in the nearby mountains. The Bedouin accepted them as convent guests and passed by with expressions of stately dignity, such as 'Blessed be thy day'; they only sought to detain them once or twice, when Mrs Bensly was asked by one of her knitting apprentices to pick up a stitch he had dropped.

By March the ground was white with almond blossom and Professor Bensly, on the morning shift, was able to replace his heavy overcoat and Homburg hat with a linen jacket and a fez. The flock of chickens and turkeys that scratched around him was steadily diminishing, and yet still the transcription was not complete. A plan to go on from Sinai to visit Jerusalem had to be abandoned, and Ahmed, who had tightly calculated provisions and had counted on Jerusalem as an opportunity to restock, was only placated by a camel dispatched to the nearest provisioner: 200 miles away at Suez. It was therefore with relief that the scholars watched the rotten binding of the palimpsest finally split. It had promised to do so for some time, but Burkitt, Bensly and Harris had been too high-minded to hasten the process. Now, instead of having to work in shifts, the men could transcribe at the same time, each from his own section.

They had witnessed the arrival and departure of several other groups of visitors. One seen approaching by camel from up the valley, mysteriously clad in white robes, turned out to be a party of Catholics from a newly established house of study in Jerusalem. This was the first visit to Sinai by the Dominicans of the *École Biblique*. They are 'a

The Prior, Galaktéon, with Professor Bensly
in a fez and Francis Burkitt in tweeds

learned set', wrote Rendel Harris to his wife. 'Fancy talking with a
Belgian on Mount Sinai who had read Codex Bezae!' This was their
prior, Father Marie-Joseph Lagrange, an Orientalist who had faced
criticism from his own Church for pioneering the scientific and
historical study of the Bible.[1] Agnes was flattered by his informed
interest in her Syriac work, and he in turn later wrote of her dedication
and expertise in photographing and cataloguing the manuscripts. Mrs
Bensly thought the young German, Belgian and Scottish men 'showed
their superior breeding by the pleasant way in which they conformed
to the wishes and habits of their hosts . . . they willingly shared the cells
and the table of the convent, and joined in all its religious observances,
merging the minor distinctions of Eastern and Western in the
community of the Holy Catholic Church'.[2]

Chaos erupted when the time came for the Dominicans to travel on
to Petra, an operation that required their transfer to a tribe of Bedouin
from there, rather than Sinai. The courtyard was filled with camels,

Bedouin, Greek monks, Latin priests and white-helmeted Britons.
Father Nicodemus, as steward, presided over the negotiations for
several hours and, says Agnes, 'plenty of bad language was flying
about. I wished to seize the opportunity of studying this department of
Semitic science, but the loud voices dropped and uplifted hands fell
whenever I tried to make my way into the centre of the throng.'[3]

There had also been a large party of Russian pilgrims: mostly kulaks,
farmers and their wives from villages in southern Russia. They had
been travelling, without tents and on foot, since early winter and now
made it across the desert with a Bedouin escort and some camels for
the women. The monks housed them all at the convent – the women
as well as the men. The men wore fur-trimmed coats and caps, and the
women, in their heavy woollen skirts, bright aprons and neat head-
scarfs, wandered amongst the tents of the British transcribers, with not
a word in common to voice a comment or ask a question. The Benslys
dined with the monks and the Russian peasants one evening – all at the
rough, uncovered tables in the refectory built for the monastery by the
Crusaders. Bowls of stewed lentils and huge brown loaves were passed
along, and over the clatter of plates and spoons a priest read a Greek
homily from a pulpit in the dining hall. Though not as dramatic as that
of the Dominicans, their departure, too, was a spectacle. Twice the
required number of Bedouin assembled at the gate jostling for
employment, and the Russians, who had no dragoman, were helpless.
Father Nicodemus stepped in, invoking the abbot's authority to select
some Bedouin and drive others off and, when necessary applying
blows with his staff, which no one appeared to resent. The party
eventually left at midday, accompanied by one of the convent's
Russian monks to arbitrate, should they have trouble with the
Bedouin. The women, mounted on camels, filed off immediately
down the valley, but the men stepped to the rocky platform at the
opposite side of the road and, lifting their arms towards the heavens,
prayed aloud for blessing on the convent.

One Russian lady was too sick to travel and remained behind, with
another to nurse her; Mrs Bensly decided to show her the modern
conveniences of the British camp. She remained stolidly indifferent to

everything she was shown, from the Union Jack to their cook's portable oven. But as they passed together through the monks' vegetable gardens her eyes fell upon a large cauliflower, which seemed to remind her of her distant home: 'She took it in her arms and pressed it to her bosom, her face suffused with smiles and her eyes brimming over with tears.'[4] In due course the two Russians, nurse and patient, were able to join another group and catch up with their caravan. But a tragedy befell that pilgrimage – Agnes and Margaret later heard that the Russians were caught in heavy rains near Nazareth and some seventy pilgrims died of exposure.

When the rains on Sinai come, they are sharp and ferocious. On the morning of the 9 March Mrs Bensly saw a little cloud like a man's hand in what was normally a seamless blue sky. 'Before noon the whole heaven was black with clouds, the mist clung in white folds to the sides of the gorge, and at dinner-time the long-desired rain descended in torrents.' The next morning wind and rain subsided, the mist lifted and the landscape around emerged freshly laundered. Only then was the full impact of the rain seen as the waters poured down from the granite cliffs to the valley below. It swept into the water courses made by the monks, and filled the convent's intricate system of cisterns and tanks. By mid-morning the paths were dry, but amongst the rocks were deep, clear pools of water. The Bedouin women washed their clothes in them and the babies paddled 'like English children in a summer sea'. The monks surrounded each tree in the orchard with a little circular ditch to save the water, and the rocky wilderness bloomed.

As the time of departure became imminent, Professor and Mrs Bensly finally made an ascent of the 3,000 irregular steps up Gebel Musa (the 'Mountain of Moses') to view from 8,000 feet the whole of the mountain desert that had been their home for forty days. The sharp granite of the path cut Mrs Bensly's stout boots to pieces, and for the journey home she was left with nothing but a pair of velveteen slippers.

Departure was fixed for Monday, 20 March – in 1893 this was the first day of Ramadan. This afforded the opportunity for a splendid goodbye party amongst the assembled Bedouin the night before their season of fasting began. The British travellers gave them a sheep and their milk

Margaret with the cook, the waiter, camel drivers
and Bedouin outside the convent walls

goat, which the camp cook prepared for them in his large cauldron. Children were given extra treats of biscuits and oranges, and the empty match boxes and battered mustard tins, from which they made their Mardi Gras on rocks nearby.

The British party, Mrs Bensly reported, had a more subdued supper. The loss of their milk goat was one thing, but her kid had become a camp favourite, visiting the tents and getting under the feet of the transcribers. 'Busy this day with packing and photographing, we had hardly missed our little pet; and it was a painful shock at dinner-time, when Ahmed himself triumphantly bore it into the tent, dished with tomatoes and covered with gravy.' Mr Burkitt took a little onto his plate to avoid offending Ahmed, but all in all, says Mrs Bensly, 'it did much to deepen the natural depression that is connected with every parting in this troublesome world.'[5] The transcription of the palimpsest, on which the men had been working so hard, was still not complete.

The next morning, even as the remaining chickens were captured and confined for the return journey, the men stayed bent over their sections of the palimpsest; 'the tents removed, they repaired to the well; tables and chairs folded up, they sat on a tree-trunk with the book on their knees; inkstands and blotting books gone, they took to their pencils'.[6] By the time the camels were loaded and the baggage caravan set off across the desert, they had managed another half-day's work on the still-incomplete task. Galaktéon put an end to their efforts by appearing in the garden, on the arms of two of his brethren, in a state of agitation. Another party had arrived and he did not want them to suppose the privilege of keeping a manuscript at the camp site would be extended to them. Mrs Bensly wrapped the palimpsest in a treasured silk cloth that she had used to wipe the brow of her dying son, and Father Euthymios bore it away, his ears ringing with pleas that it be kept safe.

Gakaktéon at last rose to the solemnity that Mrs Bensly thought fitting in one of his rank by summoning them to his rooms and receiving them in the weighty prior's robes and cross. He had assembled on a table ancient relics and charters of the convent, and a silver dish contained sweet, turpentiny beads of 'manna'. Each guest was given a little ring with the monogram of the convent and a box of sweet manna. Mrs Bensly was delighted to be the first German woman to lay her name down in the monks' august visitors' book.

All were loath to leave. They set out on foot, the riding camels having gone ahead. The most melancholy parting was reserved for Agnes and Margaret. Galaktéon walked with them a little of the way, his need for a staff being more than ceremonial: 'The hand of death was almost visibly on our kind friend, Father Galaktéon,' wrote Agnes:

Something told us . . . in his manner that we should never again see the priest and enlightened Hegoumenos to whose frank generosity we owed so much, and it was natural to suppose that this convent and all its courteous inmates with whom we had spent so many pleasant hours were now as a closed chapter in our history. The rest of the party started before us, even Mr Harris, at Galaktéon's request, then he himself accompanied us slowly and heavily, a very short way. We parted with hardly a word of farewell, for our hearts were too full to speak . . .[7]

The Cambridge visitors turned back, as had the Russian pilgrims before them, to take a last look at the convent: the white roofs and blossoming trees clustered beneath the granite cliffs. Their garden camp site already had new occupants. There was a new cook and cook tent, a new dragoman dealing with Nicodemus, and the Stars and Stripes had been hoisted in place of the Union Jack.

Agnes's friends were wont to say that this must have been a time of great happiness for her. 'It ought to have been so,' she wrote:

for I was returning home with the fruits of a discovery which had only to be known to the Bible reading world to be welcomed with delight. But I could not shake off the heavy depression which had weighed down my spirit ever since the beloved partner of my life had been so suddenly snatched away. I had sought to drown it with work, and now when a great joy had come to me, a joy which *he* would so thoroughly have appreciated, I could not restrain the thought. 'Oh, if it had been only nine months earlier!' But this was ingratitude to a kind Providence, and events occurred after our return to Cambridge which made me shake off my lethargy and take a more active interest in the affairs of life.[8]

CHAPTER 19

The devilish press and the Highland Regiment

The events that shook Agnes from her lethargy were already in train as they departed from St Catherine's, but no one could have anticipated the series of mishaps that got Agnes and Margaret into such hot water once they were back home. Difficulties of transmission, they were to learn, were not restricted to the transmission of ancient texts.

The twins were the first to get back to England, arriving on 8 April 1893, and were the only members of the transcription party to have returned when on Thursday, 13 April, the London *Daily News* ran this breaking story from its Berlin correspondent:

Discovery of a Syrian Text of the Gospels

Berlin, Wednesday night

It will be remembered that last year Professor Hanak surprised the theological world by his discovery in an Egyptian tomb of a fragment of the Gospel and Apocalypse of St Peter.[1] Now another discovery reported by Professor I. B. (*sic*) Harris of Cambridge, who is now staying in Egypt, and who has given an account of it written from Suez to Professor Nestle at Tübingen. Two ladies – Mrs Lewis and her sister, Mrs Gibson – both conversant with oriental languages, and speaking Arabian and modern Greek fluently, went last year to Mount Sinai, after being thoroughly instructed by Professor Harris in the photographing of handwritings. Although the Convent has been searched for written treasures since Tischendorf's great discovery there – and even by Professor Harris only three years ago – the present discovery remained hidden from previous investigators.

It is a palimpsest manuscript. When Mrs Lewis first saw it, it was in a dreadful condition, all the leaves sticking together and being full of dirt. She separated the leaves from one another with the steam from her tea-kettle, and photographed the whole text – from three to four hundred pages. It turned out to be a Syrian text of all the four Gospels, closely related to the one known to theologians as Cureton's 'Remains of a very ancient Rescensions of the Four Gospels in Syriac', and among all the preserved testimonies contains the oldest authenticated texts of the Gospels. Only fragments of the Syrian have hitherto been known, these being in a single manuscript in the British Museum, and in two leaves of it which came to Berlin. Now all the four Gospels in this text are nearly complete.

Professor Harris, himself, on hearing of the discovery, set off for Mount Sinai, and for forty days he and the two ladies sat in the convent deciphering the palimpsest leaves. They are now on their way home with the results.

If not entirely false, the article was at least highly misleading. No mention at all was made of Professor Bensly and Mr Burkitt, which gave all the glamour and glory to Rendel Harris and the sisters! They could all too well imagine the fury of their already hostile camping companions. And why had the *Daily News* ('not a paper we take,' said Agnes) broken the story, and not the London *Times*? They had suspected while still at Suez that *The Times* had failed to receive the joint letter from Cairo, for none of the expected expressions of astonishment and admiration, or warm telegrams of congratulations, had awaited them at their hotel. This now seemed confirmed. The next day the story was printed up in the *Cambridge Chronicle* and there was no escaping the limelight.

On their last Sunday at St Catherine's, after weeks punctuated by explosions of temper, there had been a final, terrible row: Agnes and Margaret on one side, and Bensly, Burkitt and wives on the other. Agnes had read out loud a letter she was then drafting for *The Scotsman* describing their joint progress, and its wording had set off a bitter quarrel as to who had found the text and who should be

involved in its future publication. Bensly and Burkitt did not dispute
the fact that Agnes had *physically come upon* the manuscript, but they
were unwilling to credit her with much more. The version favoured
by the men (and adhered to loyally by their wives) might be
summarised thus:

> the twins, lady-travellers, had found at St Catherine's, amongst other
> things, an old palimpsest which they thought might be of interest to
> scholars, although they were 'not sure what it was'. It was then Burkitt
> and Bensly who discerned from a few pale photographs of a shimmery
> palimpsest that here lay a copy of the old Syriac Bible, known otherwise
> only from the sadly incomplete Curetonian manuscript. Bensly and
> Burkitt had put together a transcription party to go to Sinai, and Mrs
> Lewis and Mrs Gibson volunteered to accompany them to assist with
> their knowledge of Eastern travel and modern Greek.

Put in this way, the story of the palimpsest made a nice parallel to
the Curetonian, whose fragments had been physically *retrieved* by
Archdeacon Tattam from the Nitrian desert, but whose real
significance was only subsequently determined by William Cureton of
the British Museum.

Agnes and Margaret saw matters quite differently. Agnes had not
'stumbled' upon the manuscript. On the contrary, she had gone to
Sinai with the express intention of searching out those Syriac texts that
Rendel Harris had said lay unseen in the dark closet. That is why she
had put so much effort into learning Syriac before their departure.
Admittedly she was still new to the language, but her competence in
Hebrew and Arabic made a good foundation. She had seen as soon as
she lifted it from its box that the manuscript – though black with grime
and its sheets stuck together by age and neglect – was a palimpsest.
After a brief examination she could see that the underwriting was the
Gospels in Syriac and concluded that it must be extremely ancient.

As far as both twins were concerned, Agnes not only found the
palimpsest, but had struggled to have its significance recognised; first
by her own sister and Galaktéon at St Catherine's, and subsequently by

the specialists at Cambridge. It was she who had assembled the team of three first-class transcribers and, with the goodwill accorded to herself and her sister by Archbishop Porphyrios and the monks, she who had secured the scholars' access to the manuscripts at St Catherine's. Agnes had no wish to claim the transcription as her own work, but neither was she prepared to become a graciously acknowledged footnote.

The twins compounded their presumption, in Mr Burkitt's opinion, by undertaking to catalogue the Syriac and Arabic manuscripts of the convent: they had no training in the decipherment of ancient texts, no expertise in comparative philology and were not familiar with the wider world of Syriac and Arabic writings. Agnes and Margaret conceded all these points; however, the fact of the matter was that Archbishop Porphyrios had entrusted them with the task. Professor Palmer and many other scholars had asked to catalogue the manuscripts before them and had been refused, for clearly anyone who did so would be at liberty to leave a few choice items off the list and pocket them for his or her own. Porphyrios and the monks at Sinai were confident in the integrity of the twins.

It had eventually been agreed that Agnes should write the introduction to the published transcription, provided it was brief. As if to underscore the scholarly unimportance he projected for her contribution, Burkitt had taken Agnes aside to say that she was *on no account* to ask Professor Bensly to assist her. Perhaps Burkitt feared she would attempt to parade Bensly's erudition as her own.

Everyone had been subdued on the camel trip back across the peninsula: the British because they were cross with one another, and the Bedouin because it was Ramadan and they were fasting. Ahmed himself took advantage of a clause that allowed the traveller to nourish himself, provided he fed six beggars a day (in the unlikely event they saw any). The Bedouin camel drivers ate nothing and did not even draw on their pipes until sunset when Ahmed sounded a gong. A prevailing north wind throughout the journey filled the travellers' eyes with sand and blistered their faces. It had therefore been a most welcome moment when, after seven days' heavy trudge, they had their first glimpse of the blue of the sea with the African mountains beyond. As if to snatch even this moment of pleasure, the view was suddenly eclipsed by the dark-yellow cloud of a sandstorm. Both Mrs Bensly and Agnes were temporarily blinded, but the storm lasted only ten minutes, leaving the air full of fine sand like tiny flecks of glass dancing in the sunlight.

As they neared 'Ain Musa, Agnes and Margaret took a decision that would lead to much misunderstanding later. The Benslys and Burkitts had their ship's passage booked from Alexandria for a few days hence, but the sisters had no fixed arrangements. They needed to get to Suez as soon as possible in order to secure berths on the fortnightly Messageries Maritimes steamer as it passed through on its way from the Far East to Marseilles.

The twins decided to press on after dinner, in order to cross the Red Sea the next morning so as to catch the dawn train to Suez. Rendel Harris, torn between his care for the sisters and his fear of offending the others, decided to go with Agnes and Margaret. They planned to travel only with their own camel drivers and Ahmed's son, but Ahmed impulsively decided to join them; the Bedouin were capable, after all, of managing alone for a few hours, and Mrs Burkitt with her fluent Arabic could meet any translation difficulties. They set out after dinner by moonlight for the two-hour ride to 'Ain Musa, and crossed the Red Sea early the next morning, as planned.

Once in Suez, Rendel Harris posted an excited letter to his friend, Eberhard Nestle, a young professor in Tübingen.[2] Harris had written to Nestle from St Catherine's after Bensly had lifted the communications embargo. Now he added this breathless sequel.

We are out of the desert now after two months' retirement, and I am sending you one of the first letters on my return. How I wish you could have been with us . . . The great thing that I think you would be interested in is the new Curetonian Gospels. I think I sent you word about them before leaving home, but now I can write more freely. The MS. is a palimpsest, and was discovered by my friends who visited the Convent last year. Mrs Lewis and her sister, Mrs Gibson, are good

Oriental scholars, and speak both Arabic and modern Greek fluently –
just the people for Sinai, you will say . . .

He continued:

> Does this not sound exciting? And do you not wish you could have been
> with us? We have had forty days of palimpsest-reading in the Convent,
> and have deciphered nearly the whole of the four Gospels. Mrs Lewis
> allows me to tell you (and you can publish the information) that the title
> 'Separate Gospels', which Cureton blundered over, is applied to the
> whole of the Gospels. There are no last twelve verses of St Mark, and
> many other Curetonian additions are wanting. In fact, the Lewis Codex
> is the most important find since Tischendorf's great discovery.
>   With best wishes,
>   Thine sincerely,
>   J. Rendel Harris [3]

What Harris could not know was that his earlier letter to Nestle – a
letter which mentioned that Burkitt and Bensly were also of the party
– had disappeared into the Ottoman postal service. Nor could he know
that the earlier, official letter approved by all the transcription party
and sent to the London *Times* had suffered a similar fate.[4] The wider
world therefore remained in ignorance of the palimpsest, its romantic
discovery and of the composition of the group that had been
transcribing it.

So it was that when Nestle hastened to relay the contents of Harris's
exciting letter to the German press, as Harris said he might, Nestle
made no mention of Bensly and Burkitt. Harris, writing in haste (and
believing that Nestle knew from his letter about the other men), spoke
only of 'we' and 'us' when detailing the adventure in his letter from
Suez, and mentioned by name only himself and the sisters. Nestle
could not know that anyone else was involved.

The story that appeared in the *Schwäbisches Merkur* of 11 April 1893,
and in the London *Daily News* on 13 April, travelled round the world
without the names of two of the world's most eminent Syriac scholars

attached. Bensly and Burkitt were, at that moment, innocently enjoying well-earned holidays with their wives in Europe before returning home.

The twins could only imagine Bensly's face, breakfasting quietly at his hotel in Rome, or that of Burkitt in some café on the Côte d'Azure, as they opened their papers and discovered the omission of their names. It could only seem a deliberate piece of treachery. Rendel Harris was heavily implicated. His apparently deliberate failure to mention Burkitt and Bensly, compounding his notice in *The Athenaeum* of the previous summer, must have seemed to aggrieved eyes final confirmation that he had hoped, all along, to take the glory of the palimpsest as his own.

Agnes was mortified on behalf of her kind Quaker friend, and terrified that an outraged Bensly and Burkitt might block publication of the transcript, or her involvement with it. A certain amount of squabbling had taken place at St Catherine's, even between Bensly and Burkitt, as to which of them should take credit for recognising the text, but this was as nothing compared to their united antipathy against Agnes and her sister. By way of a compromise, it had been agreed while still at St Catherine's that the transcription should be published by the gentlemen, and that Agnes should write the introduction. Nevertheless, Bensly and Burkitt were in a position of considerable power. Professor Bensly had only to mutter a dismissive word to the Cambridge University Press to scupper the project. Equally, since no contracts had been signed, both men could simply withdraw their portions of the transcription. Burkitt had taken Agnes aside and told her than she could on no account consult Professor Bensly about her introduction, fearing perhaps that she would overload the old man and take the credit as her own. The need to keep both Burkitt and Bensly on their side if at all possible was considerable, but the likelihood was becoming increasingly remote.

The twins had been dwelling on these difficulties on their trip back from Marseilles, even before the fateful publication of the report in the *Daily News*. Immediately on their return to England they had sent a series of urgent letters to Rendel Harris asking his advice. They had also called at once on the support of their Cambridge friends. 'The Macalisters [Alick] and Sir Robert Ball were entertained with the story yesterday afternoon,' Margaret wrote to Rendel Harris, only two days after she and Agnes got back home:

> Mrs M. said they are all determined the codex shall be called 'Lewisian'. Sir R. Ball said there was no doubt on the subject, & Prof. Macalister thinks it is a very unimportant matter which of our two friends deciphered it first. He would let them fight it out between themselves – but then he does not know how angry they were with us about it. He (Prof. M.) was really angry when I told him how you had been asked to retire from the work. Our friends had better take care & not bring down a Highland Regiment on their heads . . .[5]

The 'Highland Regiment' to which Margaret referred in her letter might better be called the Celtic fringe: the Irish and Scots Presbyterians prominent in the university, who were their friends from church. Even before the press had got hold of the story, Alick Macalister, the Professor of Anatomy, had impressed upon Agnes 'the necessity of having that introduction written before "our friends" [Burkitt and Bensly] have time to settle down'. She had begun a rough copy, leaving gaps to be filled in when she could consult Rendel Harris.[6] Professor Robertson Smith, whose early advice to publish a notice in *The Athenaeum* now seemed prophetic, was able to pilot Agnes and Margaret from the side.

After the misleading press coverage, and at Professor Macalister's 'earnest advice', Agnes sent a correct account of the joint trip to *The Academy* and *The Athenaeum*, laying special emphasis on the presence of Bensly and Burkitt. On 14 April Margaret was able to write to Rendel Harris expressing relief that the errors were now corrected, and her confidence (mistaken, as it turned out) that all would now be well: 'I am glad that Agnes wrote to the Athenaeum & Academy, though we did it in a hurry, I think full justice is done to every one, and our friends will care more for what appears there than anywhere else.'

But the Providence that had guided their steps to Sinai appeared now to have abandoned them. *The Athenaeum* had, for reasons of its own, omitted the first two paragraphs of Agnes's letter in which she spoke of Bensly and Burkitt, with the result that, once again, the two scholars remained absent from the account. The press seemed to prefer it that way anyway.

The story was improbable – sensational: that two ladies well on in middle years should have plucked from a monastic house in the Sinai desert a manuscript of incalculable value, possibly second in importance only to the great Codex Sinaiticus itself! The whole of Western Christendom had been mad for such finds for decades, and yet here a woman, not twelve months into the study of Syriac, had found a lost treasure. At some stage the detail began to circulate that they had

Agnes Smith Lewis, after she was married

found the palimpsest when the monks used a sheet of it as a butter dish for their lady visitors' morning meal. As the fat had soaked into the parchment, Agnes had seen the letters of the Gospels rise up before her.

The *Cambridge Chronicle* had an interview with Agnes, published as a lengthy, congratulatory editorial – the little tea-kettle with which they had steamed apart the pages of the palimpsest becoming a mark of their resourcefulness. Letters of invitation and requests for enlightenment from scholars began to pour in. Agnes was invited by the Earl of Northbrook to address the following month's meeting of the Royal Asiatic Society in London. From total obscurity, the twins – especially Agnes – were rapidly becoming public figures. Professor Bensly, reading his papers in Rome, was, as they had predicted, outraged.

The Benslys had not had an easy time getting to Europe. They had reached 'Ain Musa with the Burkitts late on the same morning as the twins left, but by then the tide was low and their ship was unable to approach nearer than twenty or thirty yards to shore. The two couples, and all their baggage, had to be carried out to it on the shoulders of (as Mrs Bensly put it) 'fine, bronze-coloured men, clad in loose white shirts and embroidered waistcoats, and bright turbans'. Once under sail, the heavily laden boat ran aground on sand banks 'midway between Asia and Africa' and had to be hauled off with ropes.

No sooner did they arrive at their hotel in Suez, where they hoped to spend a few days resting and cleaning up, than they received a telegram saying that the boat on which they had booked passage from Alexandria was to depart early – in fact the very next morning. The exhausted Benslys had to pack up immediately and throw themselves and their extensive luggage onto a local train, only to be set down at sunset at a provisionless station in the desert, where they had to wait many hours for a connecting mail train. Hungry, tired, without Arabic or the Burkitts (who had stayed on at Suez), Professor and Mrs Bensly (in her fraying velveteen slippers) had wandered in the darkness towards an Arab coffee house and managed – by gesturing – to get some coffee and a heavy chunk of coarse bread, which was undoubtedly the waiter's own dinner and for which he refused to charge. They must have made a wan and pitiful sight: two Europeans, older than most, she with pebble-thick glasses and inadequate footwear, waiting for their train until two o'clock in the morning.

It was a hard thing, having climbed the greasy pole of academic renown with painful slowness over many years, to find oneself joined at the top by a fifty-year-old Scottish widow, who has vaulted to this height almost by accident in a matter of months. As the press fed happily on the more saleable version of the facts, Bensly and Burkitt might have been forgiven for thinking themselves the victims of a conspiracy or even an elaborate practical joke. Agnes and Margaret, for their part, had not sought the attention and did not relish vaudeville notoriety. The need to write almost daily letters to the press, each one attempting to clarify misunderstandings and each one making things worse, was an unwanted distraction. But now, given all the publicity, it would be impossible not to include Agnes in the publication; and equally impossible, given the expectation raised in the papers, not to publish at all. Bensly and Burkitt found themselves well and truly cornered.

The Benslys got back to England on 20 April, and Professor Bensly, finding his name absent from the coverage in the English papers as it had been from the European ones, set out to write at once to Eberhard Nestle to set the record straight. But before he could complete his letter, he was beyond caring. Margaret broke the news to Rendel Harris:

Castlebrae, Sunday 23rd April, 1893

Dear Mr Harris,

I am sure you & Mrs Harris will be dreadfully grieved to hear that Professor Bensly is no more. We heard from Mr Francis last night at Christ's Lodge that he was seriously ill . . . As we were coming from church Dr. Bensly from Norwich came up to us and told us his brother wasn't expected to survive the day. Mary Kingsley, who is staying with us . . . has just come in to tell us that all is now over. So God's will be done! I cannot help thinking of his many little gentle acts of kindness while we were travelling & had one of our party stayed at home I am sure we should have understood each other better.

His brother said it was in Rome he got a chill. Mary Kingsley reports . . . that Prof. Bensly climbed the Palatine Hill without an overcoat in the afternoon, that he had attended a college meeting on Friday & eaten oysters & drunk beer, also stout when in Rome, which was simply poison to him. It was not pneumonia but gout in the heart. He had dreadful pain & whenever it went, he collapsed.

Dr Bradbury is afraid about Mrs Bensly.

> I am just off to church,
> > Yours very truly,
> > > M. D. Gibson[7]

Bensly's life had passed its quiet decades in laborious efforts to remove corruptions and gaps from old manuscripts, much of it given away in help to other textual scholars. By his standards, the Sinai trip was a reckless stampede into the unknown, and had now resulted in a not inglorious end. Of his own work little appeared in print. This was true even of his proposed edition of the Curetonian Syriac Gospels. When Burkitt undertook to finish the edition on which Bensly had been working for years, he found that Bensly had committed almost nothing of it to paper. He had carried it in his head and with him, alas, it died.

CHAPTER 20

The Cambridge cold shoulder

Mrs Bensly wrote to Eberhard Nestle less than a week after her husband's death. Whether through grief or the strain of desert travel, Mrs Bensly was now almost completely blind, her smudged script veering wildly across the black-edged mourning stationery. She exonerated Nestle from any blame, laying this firmly on Rendel Harris.

28 April, 1893,

Dear Professor, I hardly know yet <u>clearly</u> that I am a widow – the loss has been so sudden and I feel so utterly desolate –

When we reached England and found in English papers the same omission of my husband's name . . . Professor Bensly's first conviction – that <u>you</u> [doubly underlined] have no part in the misrepresentation was fully confirmed – he was going to write to you to tell you so – he sat down with the pen in his hand when the physician's visit interrupted him. It was the first day of his short illness – which lasted 48 hours only. Twice during that time he called for paper to write to you, but paroxysms of pain or faintness prevented him.

I feel compelled to tell you exactly the facts of the great discovery and subsequent work.

The facts were, according to Mrs Bensly, that Mrs Lewis and Gibson had travelled to Sinai and, through befriending the monks, 'got access to all their treasures'. They returned with photos of a codex which they recognised as the Syriac Gospels and had shown these to various people, but: 'it was my husband, together with his most distinguished pupil, F. C. Burkitt of Trinity College, Cambridge – who <u>first and alone</u> [doubly underlined] discovered the true value of the Palimpsest.'

Rendel Harris was a last-minute addition to the party. At Sinai the three men had worked on the transcription in equal shares: 'I expected,' continued Mrs Bensly, 'I suppose we all expected, that as soon as we reached England, a joint account of the work would be published.'

To Mrs Bensly it was nothing short of treachery that Harris, who had 'a smaller share in it than the others', should communicate the find to the rest of the world without so much as a whisper of his intentions to his co-workers:

> I wish to make no further comment on his conduct – it embittered (<u>no, Mr Bensly was never bitter</u>) it saddened my husband's last days – not that he feared for his own reputation (that is firmly established here) but that he felt the unkindness of Mr Harris very deeply . . . Mr Bensly never doubted you but knew that you would with perfect fairness give the honour to whom it was due.
>
> Forgive me if this troubles you at all – I am your friend's broken-hearted widow
>
> Agnes Bensly

Mrs Bensly was not alone in feeling betrayed. From letters they were receiving, it was becoming apparent to the twins that they had not been privy to important details of the transcript that Burkitt and Bensly had shared with others.

One of the most troubling requests was from Mrs Humphrey Ward, infamous to the faithful on both sides of the Atlantic for her novel of religious doubt, *Robert Elsmere*. Mrs Ward wanted clarification as to whether discovery of the palimpsest put into question the Virgin Birth. She had learned that the palimpsest contained a controversial variant of the genealogy of Jesus at the beginning of Matthew's Gospel: the famous list of 'begats'. Whereas orthodox versions of the New

Testament do not list Joseph as 'begetting' Jesus, but, more vaguely, as
the husband of Mary 'of whom Jesus was born', the palimpsest seemed
to imply that Joseph was the biological father. This was not only news
to Agnes, but it was also attention from entirely the wrong quarter.
Mrs Ward was an acknowledged leader in the free-thinking party that
advocated stripping Christianity of its miraculous content to focus
instead on its moral teachings. Agnes was incensed by the suggestion
that *her* Gospels might be heretical, but even more galled by the fact
that either Mr Burkitt or Professor Bensly had transcribed this
momentous variant, without seeing fit to mention it to either Rendel
Harris or the twins. Burkitt had even written to Robertson Smith about
it from Sinai, without breathing a word to Agnes. Was this an
indication of their 'good intentions'?

What had started as a heated but private misunderstanding was now
doing the rounds in Cambridge gossip as an open dispute. Agnes wrote
to Helen Harris, over another unusual reading, 'I wrote to Mr Burkitt
to ask if that passage really occurs in our codex, as if it does not, some
one ought to contradict the statement. In reply, I have received a very
rude letter from his wife saying that he does not consider the matter of
any importance . . .' And she added, 'You see the Burkitts are talking
everywhere they can'; 'now people are taking notions without taking
the trouble to enquire about them . . .'[1]

While it was not possible to be publicly angry with someone so
recently deceased, Professor Bensly's behaviour was not beyond
criticism. While binding them to the strictest secrecy, he himself (the
twins now discovered) had talked freely to other scholars about the
palimpsest before they set out together, including (more presumptu-
ously) his own intentions for it.

Spurred on by the need to clear their names, the twins put together
a small volume entitled *How the Codex Was Found*, the title suggesting
what a cause célèbre the manuscript had become even before its
publication. Published on 1 June 1893 under Margaret's name, its clear
intention was to show that Agnes had been well aware of what she had
discovered at St Catherine's and had advertised the fact, before Bensly
and Burkitt had even examined the photos. The book mostly consisted

of Agnes's travel diaries from their first Sinai visit. Margaret's introduction pointed out that these had already been printed in the *Presbyterian Churchman* of the previous summer, but since 'many inaccurate statements have been made by too hasty writers in our public prints', it was best that they appear again.

The very day that *How the Codex Was Found* appeared, Agnes received a letter from the Cambridge University Press – clearly the result of Robertson Smith's efforts on their behalf – expressing a delighted willingness to publish the transcription and offering generous fees for the transcribers' services. Agnes herself was named as the person with whom the Press would negotiate, and their friend, Robertson Smith, as the officer who would negotiate on behalf of the Press. Relishing what seemed an unconditional victory, Agnes wrote to Rendel Harris, 'Is it not a pity that our quondam friends [the Burkitts] should be making such a row over it!'

But as the dust settled on this triumph, it became apparent to Agnes that she was now more vulnerable and exposed than ever before. Overall responsibility for preparing the manuscript for publication was hers but Burkitt – who controlled not only his own part, but also Bensly's part of the transcription – was not even answering her letters. He had not signed a contract and neither had Rendel Harris, who, still raw from the verbal savagings he had received from Burkitt and Bensly at St Catherine's, now wanted to withdraw from the project altogether. One-fifth of the palimpsest had not even been transcribed.

Agnes had to balance on a knife-edge: she was not, she knew, a scholar. The exotic nature of the discovery of the palimpsest and the surrounding press attention meant an eager audience awaited the book's publication. Should it fail to appear or – even worse – appear and be judged a second-rate production, then criticism would crash down upon her head as an amateur who had the presumption to undertake what she could not possibly deliver. The most sensible course for Agnes was to withdraw gracefully and cede editorial control to Burkitt.

Agnes did not choose the sensible course.

All her life she had been an outsider: excluded from the social circles of the landed gentry in Ayrshire; apart from the 'English roses' at boarding school; outside of the Anglican elites of Cambridge; and pervasively, as a woman, exiled from the life of the mind. She had enjoyed three sociable and intellectually stimulating years with Samuel Lewis, but on his death feared losing it all. Now she had been given a second chance. Like St Catherine rescued from the wheel, Agnes had been seized from the 'jaws of death', transported to Sinai and 'established at a great height'. What better tribute could a widow pay to a deceased husband – librarian, antiquarian and clergyman – than to lay an important new codex of the Gospels on the altar of his memory? To withdraw from the publication process now could only look like an admission that the Burkitts and the Benslys had been right all along, in deeming her an upstart and Rendel Harris an academic bandit. She wrote to encourage the wavering Harris: 'Our Shorter Catechism says that "the ninth commandment requireth the maintaining and pre-serving of our own and our neighbour's good name". Surely one of God's best gifts to us is worth cherishing?'

Far from backing down, Agnes determined to acquire the scholarly knowledge necessary to produce an edition that would pass muster. It would not be easy, but she was undaunted and not afraid to lean on her friends whenever necessary.

It is greatly to Harris's credit that he did not abandon Agnes. He had many other projects under way, and to be accused of trying to steal the glory for this one was humiliating. Nonetheless, to hand his portion of the transcription over to Burkitt and withdraw from the publication would be to crush Agnes's dreams, as well as going against his own sense of truth and fairness.[2]

Still, it took a man of patience and generosity to deal with Agnes's relentless determination. Harris appears to have been only mildly affronted when she decided that he should return to Sinai in November to transcribe the missing portion of the text. Before she secured his agreement, Agnes wrote to Archbishop Porphyrios, enclosing a copy of *How the Codex Was Found* and asking whether the palimpsest might be transferred for a period from Sinai to Cairo to spare Harris the desert crossing. Harris was less than keen to go, particularly if his visit was to take place (as Agnes was apparently suggesting) without Burkitt's knowledge. Undaunted, she wrote to urge him on:

> I cannot see that we are under any obligation to tell Mr Burkitt about it. If we do not take this opportunity . . . then we fall back on Mr Bensly's plan to let any stray scholar who goes to Sinai copy and publish a stray page or two . . . You have a right to spend your holiday as you please & write on what you please without consulting anyone. If we were to let him [Burkitt] know anything about it beforehand, the probability is that he would withdraw his own and Dr Bensly's transcriptions and break up our edition . . . While we were working <u>with</u> Mr Burkitt, we were bound to tell him everything, but now I hope we shall do so no more than is necessary.[3]

In the days that followed, Agnes barraged Rendel Harris with letters begging him to return to Egypt. She wrote that she had even taken the liberty of approaching 'in strictest confidence' various university authorities to see whether he might get some time off his duties for the purpose. What was more, she had got the monks to agree to her plan. It would be the greatest pity, she said, if the brothers were to bring their treasure to Cairo for no purpose. The thought of Burkitt going was almost too much to bear.

Before Harris could capitulate, a letter to Agnes from Archbishop Porphyrios put a stop to all these schemes. She relayed its contents in two letters to Harris on 26 July 1893:

> I am sorry to say I have got into a fresh trouble. I have received another letter from the Archbishop of Mount Sinai, and he is <u>very</u> angry at me for some of the things I said in my book . . . the consequence is they will not send the codex to Cairo . . .
>
> I cannot think how I was so desperately stupid as to send that book! – for it is all my doing, not Maggie's . . . I shall write (to the University Press) . . . to say that the monks have withdrawn their offer owing to unexpected difficulties. I shall not tell the reason as it would be 'nuts' to

our friends in Harvey Road [the Burkitts] if they knew! But it is a disappointment.[4]

Agnes feared that neither she nor anyone connected with her, would ever see the palimpsest again.

CHAPTER 21

A lightning course in text scholarship

Agnes and Margaret had been over-hasty. In the rush to vindicate themselves, they had not written *How the Codex Was Found* with monastic sensibilities in mind, and Archbishop Porphyrios was gravely offended by some of its contents. Amongst them (his letter gives page citations) were Agnes's account of meeting the monks in procession in the garden and being obliged to venerate the cross and her remark 'that the Syriac manuscripts had been stored in vaults beneath the convent for safety . . . and there "exposed to damp" and "allowed to dry without care" '. He was dismayed by her suggestion that the brethren had neglected their Christian duty to instruct the Bedouin in Scripture; by her claim that, despite fifteen centuries of liturgy and sacraments, as 'for being a centre of light to the population around it [the convent] might as well never have existed'; and finally by her observation that the brethren were 'sleepy, useless, and miserable' during their Lenten fast. The palimpsest, then already on its way to Cairo, was sent back to Sinai and permission to consult it withdrawn. At least, said Agnes – drawing what solace she could – they were now spared the trouble of anyone going to transcribe the final pages, but still, ' *"Der alt böse Feind"* [the Devil] has had something do with it!'

Not to be defeated, Agnes and Margaret threw themselves into the study of Syriac. Throughout July of 1893, Robert Kennett, who had previously taught Agnes, sacrificed his research time to give Margaret lessons in what was, for her, an entirely new language, and Agnes visited the British Museum to make her own comparison between the Curetonian Codex and the Sinai Palimpsest.

In August, Kennett invited the twins to join him and his young wife in the Lake District, where they were taking a party of undergraduates on a reading holiday.[1] In the morning Kennett lectured his students on Hebrew (assisted by Margaret and his wife, Emily) and in the afternoon took them off for long walks on the Fells. The twins took rather shorter walks and spent the rest of their time poring over the transcriptions.

They wrote almost daily to Rendel Harris. Despite being a published editor of Syriac texts, Harris was having doubts about the quality of his own transcription. The saintly Kennett, assisted by Agnes, offered to check all his drafts. Agnes wrote to Rendel Harris:

> Watendleth Farm, Borrowdale by Keswick
> 11 August, 1893
>
> Dear Mr Harris,
>   . . . Mr Kennett has read 20 pages of your transcription with me, and I have translated into English 35 pages by myself. I am greatly delighted with it, for it seems a grand witness to the accuracy of the Gospels as we possess them, and you really have done a great work in writing down so much of it. If only Messrs Bensly and Burkitt have worked as well as you, it will be a glorious volume.

As Kennett's scrupulous corrections rained down on Harris, Agnes had to reassure him:

> I hope you will not be too alarmed at the apparent number of Mr Kennett's emendations. In the first place, no doubt Mr Bensly made as many in Mr Burkitt's copy at Sinai, and he ought to have looked over yours in the evenings . . . Mr Kennett is off to the top of the Helvellyn with four young men . . . Still, it is most important that a critical eye like Mr Kennett's should go over the text, before it comes under eyes that are not so friendly, as he says, we must give the enemy no cause to blaspheme . . . The mountains are looking glorious after their shower-bath. I feel stronger for being here already.[2]

No self-doubt afflicted Agnes. Emboldened by her own audacity, she wanted to do a translation of the palimpsest into English, for otherwise the transcription would appear only in Syriac and be of little use to ordinary people. Even the kindly Kennett thought this a step too far; she was only three years into the study of the language and risked severe criticism – 'of course entirely unjust!' he hastened to add. Agnes sought the advice of Donald MacAlister who, in a letter of encouragement, swept away all hesitations with his scornful hilarity – although how, as a medical doctor, he was in a position to advise is unclear.

Agnes complained to Harris that when visitors came to stay, Kennett 'tramped over the country in melting heat or splashing rain at the rate of 24 miles a day, starting at 8 a.m. and returning sometimes at 10.30 [p.m.]. When this sort of thing goes on, there is no time for Syriac . . . I have only gone on one afternoon's expedition with them, it does not quite suit me to spend a whole day jumping amongst wet bogs.'[3] She was, in the main, however, highly satisfied with the way the work was going. 'It is a great benefit to us all,' she continued, 'that Mr Kennett is revising yours so carefully, and as nearly all his suggestions have been confirmed or negated by the photographs we shall not have much room for the critics . . .'[4]

Back in Cambridge for the autumn term, Rendel Harris bent the university's rules by allowing Agnes and Margaret to attend his classes in palaeography. He made the difficult discipline of reading ancient texts a delight. An undergraduate memoir described the class as:

like no other. We were older and younger men, and among us were Mrs Lewis and Mrs Gibson, the discoverers of the Sinai Syriac MS. Every one was given, lecture by lecture a photograph of some page of MS.; and the rule was that whoever first caught the initial word should read on till he or she blundered, and the turn passed to whoever caught them out. It was great fun, a real adventure, and (it is to be remarked) it was doing the actual thing itself, not hearing about it, though, of course, we did hear about it, the brilliance and wit of Rendel Harris playing all over the work.[5]

Under pressure to check the transcriptions, Agnes and Margaret had devised a technique to help them read the manuscript more efficiently: they turned their photographs into lantern-slides, a procedure that enabled them to verify 'many passages in them with the aid of the electric lamp'.[6] In what little spare time remained to them and at the encouragement of Robertson Smith, the twins also began to work on several other Syriac and Arabic manuscripts they had photographed on their first visit to Sinai. With his help they negotiated a new book series under their general editorship with the Cambridge University Press, *Studia Sinaitica*, in which these and other Sinai-related texts could be published. The sisters partly subsidised the series – on condition, of course, that they receive profits from the sales.

Come December, neither Rendel Harris nor Francis Burkitt had signed their contracts. Burkitt was maintaining a frosty distance. Harris told Agnes that he wanted to wait until a certain Mr Stenning could return from Sinai with some further confirmations about the text. Once again Alick Macalister weighed in on the twins' behalf. He thought it would be a great mistake for Harris to delay in signing, or so Agnes wrote to Harris:

> Waiting till after Mr Stenning's visit to Sinai allows the Burkitts to say 'Well, were we not justified in asserting that Mr Harris was not equal to the task he undertook and that he might have left it entirely to Professor Bensly and Mr B? It will be one of the greatest errors of tact and judgment you can commit. You are too simple a nature yourself to estimate the ways of the people with whom we have to do, and it has come to my ears that last summer they did make a determined effort to throw us over. Now please do not furnish them with a valid excuse for doing so which will be 'Mr Harris hesitates about signing the agreement, so we are free.[7]

More influential on Harris was the understated but steady support of Robertson Smith. Now confined to bed with tuberculosis of the spine, an excruciating illness that would soon kill him, Robertson Smith was nonetheless able, as the Press's official representative and someone respected by all the feuding parties, to move things quietly along.[8]

Harris finally signed a contract and in April 1894 and, to Agnes's great relief, Burkitt – unwilling to disappoint his former mentor, Robertson Smith – finally handed over his completed sections of the transcription at about the same time, enabling her to finish her own translation and refine her introduction with the deadline for the submission of copy to the Press only weeks away.

In October of 1894 *The Four Gospels in the Old Syriac Version transcribed from the Palimpsest on Mount Sinai* was finally published. It was a triumph. The exotic tale of its discovery – by a lady – ensured the interest of the general public, but, as a glowing and lengthy review in the *Expository Times* pointed out, 'the work itself seems to have an importance that will make its publication memorable after the romance has been forgotten'. Agnes and Frank Burkitt were much in demand (separately, of course) as speakers, and a flood of correspondence and debate ensued. Even Burkitt wrote that 'few manuscripts of any part of the Bible have led to such a volume of discussion'.[9] Nearly all the reviews and articles – apart from a lengthy one in the *Church Guardian* by Burkitt himself – gave prominent place to Agnes.

Agnes's introduction was a masterpiece of ingenuity. By depriving her of his assistance and, indeed, keeping from her the contents of his sections until the very last moment, Burkitt might have hoped for a short and homely account of how she found the manuscript. Instead what Agnes provided was fairly lengthy and certainly scholarly.

She began by discussing, with extensive quotation of the Syriac, the text of the overwriting of the palimpsest – the martyrology of female saints. Readers may have been surprised that the introduction to the one text should deal almost exclusively with another, but at least the essay made it abundantly clear that Agnes could read Syriac and navigate her way through the language of ancient manuscripts. She then went on to provide a physical description of the palimpsest: its length and its pages, its quires and its vellum, its colophons and its dating, before turning finally to the Curetonian. Here she mentioned only those details already in the public domain, such as which parts of the New Testament were present and which missing, and the overall importance of securing these recensions of the Old Syriac text. To speak further of its interesting readings would, she said (neatly veiling her ignorance as modesty), 'carry us beyond the scope of the present introduction'.

Having established her credentials as a scholar of Syriac, Agnes did not neglect her role in the palimpsest's discovery; the manuscript 'was found by me in the Convent of St Catherine on Mount Sinai, in the month of February, 1892'. In her first two sentences 'me', 'my' and 'I' appear six times, leaving the reader in no doubt where credit was due.

In conclusion, she mentioned two great losses: Professor Bensly, 'who held a foremost place amongst European scholars', and Professor Robertson Smith, who had presided over the arrangements for publication and died as the sheets were passing through the Press. The roles of Bensly, Burkitt, Harris and Kennett were openly acknowledged; so, too, were those of others – not least her sister and most especially Galaktéon, the librarian of St Catherine's. But Agnes was able, via an artful locution, just to avoid thanking Burkitt: 'Of the work done by Professor Bensly, by Mr Rendel Harris and by Mr Burkitt I can only speak with sincere admiration, and my cordial thanks are due to the friends who have helped us with their advice.'

Other than recovering a Syriac translation earlier and more complete than any hitherto known, perhaps the most significant discovery in the palimpsest concerned the ending of Mark's Gospel. In the King James Version (and still in most modern bibles) the final chapter of Mark is twenty-one verses long, describing Christ's appearance to Mary Magdalene after his resurrection and providing, uniquely in the New Testament, an account of certain post-resurrection teachings to his disciples, including the promise that they may pick up snakes and drink poisons without coming to harm. But in both the Codices Vaticanus and Sinaiticus – the two oldest copies of the Bible – this chapter, Mark 16, stops after only eight verses, ending with the puzzled women leaving the empty tomb of Jesus and telling no one, 'for they were afraid'.[10] In neither the Vaticanus nor the Sinaiticus was it clear whether the final verses of Mark had ever been there in the first place, or were missing because a page had fallen off. Here the palimpsest was decisive: as Agnes wrote, in it 'there can be no doubt that they never existed'. Mark ends and Luke begins within the same column of text. Between the two gospels a colophon in red ink declares 'Here endeth the Gospel of Mark', followed immediately by the heading 'The Gospel of Luke'.

Were Agnes and Margaret distressed by this loss of Mark's resurrection? Not really. Despite her own conviction that the doctrine of the resurrection was the mast to which the disciples 'nailed their colours', Agnes seems to have been delighted to find that the palimpsest did not contain Mark's resurrection appearances.[11] The absence of these verses was confirmation of the antiquity of her find and of the priority of the 'Lewis' Codex over the rival Curetonian (favoured by Burkitt), which did include the full ending of Mark. And there was no loss from the point of view of faith, since the resurrection was well attested in the other Gospels. In any case, Agnes would later write, the addition of the verses does not prove them unreliable reminiscence – a position roughly shared by those text scholars today who think that verses 10–21, if not original, were added very early on.

What still rankled most with Agnes was the suggestion that the palimpsest was heretical in implying that Joseph was the biological father of Jesus. She was unable even to contemplate this. Margaret wrote, loyally, to *The Times* to suggest that it had been a misreading by the transcribers. To be more precise, she suggested that Mr Burkitt might have simply misunderstood this section and that, had 'Mrs Lewis been requested to apply her chemical to the page', perhaps a letter might have come up to show that it was Mary, not Joseph, who was stated as 'begetting' Jesus.

This was unsustainable. As the erudite and anonymous reviewer in *The Times* pointed out, it must have been the intention of the writer-translator to throw some doubt on the Virginal Conception, since two other verses in the first chapter of Matthew had been altered in the same direction. For instance, the final verse – which in most versions reads 'but [Joseph] had no married relations with her until she had borne a son' – in the Sinai Palimpsest reads simply, 'And she bore him a son.'

We catch a little of the residual amateurism that annoyed Burkitt in Agnes's dogged insistence on the *orthodoxy* of the palimpsest at every point, seemingly for no other reason than that she had found it. For text scholars like Burkitt and Bensly, of course, a heretical manuscript was not of inferior interest so far as it provided, just the same, a footprint of the development of the early Church and its rival views. Even Rendel Harris was of the opinion that the palimpsest was the product of a scribe, or a group, who deliberately tried to downplay or erase the Virgin Birth. This was, from Agnes's point of view, 'bad'. 'Good', on the other hand, was the fact that the scribe had been neither thoroughgoing or successful. Mention made elsewhere in the palimpsest to the 'Virgin' Mary contradicted the scribe's general tendency, since the word 'virgin' in Syriac – unlike Hebrew – is always used in its strict (that is, biological, not merely social) sense: proof that the very earliest texts did maintain the Virgin Birth of Jesus, and that the palimpsest scribe was deviating from them. Why he made his revisions is unclear. It could not be that he objected to the miraculous nature of the Virgin Birth, for other high-voltage miracles remain intact elsewhere in the palimpsest. Rendel Harris's view was that the palimpsest might have been copied for 'Adoptionists', believers who held that Jesus was born a man like other men but who, at his baptism by John, was lifted or 'adopted' into divine status.

Agnes and Margaret did not, in the end, have any difficulty with the idea of rival sects in the early Church. Agnes believed that God could of course have provided us with perfect copies of the Bible, but instead allowed human scribes to make their errors and their variants. Demonstrating her robust certitude in an age of gathering doubt, she argued that even our mistakes redound to the praise of God, 'for the very variants which frighten the weak minded among us act as a stimulant to others, inciting them to search the Scripture more diligently, to eliminate the mistakes of mere copyists, and to ascertain what it was that the Evangelists actually wrote'.[12]

As for the idea that every word of the King James Bible was as the Holy Spirit had dictated it – a view that commanded prominence in Britain in the early nineteenth century – 'no one,' wrote Agnes, 'who has ever read two out of the 3829 extant MSS [of the New Testament] and has observed the many slight variations in the order of their words . . . can continue to hold this theory for a single moment'. Most of these variants do not affect the substance. Agnes knew of thirteen manuscript alternatives for the phrase 'Jesus answered and said unto him':

> Jesus answered, and said unto him,
> Jesus answering, said unto him,
> Jesus answered him, saying,
> Jesus said unto him,
> Jesus answered, saying,
> Jesus, answering, said,
> And Jesus said unto him,
> And Jesus said,
> Jesus said,
> Jesus answered, and said,
> And Jesus answering, said unto him,
> And Jesus answered him, saying,
> And Jesus answered, saying,

Verbal inspiration (at least in the form that held that the Bible as it has come down to us is divinely inspired, down to the last word) had been, said Agnes, a 'comfortable and convenient theory', but its age had passed away.[13]

CHAPTER 22

In the company of Orientalists

When Samuel died, Agnes was described in his obituaries as simply a writer of travel books, and so she was. Now, just three years later, amongst her personal correspondents were Theodor Nöldeke, translator of the Koran and Professor of Oriental languages at Strassburg, and the great Friedrich Max Müller, Professor of Comparative Philology at Oxford and President of the International Congress of Orientalists.

In addition to publication of the palimpsest and, in a separate volume, Agnes's translation of it, 1894 saw the appearance of the first four volumes of the sisters' new series for the Cambridge University Press, *Studia Sinaitica*: these comprised the catalogues of the Syriac and Arabic manuscripts in the convent on Mount Sinai (the work of Agnes and Margaret respectively), a tract of Plutarch also found at Sinai by the sisters and edited by Eberhard Nestle, and an edition of a ninth-century Arabic copy of some Epistles of St Paul, found and photographed by the twins and edited by Margaret.[1]

After what must count as one of the most remarkable of middle-aged retraining exercises, Agnes Smith Lewis and Margaret Dunlop Gibson stepped onto the world stage as oriental scholars of international repute.

It is difficult to recapture the prestige and even glamour of the intellectual milieu into which the twins now moved. In the quarter-century since Agnes and Margaret first sailed up the Nile, huge strides had been made in understanding the ancient Near East. The translation of Egyptian hieroglyphics and then of cuneiform, and the finds of hoards of tablets and temple wall inscriptions had opened up a heretofore unknown world of official letters, trade agreements and diplomatic exchanges. Newspaper column inches were regularly devoted to new discoveries. Where before, the Old Testament had reigned supreme as the factual source for the ancient battles and victories it describes, new voices were now being heard from the other side of the intervening millennia. A stone found in 1868 near the Dead Sea, for instance, recorded the triumphs of King Mesha of Moab – from the Moabite perspective. This inscription corroborated the fact of the rebellion as described in II Kings 3. But it also recounted that Mesha had slaughtered 7,000 men, women and girls, and dragged the altar hearths of Israel's God, YHWH, before his own God, Chemosh – a detail, whether true or not, that the Bible left out.

Advances in Egyptology filled in a puzzling gap in the chronology of Egypt's pharaohs, but also held implications for the accuracy of the Bible. One pharaoh had been literally effaced from Egyptian history, his name scrubbed off any stones that bore it. Akhenaten's heresy had been his attempted suppression of Egypt's many gods in favour of one, the sun god, Aten. In the 1880s an immense rock-cut tomb was discovered at Amarna, in the ruins of his abandoned capital. Its rock carvings depict the pharaoh, his beautiful 'Great Wife' Nefertiti and the royal children with the peculiar banana-shaped heads of the 'Amarna style'; on another wall of the tomb is inscribed a hymn to Aten that is remarkably similar to Psalm 104. The likeness between the Psalm and Akhenaten's song in praise of the one god and all living creatures was in fact so great that the discovery was used to clarify several readings that had been uncertain in the Hebrew text. But Akhenaten's verses had been inscribed on the rock in the fourteenth century BC, many centuries before the life of King David, the supposed author of the Psalms. Had the Hebrew scribes borrowed an existing Egyptian song and adapted it for their own?[2] These discoveries were exciting and unsettling to a world long accustomed to regarding the Old Testament as the only source for the history of Israel.

Rendel Harris, Francis Burkitt and Eberhard Nestle belonged to a new and energetic generation of young scholars known as the

'Orientalists'; archaeologists, linguists and lovers of the East, they were 'men who have proved themselves able to handle their own spade, and who have worked in the sweat of their brow in disinterring the treasures of Oriental literature', according to Friedrich Max Müller's presidential address to the Ninth International Congress of Orientalists in London in 1892. Editor of the Rig Veda, and virtual inventor of the disciplines of comparative mythology and the study of religions, Max Müller was now Professor at Oxford and had seen through that university's press a fifty-volume series of *Sacred Books of the East*: classics in Sanskrit, Chinese, Arabic and Pali. Students came from as far afield as Japan to work with him. The year 1892 marked the 400th anniversary of the discovery of the New World and, in his presidential address, Müller seized upon this fact to say from the podium that, after centuries looking west, Europe was now looking to the east. Instead of the New World, it was rediscovering the Old. Each clay plate deciphered, each manuscript found, each grammatical conundrum resolved rolled back the cloud of ignorance that had obscured our common heritage. What lay revealed to us was not the dead past, but a living human world of thoughts, fears and hopes:

> Think only what ancient Egypt was to us a hundred years ago! A Sphinx buried in a desert, with hardly any human features left. And now – not only do we read the hieroglyphic, the hieratic, and the demotic inscriptions, not only do we know the right names of kings and queens 4000 or 5000 years BC, but we know their gods, their worship; we know their laws and their poetry; we know their folk-lore and even their novels. Their prayers are full of those touches which make the whole world feel akin.

The same is true of the ancient writings of Babylon and Nineveh, of the Vedanta and the Upanishad. The ancient oriental kingdoms have been 'made to speak to us, like the gray, crumbling statue of Memnon, when touched by the rays of the dawn'.[3]

Martial imagery suffused Müller's speech. Serried ranks of Orientalists stood before him – from France, Germany, Italy, Sweden, Switzerland, Holland, Russia and even India. He was proud to 'serve as a comrade who has fought now for nearly fifty years in the ranks of the brave army of Oriental scholars in England'. Since their first International Congress in 1873, the Orientalists' meetings had been supported and attended by princes and potentates from St Petersburg to Paris. In Stockholm, King Oscar himself had addressed the gathering in five languages! Now, in London, assistance had come from the Secretary of State for India, and one of the congress's vice-presidents was Gladstone, then Prime Minister.

A cynic might note that Europe's royalty and Britain's Secretary of State for India had every reason to delight in the 'treasures of the East', having appropriated so much of that wealth for themselves.[4] But that history did not trouble the idealism of Müller's address to his 'brave army' of scholars. He admitted to no tension between ruling the oriental nations and learning to love them. Indeed, the English must themselves be 'Orientalised', he said, for it was one thing to conquer and rule Eastern lands and quite another to understand them.[5] Out of their warm love for all that is beautiful in the East, the Orientalists must make it their object to bring the East as near as possible, to ease 'the strangeness between the West and the East, between the white and the dark man, between the Aryan and the Semite, which ought never to have arisen, and which is a disgrace to everybody who harbours it'.[6]

There is something strangely familiar in the grainy brown photographs of the young Burkitt and Harris at Sinai with their stout boots, coarse cotton trousers and unkempt beards. Only put a pick or a spade in their hands and the resemblance is clear – they become men of the Klondike gold-rush, clad in the heavy, denim trousers of M. Levi-Strauss. The decade is the same. And, like their contemporaries in the Far West, these men were searching for treasure at considerable risk to life and limb. There was romance in the life of the text scholar, a calling that combined the skills of a code-breaker with the danger of foreign travel and childhood fascination with opening long-undisturbed trunks in the attic. It was a heady mix of high scholarship and hard life, of international congresses before the crowned heads of Europe, with learned exchanges in French and Latin, Greek and Arabic, Hindustani and Coptic, and cold nights in the desert with a hard bed roll. It was all Agnes and Margaret could have desired.

CHAPTER 23

Burying the hatchet

Even with praise and speaking invitations showering down upon her, Agnes could not rest until the remaining pages of the palimpsest were transcribed. Every time she looked at their published edition – and even more when she looked at her own translation of it into English – she was aware of blank spaces, which amounted to about one-fifth of the whole. Until these were filled, there was always the risk that another scholar might venture to Sinai and make good the lack, and who knew what secrets lay as yet undiscovered in the remaining pages? Someone must return to St Catherine's, but who? Rendel Harris refused to go; Francis Burkitt was not to be trusted; and the sisters themselves were in disgrace with the archbishop.

Agnes continued to rue her tactless remarks in *How the Codex Was Found*. Archbishop Porphyrios had been repaid badly for all his kindness and Agnes had forfeited, it seemed, any chance of ever getting another look at the palimpsest. The monks were known for having, like camels, long memories when it came to those who had offended them, but the twins nevertheless resolved, if at all possible, to visit Sinai again.

Before her fall from grace Agnes had sent the convent a handsome box to hold the palimpsest, commissioning it from the same Cambridge firm that had made her late husband's elaborate coin cases. Of Spanish mahogany and lined with cedar, it was incised with crosses and Catherine wheels. An outer lid of wood opened to reveal an inner lid of glass, enabling the manuscript to be shown to visitors without removing it from its protective housing. A silver plate on the outer lid bore the inscription, in Greek:

> The Four Holy Gospels in Syriac.
> Agnes, the foreigner, has given this casket for the Sacred Scriptures,
> Not without gratitude,
> To the famous monks.

Now Agnes bombarded Archbishop Porphyrios with emollient letters, including press clippings, all of which put St Catherine's and its brethren in the best light. In an unguarded interview of the previous year she had said that the convent's manuscripts were kept in chests and that 'no very great care has been bestowed upon them, and dust and mice have played sad havoc'. Now, sincere in her remorse, she expressed herself more tactfully. In a letter to *The Times*, written to raise funds for the convent library, she wrote that although the manuscripts *were* kept in chests and 'it is now well known that confinement in a box is as unsuitable to the wellbeing of books as it is of living creatures', this less-than-ideal arrangement was not the monks' fault, for they 'have positively no space in which to arrange their treasures'. The monks were 'by no means the unlettered men that some travellers, unacquainted with modern Greek, have represented them to be. Some of them read cursive manuscripts with ease, if written in their own tongue, and we suspect that we were not the first travellers who have experienced their ready help and courtesy.' Agnes added a slightly Presbyterian twist to the monastic outlook as she continued:

> They are now fully alive to the responsibility laid on them by Providence of 'not keeping their light under a bushel' . . . But the whole monastery does not contain a single room suitable for a library. It is such a jumble of apartments, approached chiefly from irregular open courts, that any one of them, with the exception of the church, the mosque, and the refectory, might well be called an outhouse.
>
> The monastery is now very poor, its landed property in Russia,

Roumania, and Egypt having become depreciated, so that it has barely enough for the frugal sustenance of its 35 monks, and of the troops of Bedaween who have to be kept by it from starving during the long months when travellers do not want their camels.[1]

Her letter continued by stating that a significant sum, perhaps £3,000–£4,000, would be required to fund a purpose-built library. Sandstone would have to be brought from two days' distance by camel, the granite of Sinai being too hard – 'harder than Aberdeen granite' – and just as unsuitable for the purpose. In conclusion, and in contrast to von Tischendorf and many others who went before, Agnes stressed that it '. . . must be remembered that all these manuscripts, Greek, Syriac, Arabic, and Iberian, are the absolute property of the monks . . . The manuscripts have lain there for centuries, safe from the risks of wars and of political disturbance . . . The interests of science and of European civilisation lead us to hope that this most interesting relic of bygone ages may long be preserved.[2]

Despite the contrite letters and gifts, nothing more had been heard from Archbishop Porphyrios since his angry letter. With no other options open to them, the twins finally determined to go to Egypt again themselves, on the remote chance of speaking personally to Porphyrios and persuading him to let them see the palimpsest once more. They set out from Cambridge, with no notice except to their friends, early in 1895.

Cairo under British occupation was a lively place, much changed since the twins' first visit. The Suez Canal was carrying huge ships toe to tail, most of them British. With little for the British officers and civil servants actually to do – or so it appeared to Agnes and Margaret – life was gay with operas, balls and luncheons *en plein air* in front of the pyramids. Two tour operators, Thomas Cook's and its arch-rival, Henry Gaze & Son, had perfected the 'packaged' Nile cruise, making it accessible to the better-off British and American tourist. Egypt was no longer marketed as the Bible Land – it was now the 'Exotic East': souks and harems, Circassian maidens and half-clad Nubian slave girls in

Turkish baths were all lavishly depicted by British artists for the enticement of the eager public back home.

Agnes and Margaret regarded these scenes of indolent frivolity with a certain contempt. It was not that they disdained comfort, or even luxury – they themselves had stopped off en route at Worth's in Paris to purchase the silk frocks and hats necessary when residing in a fine Cairo hotel. They were, however, in Egypt for business.

After settling into the Hôtel d'Angleterre, they went immediately to the Sinai convent's Cairo headquarters with the object of speaking to Archbishop Porphyrios. He was not there. They found instead Father Nicodemus, the monk so admired by Mrs Bensly, who told them that the archbishop had been at Sinai since the previous May setting the library in order. Agnes and Margaret were disappointed, but drew comfort from the discovery that all their letters and newspaper clippings lay unforwarded in the archbishop's Cairo rooms. Perhaps this explained his silence? Nicodemus was able to grant them permission to visit St Catherine's, but could give no assurance that the archbishop would receive them or allow them to see the palimpsest again. He told them that there had been more thefts from the library and that the brethren were now deeply suspicious of all visitors.

With not much hope, but slightly more than they had on arrival, Agnes and Margaret made preparations to cross the desert once more. They hired a young Lebanese dragoman called Joseph, a Protestant who had studied at the American College in Beirut, and while Joseph set about organising their caravan, Agnes and Margaret took the opportunity to examine some of the manuscripts on sale in the city.

Since their last visit to Cairo, and after two years' hard intensive labour on the palimpsest and other ancient writings, the sisters were now in an entirely altered position when it came to examining ancient manuscripts: no longer lady amateurs, but professionals with a good working knowledge, not only of Greek, Hebrew and Arabic, but of Syriac and several other Aramaic dialects. Under the tutelage of Rendel Harris, while cataloguing at St Catherine's and through his Cambridge palaeography classes, they now knew what to look for amongst the manuscripts in the souks of Cairo – and had an idea what things were worth.

This knowledge could not have been more timely. To their horror Agnes and Margaret found that manuscripts were being dismembered and sold by dealers, leaf by leaf. It happened that one of the unfortunate side effects of the 'Second Army of Occupation' (as Agnes called the tourists) was to create a market for old curios amongst these sheets of ancient writing.

One day a dubious-looking dealer in manuscripts appeared at their hotel, directed ('I cannot say recommended,' wrote Agnes) by a learned Syrian gentleman of their acquaintance. He had a Palestinian Syriac lectionary to sell, very small and missing the last ten pages. Fresh tear marks indicated that these had been removed only recently. It was very like two Syriac lectionaries the twins had photographed during their first visit to Sinai. Agnes had never bought a manuscript before but she could not resist this one. She paid £100 – a large but not inappropriate sum. However, it was a manuscript she did not buy that was most to influence their fortunes.

The water-stained Maccabees

One Sunday, two days before their intended departure for Sinai, an itinerant dealer appeared at the Hôtel d'Angleterre. He must have promised great things to persuade the twins to look at his wares on the Sabbath.

The dealer placed a Syriac manuscript in Agnes's hands. It was instantly familiar. Agnes well remembered that a beautiful sixth-century Syriac copy of Maccabees, which Rendel Harris had photographed on his first visit to

St Catherine's with Frederick Bliss, had disappeared by the time he
returned with Agnes and Margaret in 1893. At Agnes's suggestion they
had used one of the photographs for the frontispiece of her published
Catalogue of the Syriac Manuscripts, in the remote hope that someone
would recognise it and report its whereabouts. The top of each page of
the manuscript she was now holding said 'Maccabai'. Even the areas
damaged by damp matched those she knew from Rendel Harris's
photograph. Without saying anything, Agnes stepped over to a side
table and opened a copy of her catalogue, placing photograph and
manuscript side by side – the two matched, even down to the minute
yellow stains. 'There were only two people in the world who could
have recognised this at a glance, Dr Harris and myself,' Agnes would
later write. Thinking quickly, she informed the dealer and her
astonished sister that she and Margaret must depart immediately for a
church service, but wished to retain the manuscript until Monday in
order to make a decision. The moment the dealer had gone, they
contacted the Cairo agent of the convent. A tense day followed while
he got in touch with some of the monks at Suez. Margaret wrote to
Rendel Harris as events were still unfolding: 'Really God is answering
your prayer and ours in a very remarkable manner . . . not yet 48 hours
ago a dealer placed in her [Agnes's] hands . . . your lost Maccabees! We
got his permission to keep it in order to examine it . . . and ever since
we have been in a chronic state of excitement, as the dealer is
constantly coming asking for it.'[3] On the Tuesday Agnes and Margaret
were able to present the civil authorities with the manuscript, tied up
in a cambric handkerchief and bound with white ribbon like a 'bridal
present'.

The twins set out with their camel caravan from Suez with
confidence. Margaret was sure that when next they met Archbishop
Porphyrios, they would be able to 'sing a paean together and bury all
hatchets'.

She was right.

They were received at St Catherine's as honoured guests. The legal
process begun in Cairo had not yet led to the return of the stolen
Maccabees, but the archbishop was aware of Agnes's prompt action

and an altogether sunnier climate prevailed. Agnes and Margaret were able to present him with copies of their published catalogues (he already possessed the handwritten ones, Greek–Arabic and Greek–Syriac, which they had created for the monks on their previous visit). They also presented him with a copy of the published transcription of the palimpsest. He could see for himself that the work needed to be completed and gave his permission for them to carry on.

The convent had changed from the genial untidiness of Galaktéon's day. The sisters had noticed it as soon as they arrived, as a Russian pilgrimage was preparing to depart. Whereas two years before any pilgrim departure entailed a whole morning of roaring camels and disputes among the Bedouin, pilgrims and priests, this leave-taking was quietly efficient. Camels were allowed between the inner and outer gates only in small batches, to be laden with the pilgrims, pans, kettles, pillows and palm branches in orderly fashion. It was typical of the tight ship now run by Porphyrios. There were new monks, who looked taller and more alert. The interior of the convent had been whitewashed and the doors and windows painted a hygienic blue. Even the thick and ancient entrance portal was now encased in sheet metal painted in this colour. Agnes remarked to Father Euthymios that this had an incongruous effect and received the reply she have been given so often in Greece: 'What can we do?'[4] Gone was the substantial wooden bench on which the twins had been accustomed to sit in the mornings, waiting for Galaktéon to arrive with the keys.

Porphyrios had also changed the way in which manuscripts were stored. Although a new library had not yet been built, the warren of dark closets off the archbishop's room had been knocked together to form two light and airy rooms. These now had glazed windows and new bookshelves, which held manuscripts in numerical order. Near the monks' dormitory stood a substantial, new whitewashed building whose upper floor, with five large sunny windows (also glazed), was designed as a place where Western visitors could study manuscripts. It was built, as Agnes would observe in her 1898 book, *In the Shadow of Sinai*, at the highest point of the convent so as to catch all possible light, and was reached by the staircase the monks most commonly used

when going back and forth to their cells. The effect was to make the
surveillance of visiting scholars as good as that achieved in London's
British Museum. What Agnes does not mention in *The Shadow of Sinai*
or any of her other writings is that this building was built with funds
sent by Margaret and herself.[5]

Asked which book they should like to see first, Agnes asked boldly
for the palimpsest, officially now 'Number 30'. Something of the older
disorder reared its head as the librarian, Father Euthymios, climbed a
ladder lying against the neatly ordered shelves only to declare, after
shuffling about fruitlessly for some time, 'We haven't got it.' Agnes
and Margaret remonstrated: the archbishop had said it was here, and
Mrs Lewis had sent a beautiful box! But Father Euthymios did not
know where the box was, either. He hadn't seen it for a long time.
Agnes began to panic. She recalled that young Mr Stenning, whom
they had asked to review the manuscript when he visited the convent
a year before, had not been able to see it. She feared it might have been
disposed of by some secret negotiation, and sat down to have 'what the
French so aptly call a bad quarter-of-an-hour'. But her sister's voice
roused her: 'Agnes, there it is! . . . It's coming!' Agnes looked up and
saw the palimpsest still wrapped in the striped silk cover given by Mrs
Bensly.

The twins settled back into a routine of work now familiar to them.
Agnes set about her transcription of the remaining leaves of
palimpsest, making ample use of the reagent whose disgusting smell
had the benefit of shortening the visits of those who came merely to
gawk. She revisited every word done by Burkitt, Bensly and Harris,
discovering to her delight several 'grotesque blunders' in their work,
although few in that of the beloved Rendel Harris. Agnes's expertise
was now such that she was able to clarify a number of standing
ambiguities.[6]

Outside the comfort of the reading room and the walls of the
convent, these January and February days were cold and violently
windy. In the garden the sisters' tents had to be pegged to the olive
trees to keep them from blowing away. Father Eumenios begged them
to move inside the convent to be out of the cold and the danger (he

cited) of wolves, but the twins, more confident of the comfort of their own domestic arrangements, politely declined. Rather than the hardship, their letters to Rendel Harris describe their deep contentment during this, their most leisurely visit to St Catherine's. 'We . . . are as happy as two little crickets,' wrote Margaret to him:

> . . . There is no warm friend like Galaktéon, to be sure, but everybody is very friendly, from the handsome and dignified Archbishop to the tall active gardener . . . the Archbishop and several monks stroll in when they have a few minutes to spare, and Euthymios sits about a good deal and reads, also an Arab servant named Ahmed comes in several times a day with coffee or sweets; indeed the Archbishop told us to call for those luxuries when we want them.[7]

One evening, as Margaret picked her way over rocks at the base of the convent walls after a walk, a loud hallooing made her look up to the battlements. High above her, Father Eumenios was waving a newspaper, which he tossed over the wall. Margaret scrambled over the rocks to catch it as it drifted down; it was a Greek newspaper containing an announcement, translated from *The Athenaeum*, of the publication of her catalogue of the Arabic manuscripts in the convent library.

A decent handful of Western visitors had now turned up at the convent: six English travellers, two young Germans, and the Hon. Whitelaw Reid, formerly American Special Ambassador to Britain during the Queen's Jubilee Year, with his wife. Agnes and Margaret decided to throw a party, their first effort at entertaining at Sinai. The plan was for little tables beneath the olive trees with a display of cakes, sweets and fruits 'more remarkable for its elegant simplicity than its luxuriance'. Americans, Europeans and Sinai monks would mingle and exchange pleasantries. The cook spent three days baking cakes in an outdoor oven that he and their dragoman, Joseph, fabricated for the purpose.

Sinai had been suffering a drought since the rains of April the previous year. Even the palms at the Oasis of Feiran looked miserable and, in the garden of St Catherine's, the olives and almond trees were drooping. The monks had received a deputation of Bedouin sheikhs from the distant northern plain of Tih. Though Muslims, they had nonetheless come to ask that the monks pray for rain. They even asked Joseph, a Protestant, to pray for them, with the stipulation that he put on a white tunic and go to the top of Gebel Musa at midnight to do so. Joseph refused.

The monks prayed, but without confidence: 'It is for our sins,' they said. Father Eumenios glumly declared that there would be no rain now for they were entering the summer season.

Working in the convent on the morning of their garden party, Agnes noticed that the light was a little less brilliant than usual. She thought nothing of it, until the wild clamour of bells and gongs from the courtyard made her put down her pen. Where the prayers of monks had failed, the simple expedient of scheduling a garden party in the British style had brought on a deluge. In their dripping tent Agnes and Margaret entertained successive parties of damp monks and waterproof-clad foreigners.

The twins left the convent on 14 March. Agnes's work of transcription was finished, but, as sorry compensation for the pains of sitting hour after hour at a desk, a carbuncle on her buttock was now causing much discomfort. She was forced to forgo the saddle and walk the last fifteen miles before tumbling exhausted into a felucca at 'Ain Musa. For two weeks she saw nothing but the mosquito nets of her bed in their room in the Hôtel d'Orient at Suez.

They had planned to proceed from Suez to Urfa in what is now eastern Turkey. When known as Edessa, the city had been the capital of Syriac-speaking Christianity in the earliest Christian centuries. Now letters from Rendel Harris warned them off. The region was drenched in blood as the Ottoman rulers suppressed perceived insurrection amongst their Armenian subjects.

The twins still wanted, before returning to England, to meet people among whom the Syriac of the palimpsest was a living language. To this end they took a steamer to Beirut and travelled with Joseph, in the comfort of a horse-drawn carriage, to some of the Syriac-speaking villages of the ante-Lebanon (now modern Syria). In villages that clung like wasps' nests to the sides of cliffs, they upbraided the Christian populace for allowing their native tongue – 'the mother-tongue of our Saviour' – to be corrupted by Arabisms.

The palimpsest now fully copied, Agnes had found no more worrying deviations from orthodoxy. Instead she was strengthened in her conviction that the text of the Sinai Palimpsest was not only more complete, but more ancient than that of the rival Curetonian.

After three trips to Sinai in four years, Agnes and Margaret now expected to stay quietly at home working on the newly transcribed portions of the palimpsest, various manuscripts they had already photographed and the Syriac lectionary Agnes had purchased in Cairo. But their plans changed when they received a letter telling of manuscripts leaking mysteriously onto the market in Cairo. They could not miss the chance, and early in 1896, less than nine months after returning from their last trip, the sisters set out once more for Egypt.

CHAPTER 24

Keepers of manuscripts

It was now clear that the palimpsest, far from being a fortuitous find and glorious 'one-off' adventure, was the beginning of a whole new life for Agnes and Margaret. While they disapproved of buying manuscripts from ancient monasteries almost as much as stealing them, when the same manuscripts turned up for sale as tourist trinkets on market stalls, purchasing them was not merely permissible, but obligatory. They would not visit Sinai on this trip, but only Cairo, and would proceed from there to Jerusalem with the sole object of photographing and purchasing manuscripts.

In Cairo they found that their mysterious informant had not misled them.[1] They purchased a considerable number of manuscripts – some not more than a page or a fragment – and, before even stopping to examine them fully, turned their sights on Jerusalem.

This was the first time in their travels that the sisters had encountered the problems created by cholera, with boats leaving Egypt's ports being regularly blocked from landing. If, as planned, they sailed from Alexandria, they would not be able to stop at Jaffa or Beirut and might face a long quarantine on a boat. This was widely thought to be more dangerous than remaining in the most infested city: should cholera develop amongst the passengers, a whole boat might soon became a floating plague pit. And so Agnes and Margaret, well used to travelling with dragomen and tents, decided to make the journey to Jerusalem overland, along the ancient Via Maris. They would go over the desert to Gaza, following roughly the route of Mary and Joseph's flight with the infant Jesus, but in reverse.

Alighting from the evening train at Suez, Agnes and Margaret found their own Joseph, and the caravan he had assembled, waiting for them on the Asiatic bank of the Suez Canal, the tents pitched so close to the great nautical freeway that they could almost lean out and shake hands with fellow countrymen standing on the decks of the steamers on their way to Bombay or beyond. The flood-lamps of these great boats, scooping a path out of the darkness before them, dimmed into insignificance the tiny illumination of the sisters' fire, with its tough Bedouin and spectral camels arrayed about it.

The journey over the bleak landscape took only six days, but was unexpectedly difficult. In contrast to the firm gravel of the southern wadis, the northern Sinai was deep sand that made walking impossible, except on the occasional dried-up salt marsh. Even the camels had trouble moving, and the water found on the way was so bad that they 'only sniffed, and refused to drink'. Circling vultures set the Bedouin on a hunt for their eggs as a dinner-time delicacy, but otherwise lent a mournful note. The path itself was usually hidden by sand drifts, with a line of half-submerged telegraph poles as rather desolate waymarks. Margaret noted that the Egyptian (British-administered) telegraph lines were taut, while the Syrian (Ottoman) lines hung slack.

Agnes extracted some poetry from the journey:

> From Egypt's fields of glowing green,
> To Gaza's gardens gay,
> Deep barren sand for ever drifts
> Athwart the traveller's way.
> Six days beneath the blazing sun
> We press the blazing sod;
> Where twice beside His mother rode
> The great Incarnate God.[2]

Gaza, once reached, with its orange groves and olive trees, was green and radiant, but scarcely welcoming. They passed through a Muslim cemetery where children, celebrating the end of Ramadan, playing on swings and merry-go-rounds amongst white gravestones, shouted at the twins as foreigners, and some older boys threw stones that hit one of the camel drivers. The sisters thought it best to look pleasantly jocular as the stones whizzed by, but were relieved to find that the cook and waiter, who had gone on ahead, had pitched their tents behind a protective hedge of prickly cacti. They decided, under the circumstances, not to visit the mosque as planned and, rather than wait to find suitable horses in Gaza, to proceed immediately to Jerusalem by camel. By comparison with their earlier treks, this was only a short distance and they could visit some biblical and archaeological sites on the way.

As was the custom for travel in Palestine, Joseph acquired two Turkish cavalrymen to act as night guards, one of whom stayed with the ladies as they travelled by day. These soldiers provided their own horses and were paid very little, but they were entitled to pasture and payment in kind from the villages they passed through; the day guard told Agnes and Margaret that he 'would just say "Bring me a chicken," and when he had eaten this, "Bring me another chicken." Then he would ask for some tobacco, and even for a little money.'[3]

On the first day in Palestine they visited Lachish, one of Frederick Bliss's excavations. Tablet letters in cuneiform were discovered here, part of a correspondence between the governors of the Canaanite cities and the court of the pharaoh Akhenaten in Amarna. On the second day they explored caves believed to have been used by King David in his shepherding days.

That evening things soured. As they descended into the valley where David had encountered Goliath, the sky became heavy with clouds. Their waiter and cook had, as usual, gone ahead to pitch camp, but no one whom the twins and their guard now encountered had seen them pass. As the moon rose they found themselves in the narrow valley of a stony, dry river bed, the going so tricky that they had to dismount. They could only grope their way towards faint lights in another valley, their Turkish guard bellowing before them in Arabic, 'A soldier, a soldier, and ladies of quality.'

After several hours they reached a walled road between olive groves, which the heavy rains had reduced to a succession of mud pools and rocks. It was impossible to ride the camels, which were unsteady on the wet ground. They could only hope that the distant lights towards which they had been heading were the comfortable camp site the waiter and cook were meant to have made, but it turned out to be a village so poor it could not house them. Now, late on a March night of 1896, they had no alternative but to raise the small luncheon tent they carried with them – little more than a parasol since it lacked sides – and make do. The cold was penetrating and the brushwood fire lit by the Bedouin did little to warm them or dry the sisters' thick skirts, claggy with mud.

Joseph managed to procure eggs and milk from the village, whisking them into scrambled eggs for an evening meal, and the Bedouin 'roasted some coffee in a shovel, pounded it in a wooden mortar, and boiled it in a little pot'. But the strong, hot coffee, though pleasing at the moment of consumption, in combination with the damp skirts and a scourge of insects attracted by the camp fire, made for a sleepless and miserable night. Joseph, overhearing one twin say to the other that she was cold, insisted on rolling the two of them up together in a bundle, using his own greatcoat.

Next morning Agnes and Margaret admitted defeat. After a weary ride over the mountains they intersected the railway line and caught, at Bittir, the Jaffa–Jerusalem Express. This was rather lowering for individuals who prided themselves as independent travellers, especially since the first-class carriage in which they made their bedraggled appearance was otherwise wholly occupied by a British party from 'Gaze's Health and Pleasure Cruising – 60 days travel for 60 Guineas. Cairo–Jaffa–Jerusalem.'

They finally found their distraught cook and waiter at Jerusalem's Jaffa Gate. The pair had set up camp at the agreed stopping point, prepared dinner and waited for the twins with increasing anxiety, before sensibly carrying on the next day to the city. It says something of the twins' thrift – tents and servants being already paid for – that despite constant rain and cold, they persisted with their original plan to lodge in their own tents outside the city's walls. Three nights later driving rain drenched Margaret's bed and set their boots and shoes

afloat in a pond on the tent floor. The women held out until daybreak
before asking the Turkish soldiers, still mounting guard over them, to
order a cab for the Grand New Hotel.

Agnes and Margaret stayed in the Grand New Hotel for four weeks.
It rained incessantly and Agnes never fully recovered from the cold
night they had spent without their tents. They photographed manuscripts in a Syrian convent and in the monastery attached to the Holy
Sepulchre (where the Greek librarian often turned them out to attend
to his Easter duties), and continued to receive dealers in manuscripts.

They liked Jerusalem no better this time than they had thirty years
ago. The unseemly barging amongst the worshippers at the Church of
the Holy Sepulchre was the same as before. Armenians had been
excluded from the Ceremony of the Holy Fire on Easter eve, as a result
of a fight with the Greeks the previous year, during which the
Armenian patriarch had his beard 'completely plucked out'. When
Agnes and Margaret attended the ceremony they were appalled by

European travellers outside the Damascus Gate, Jerusalem

some Arabic-speaking Christians who, while waiting for the fire to
appear, amused themselves by standing on each other's shoulders to
make a human pyramid and singing, in Agnes's rough translation:

> Your feast, O ye Jews!
> The apes they would choose.
> Our feast is the feast of the Christ!
> The Christ He hath sought us,
> With His blood He hath bought us.
>   Right merry are we
> When doleful ye be,
>   O Jews![4]

What a 'travesty of the Christian spirit', wrote Agnes, 'when compared to our Lord's lament as recorded in Matthew 23:37: "Jerusalem,
Jerusalem, the city that kills the prophets and stones those who are sent
to it! How often have I desired to gather your children together as a
hen gathers her brood under her wings . . . ." '[5]

By mid-April they were ready to leave. They had acquired some
Hebrew fragments from a dealer on the Plains of Sharon and in
Jerusalem they had bought a large and valuable Hebrew Pentateuch,
said to originate in Yemen. Together with what they had gathered in
Cairo, this made more than 2,000 manuscripts; some of which as little
as a page, others full books. All nearly came to grief on the day of
departure when Ottoman customs officials at Jaffa port announced
they were impounding all the sisters' purchases. Joseph was quick-
witted enough to remember that the Bible and Koran were exempt
from confiscation. 'Do you not see that these are in Hebrew, and the
ladies say their prayers in Hebrew. Do you want to prevent them
saying their prayers?' The officials vented their frustration by rumpling
up the contents of the ladies' packing cases, placing 'a heavy pair of
boots on the top of a broche silk evening dress, and treating fancy
creations of French millinery art as if they were like their own ragged
uniforms'.[6]

These inconveniences were as nothing to the plight of the Armenian emigrants they saw being bullied and separated from their families by the Jaffa officials as they tried to join their boats – only a fringe of the oppression that, Agnes wrote, 'was even at that moment, drenching the churches and valleys of Armenia with blood'. Rendel Harris and his wife Helen had been travelling on horseback through Armenia since early March, assisting with the distribution of aid given by British and American evangelicals in response to news of the slaughters of the previous autumn and winter. They found cities ruined, sons slain, villages plundered, vineyards abandoned. In the Syriac-speaking region of Mardin, most monasteries were in ruins. Some monasteries – and their ancient manuscripts – had only recently been destroyed by wandering tribes who, taking advantage of the Sublime Porte's indifference to its Christian populace, looted with impunity. 'It is fortunate,' wrote Rendel Harris for whom the human tragedy far outweighed the devastation of manuscripts, 'that we do not live by books alone.'[7]

CHAPTER 25

Solomon Schechter and the Cairo genizah

This last-minute trip to Cairo and Jerusalem in the spring of 1896 had been the twins' most demanding so far and not one of their most productive, or so they thought. Margaret set about sorting through their recent Hebrew acquisitions. She identified the fragments that formed part of the Old Testament, and thought the rest must be either portions of the Talmud or other Jewish writings. The sisters resolved to ask their irrepressibly curious rabbinical friend, Solomon Schechter, to take a look at them. Schechter was keenly interested in new manuscript finds, and especially any that might shed light on the history of Judaism. He and his wife Mathilde had taken a personal interest in the twins' recent journey, and had dined with them at Castlebrae, along with Mr and Mrs Kennett, only a few days before their departure.[1]

Feeling no particular rush about what seemed to them a lacklustre collection, the twins did not speak to Schechter until 13 May, a fortnight after they were back, when Agnes bumped into him on King's Parade. She told him they had some things at home 'which awaited his inspection'; by the time she returned with her shopping Schechter was already in her dining room surrounded by sheaves of manuscript. Amidst the fragments he had found a rare and interesting leaf of the Talmud and a very dirty scrap of Hebrew writing that he asked if he might take away to examine.

Within the hour he had drafted the twins a letter from the library: 'I think we have reason to congratulate ourselves . . .' He added that he would meet them the next day to say more. Clearly he could not wait that long. Dashing back home, he called out to Mathilde, 'as long as the Bible lives, my name shall not die. Now telegraph Mrs Gibson and Mrs Lewis to come immediately.' Within the hour the twins had received the message: 'Fragment very important; come to me this afternoon.'[2]

Schechter had made a momentous discovery in Hebrew Bible scholarship, and one that had the effect of restoring a biblical book whose status was long a matter of debate for both Jews and Christians. The tatty fragment from Cairo was in fact a section of the Hebrew scriptures known to Christians as Ecclesiasticus and to Jews as the Wisdom of Ben Sira. This was one of fourteen books included in the Greek Old Testament, but whose Hebrew originals were lost.

Ben Sira had largely dropped from Jewish usage, but remained in Christian use until the sixteenth century when the Reformers dropped it and other books like it from their bibles, for lack of a Hebrew original. The Church of England, striking a middle way as always, retained them in the King James Version, as 'Apocryphal'. But the more austere Westminster Confession of the Presbyterian Church (1647) had gone further, actually banning the Apocryphal books, so it was not surprising, as Margaret said, that she did not recognise the fragment when combing through her purchases. A number of scholars believed that the books of the Apocrypha (which also included Tobit, Judith, the Wisdom of Solomon, Bel and the Dragon) never existed as Hebrew originals in the first place, and so were something worse than apocryphal.

As if to show that the 'Greater Providence' favours not only Presbyterians but Orthodox Jews, Schechter turned out to have been at that time engaged in a heated dispute on just this matter. His academic arch-rival, Professor David Margoliouth of Oxford, believed that Ben Sira/Ecclesiasticus had been written first in Greek and then translated, in portions, back into the Hebrew. But Solomon Schechter was convinced that Ben Sira *must* have had a Hebrew original. He could point to the fact that it sported a preface by the translator, who identified himself as the grandson of the book's author, Ben Sira, and said that he undertook to translate his grandfather's book while living in Egypt in around 132 BC. This preface, of course, could be a fiction added later to create verisimilitude, but it had the markings of truth in its frank, no-nonsense discussion of the difficulties of finding the exact Greek equivalents for the original Hebrew. Furthermore, St Jerome in the fourth century AD had also mentioned possessing a Hebrew original of this book.

Decisive for Schechter, however, was the fact that Ben Sira, while not included in the later canon of the Jewish Bible, was cited extensively by rabbis in the classic period of rabbinic Judaism (*circa* AD 200–500) and was often quoted in the Talmud and in medieval Jewish writings. The rabbis would not, Schechter was convinced, give reference to a book not initially written in Hebrew.

Professor Margoliouth knew that the rabbis had quoted the book, and in Hebrew, but he thought these citations were not pure frag-ments of an ancient Hebrew text, but a 'rabbinic farrago' worked backwards into a degraded sort of Hebrew from Latin or Greek originals. In his inaugural lecture as Laudian Professor at Oxford, entirely devoted to Ecclesiasticus/Ben Sira, Margoliouth threw down the gauntlet by saying that the best guides to the book were the Greek and Latin texts.

Margoliouth's dismissive Oxford attitude to the rabbis and their so-called 'farrago' was bound to infuriate the observant Jew, Schechter, who was also alive to the fact that Margoliouth was a member of a Jewish family only recently converted to Christianity.[3]

Now, courtesy of Agnes and Margaret, Schechter held in his hand something no one had seen for perhaps 800 years, a chunk of a manuscript of Ben Sira in Hebrew. It was a medieval copy, eleventh- or twelfth-century, but the text it bore corresponded to the rabbinic citations and Schechter was confident that it would prove to be different from, and pre-date, the Greek and Latin versions. He instructed Agnes to write immediately to *The Athenaeum* and *The Academy*, which she did that afternoon.[4]

Her letters, published three days later on 16 May 1896, prompted a frenzy of activity in the manuscript-hunting world. Within days, scholars at Oxford reported that they had found another nine leaves of the same Hebrew manuscript amongst treasures recently brought back from Egypt by Archibald Sayce, a part-time professor of assyriology at that university.

Significant as this discovery was, the ever-vigilant Solomon Schechter was privately mulling over a more breathtaking possibility: he thought it too much of a coincidence that Sayce should have returned to England within weeks of Agnes and Margaret with pieces of the same manuscript. Someone in Cairo must be dismantling a copy of Ben Sira and feeding the leaves onto the market. Poring over the remainder of the sisters' recent acquisitions, Schechter was struck by the recurrence of the word 'Fustat', the medieval name for Cairo. He suspected that not just one, but a hoard of Jewish manuscripts was being gradually dispersed to Cairo's dealers; he had a hunch just what this hoard might be, and where it could be found. Keeping his plans from all but a few of his closest friends (including of course the twins and their friend, Donald MacAlister), he made plans to go to Cairo as soon as possible. So great was his need for secrecy that Schechter did not even risk alerting rivals by applying for a university travel grant. His friend, the Christian Hebraist Charles Taylor, then Master of St John's College, personally underwrote much of the cost of the trip.

Schechter's departure was planned for December 1896, and Agnes and Margaret were invited to accompany him. They had to decline. Shortly after her propitious meeting with Schechter in King's Parade, the illness that she had been fighting since Jerusalem caught up with Agnes and, from June, she lay for three months in bed, partly paralysed by fever and rheumatism. In more jocular moments she attributed this illness to microbes inhaled from the Ben Sira they had brought home with them, for its author was a famous 'woman-hater' who had written: 'Better is the wickedness of a man than the goodness of a woman.' (Ben Sira 42:14). Not until October did she begin to recover the use of her limbs.

Agnes's convalescence was not assisted by the publication, in September 1896, of Mrs Bensly's *Our Journey to Sinai*. This slim volume was the first full account of their joint trip and was judged significant enough to be chosen as one of the *The Times*' 'Books of the Week' on 17 September 1896. A paean of love for her lost husband and lost sight, it was made all the more touching by the fact of having been first written in Braille.

For Agnes and Margaret, it was a nightmare. What read to the uninitiated as an innocent, tender-hearted account of a journey to St Catherine's read, to Agnes in particular, as insult from first to last.

The twins were effectively erased from the story and, on those few occasions when they did make an appearance, it was not usually to their credit. Mrs Bensly mentioned Mrs Smith and Mrs Lewis briefly at the beginning of her account, but in their capacity as travel guides – Scottish ladies who had brought back photographs of an early Syriac palimpsest whose significance they knew not, and who subsequently agreed to return to Sinai with the professional scholars 'to assist the party with their experience in Eastern travel and with their knowledge of modern Greek'.[5] By the selective use of 'we' and the evocative initial framing – wandering hand in hand in the desert with her beloved – Mrs Bensly seemed always to be enchantingly alone with her professorial husband.

To be fair, the Burkitts and Rendel Harris were not much mentioned either, yet the omission of Agnes and Margaret at crucial points cannot but have been deliberate. Mrs Bensly, for instance, treats her readers to a lengthy account of the meeting that she and her husband had with Archbishop Porphyrios in Cairo: a description of his quarters, his bearing, his throne and his episcopal robes; his joviality, his tête-'a-tête with Professor Bensly over new discoveries of biblical manuscripts, the sweet-meats proffered, the coffee drunk . . . 'We conversed with him by an interpreter,' she says, not mentioning that the interpreter was Margaret or that the twins were present throughout; or that it was indeed only through their good offices that the meeting had been arranged.

But it was not so much what was left out as what was inserted that prompted Agnes's seething letter to the *Cambridge Chronicle*. Mrs Bensly had written that, on the return journey, Agnes and Harris had led Professor Bensly on 'forced marches', eventually pushing on ahead and 'deserting' their fellow travellers.

Agnes well knew that many readers of Mrs Bensly's book would be aware that her husband reached home only to die, and might readily draw their own conclusions from talk of 'forced marches' and 'desertion' in the desert. Those who had been party to the dispute over the honour of finding the Syriac Gospels – not a great many, but influential people – would also note Mrs Bensly's explanation for the haste of Agnes and Harris: it was 'to post certain letters . . . by an earlier mail', postings by which, so Mrs Bensly believed, Harris and the twins aimed to secure all the glory of the find for themselves.[6]

Running to more than 2,000 words, Agnes's letter to the editor outlined their travelling contract and maintained that she, her sister and Rendel Harris had gone ahead solely to catch the fortnightly French boat from China to Marseilles. She denied outright that their intention was to make an early post – a claim she never encountered before reading Mrs Bensly's book. The twins had rushed back to Cambridge after the trip, not to monopolise the glory, but to receive a deputation of church leaders from London who were to examine the proposed site of the Presbyterian college. Further, they had had business to accomplish at Suez: 'was a short afternoon too long to get our circular notes cashed at the bank, to settle with the dragoman, repack our boxes, and secure berths at a season when the boats from Egypt to Europe are notoriously overcrowded?' As it was, they had to make do with a berth only recently vacated by bananas, whose walls were 'swarming with microscopic insects'. They had intended to take only Ahmed's adopted son, Surur, with them on their midnight camel ride to 'Ain Musa, but Ahmed insisted on coming too.[7]

There had been no selfish haste to depart: *everyone* had agreed to delay leaving Mount Sinai to squeeze in a final morning's work on the palimpsest. En route the travellers had observed full Sabbath rest at the insistence of the twins, who had in no way 'forced the pace'. 'I had no idea, until now,' wrote Agnes, 'that Mrs Bensly, whom we all love and respect, failed so greatly to understand our conduct on that occasion. I can only attribute it to the terrible affliction which she suffered in the loss of her sight: a calamity whose approach was even then discernable. This makes her perhaps ready to believe in random thoughtless statements, which she has not the power of verifying.'

And there was one more score to settle. Mrs Bensly had also written of the edifying suspense with which she and her husband had awaited Father Galaktéon, before their first meeting. They wondered who this holy man, abbot of the ancient house of St Catherine's, might be. 'Had the rules of the convent required it, we would willingly have knelt on his threshold or kissed the hem of his garment; but our pious exaltation was doomed to some disappointment.' Instead, a 'stout, red-faced monk, in the plain black garb of the priesthood (rather greasy in this case), rushed forth with loud shouts of merriment, and fell on the neck of Mrs Lewis.' Mrs Bensly records her discomfort as Galaktéon patted Agnes and made her sit next to him, placing his arm around her shoulder and chatting all the while in lively Greek – which none of the others could understand – punctuated by bursts of laughter. 'His excessive friendliness,' she concluded, 'augured well for his readiness in producing his literary treasures. The good old man had to be propitiated, yet we did not relish the thought that we might have to submit, in our turn, to similar familiarities.'[8]

Agnes fumed over this vague allusion to fondling of garments and some unstated priapic rite as a quid pro quo to hand-over of the palimpsest. Galaktéon 'did not "fall on my neck," ' she said, adding, '. . . It is true that he spent nearly half-an-hour in kissing my hand, and stroking me on the shoulder, but the former of these salutations is a common one amongst Oriental Christians and [she adds picturesquely] even the Emperor of Russia is reported to have done the same thing to a Quaker maiden, for whose family he wished to show respect.'[9]

Writing to the editor of the *Cambridge Independent*, Agnes was even more intemperate: 'To introduce such complaints about one's fellow travellers into a book which is meant to be instructive, seems to me beneath the dignity of literature', she wrote, adding that it was 'a pity that so interesting a book . . . should have been spoiled by reflections on the conduct of the authoress's fellow travellers . . .'[10]

After such an experience the twins could be forgiven for their wariness of joint expeditions, but there is nothing to suggest that they declined Schechter's invitation to Cairo for any reason other than Agnes's ill health. They took an active interest in his plans.

Schechter was able to set out for Cairo in December 1896, immediately after the autumn university term ended, armed with a letter of introduction from the Chief Rabbi of London, Hermann Adler, to the Chief Rabbi of Cairo, Aaron Raphael Ben Shim'on. Once in Cairo, it was still necessary for him to spend many hours, stretching into days, smoking cigarettes and drinking coffee with the Chief Rabbi until this patient nurturing was rewarded with trust and the rabbi took him, by carriage, to Cairo's oldest synagogue, the Ben Ezra.[11] At the end of one

The Chief Rabbi of Cairo

of the galleries was an opening high in the wall and accessible only by ladder. Schechter climbed up and peered down into a 'windowless and doorless room of fair dimensions'. The sight that met his eyes was one to thrill and appal the scholar: a chaos of books and papers, manuscripts and printed texts, tossed in at random over eight centuries. He had found, as he suspected he might, a *genizah*.

A *genizah*, as Schechter explained in a letter to *The Times* is an institution that takes its name: 'from the Hebrew verb "ganaz" and signifies treasure-house or hiding place. When applied to books it means much the same thing as burial in the case of men. When the spirit is gone, we put the corpse out of sight to protect it from abuse. In like manner, when the writing is worn out, we hide it to preserve it from profanation.'[12]

Developed Jewish law determined that no document containing the four letters of the Holy Name, or Tetragrammaton, should be destroyed. In many places documents were buried reverentially, like human remains, and in damp climates this led quickly to natural decomposition. In warmer southern lands *genizot* (plural) were sometimes placed in caves, tombs or sets of jars and, thus laid down, the documents might survive their burial by many years – even centuries, as was the case at Ben Ezra in Cairo.

As well as 'dead' books, Schechter explained, *genizot* became home to ailing or invalided books (some of whose pages might be missing) and to 'disgraced' books whose contents were deemed not entirely orthodox. In time, any document written in the sacred language – love songs and wine songs, wills, marriage contracts, letters of divorce – might find its way into a *genizah*. The window high in the wall of the Ben Ezra synagogue was a postbox to nowhere that, for 800 years, had received the offcast Hebrew writings of Cairo's Jewish community.

In his letter to *The Times*, Schechter described the dark chamber in Darwinian terms:

It is a battlefield of books, a battle in which the literary productions of many centuries had their share, and their *disjecta membra* are now strewn over its area. Some of the belligerents have perished outright, and are literally ground to dust in the terrible struggle for space, whilst others . . . are squeezed into big unshapely lumps, which even with the aid of chemical appliances can no longer be separated without serious damage to their constituents. In their present condition these lumps sometimes afford curiously suggestive combinations; as, for instance, when you find a piece of some rationalistic work in which the very existence of either angel or devil is denied, clinging for its very life to an amulet in which these same beings (mostly the latter) are bound over to be on their good behaviour and not to interfere with Miss Yair's love for somebody.[13]

Since the *genizah* had already survived the invention of printing by some 400 years, the vast bulk of its papers were printed works. Schechter had no interest in these troublesome documents, which nonetheless clung 'to the old nobility [the manuscripts] with all the obstinacy and obstrusiveness of the *parvenu*'. The task of sorting and separating them was immense. Schechter decided that the only possible recourse was to load the papers into sacks and transport them back to Cambridge, where they could be studied more effectively. By who knows what powers of sacred eloquence he had been authorised by the Chief Rabbi to take from the *genizah* 'what, and as much as, I liked' to deposit in the Cambridge University Library. 'Now as a matter of fact, I liked all,' said Schechter.[14] He must have been able to demonstrate beyond doubt to the rabbi that the genizah's contents were slipping away illicitly to dealers, although even this would require tact, since the person or persons responsible must have been synagogue insiders, very likely the beadles who were supposed to be its keepers.

When she learned, through Schechter's letters to Mathilde, of his success in finding the *genizah*, Agnes could restrain herself no longer. She was determined to join him. After doing what they could in Cairo, she proposed travelling on to St Catherine's to compare the Syriac lectionary she had purchased in Cairo with the two they had found earlier at the convent, all three written in the extremely rare dialect of Syriac known as Palestinian Syriac.

Margaret worried about the consequences of another trip for her sister's health, but Agnes 'had the feeling that my aches would all be coaxed away if I could once get my feet on the warm sand'.[15] The scales were tipped by Donald MacAlister's shrewd observation that Agnes would be all the better for another trip to Sinai. As a medical man, he was able to equip Agnes and Margaret with a special respirator for Schechter, who was suffering from the choking dust, heat and fleas of the *genizah*, and bless the twins on their way.

CHAPTER 26

In Cairo with Schechter

The twins reached Cairo in January 1897. Schechter took them immediately to the synagogue, a plain building in one of the most densely populated parts of the city. They saw for themselves the window high in the white-washed wall above the gallery. At first Agnes did not dare ascend the ladder, whose rungs were very widely spaced, but a synagogue servant did and leaped through the window to the sound of scrunching vellum on the other side. Lured by what lay beyond, both twins eventually mounted the ladder and descended into the pit of papers. The mess, compounded by fallen whitewash, desert sand and the odd dousing of water, was, Agnes reported, 'simply indescribable'.[1]

Schechter was in the process of packing the 'whole mass of rugged, jumbled, dirty stuff' into huge sacks. He judged he had at least 40,000 separate documents.[2] The *genizah* was very dark and emitted clouds of dust in protest when it was disturbed. The difficulty of the work meant that Schechter had to accept the assistance of the keepers of the *genizah* who, he noted wryly, 'had some experience in such work'. As 'no self-respecting keeper of a real Genizah would degrade himself' by accepting pay, these assistants insisted on *baksheesh*, which 'besides being a more dignified kind of remuneration, has the advantage of being expected also for services *not* rendered'. Some texts escaped, only to be offered back to Schechter, for an exorbitant price, by a dealer in antiquities. Schechter bought them.[3] Agnes and Margaret, with Schechter's approval, also bought a quantity of stray fragments in the souk and cleaned them off with water in their hotel bedroom, a messy process that meant their floors were covered with drying sheets of vellum. They kept those manuscripts that contained the canonical books of the Old Testament and gave Schechter the rest. He took them to tea with the Chief Rabbi.

The quality and variety of the finds were astonishing: fragments of old Talmuds; old and forgotten hymns; rabbinic Midrash; a draft copy in his own hand of the *Guide to the Perplexed* of the famous medieval physician and philosopher, Moses Maimonides (or Rambam), an important influence on Thomas Aquinas. Most touching and interesting to the non-specialists were the many personal documents, such as a letter to Maimonides from his brother, written from a Sudanese port, which describes his caravan trip across from the Nile and tells Moses not to worry about him, and that he intends to sail to India on business; he would never return.

There are fascinating glimpses into daily life: a letter from a schoolmaster about a child's bad behaviour, 'As soon as he comes in, he starts fighting with his sister and cursing her incessantly . . . Perhaps you

The entrance to the windowless, doorless room that housed the Cairo *genizah*

could threaten him with a little spanking . . .'; from a father to a schoolmaster, 'Please don't spank my son for being late. His homework delayed him,' There are a young child's doodles from the eleventh century; letters from wives to distant husbands, 'We have weaned the baby. Do not ask me what we suffer for him: trouble, crying, sleepless nights, so much so that the neighbours – God is my witness – are complaining.' A woman from Jerusalem writes, in Yiddish, to her son in Cairo asking him to bring the grandchildren to see her, adding, 'Thank God, everything is cheap here.' The date was 1567.[4] It was the richest archive of medieval Jewish materials in existence.

Having helped where they could, Agnes and Margaret left Solomon Schechter to his dusty treasure trove and headed once more for Sinai.

It was as true internationals, and as women finally assured of their place in the scheme of things, that Mrs Lewis and Mrs Gibson boarded a vessel of the Khedival Steamship Company at Suez: wives, widows, and now scholars of repute.

So many puzzling features of their lives now made sense. Their money, for instance – never unwelcome, but what was it for? Giving it all away, St Francis-like, had never been a Presbyterian option. Riches (especially riches, like theirs, acquired almost accidentally) must be intended to play some part in the providential plan.

Now it was clear that they *did* have vocations, and ones for which their life experiences entirely suited them. They knew the East, the monks, the network of manuscript dealers in Cairo and Jerusalem. They had the languages, the money and, just as important, the leisure to travel with an eye to photographing, studying and collecting ancient manuscripts, just at the time when these were imperilled. They could even bless Mr Burkitt's efforts to exclude Agnes from any significant role in the publication of the palimpsest. Painful though it had been at the time, it was his hostility that had pushed them to acquire the scholarship that was now theirs to command.

As the only women in first-class, Mrs Lewis and Mrs Gibson were chivalrously attended by the ship's captain and officers. Eight Turkish gentlemen, the only others travelling in such style, were surprised to learn that Agnes and Margaret were on their fourth visit to Mount Sinai in the space of five years, and equally astonished that two ladies – and Protestants at that – should have made good friends of the Sinai monks. 'They did not in the least understand,' wrote Agnes, forgetful of her own upbringing in a Scottish town so riven by religious factionalism that one would not even buy eggs from a rival kind of Presbyterian, 'that there is a common bond between Christians even when they follow very divergent ways of life'.[5] The twins had further reason for quiet satisfaction: the Synod of their church has accepted the 'Cambridge plan' and with it their offer of land and money for the new Presbyterian college to be built in that city of great biblical scholars – which now included them.

It was with such comforting thoughts, and the hurt caused by Mrs Bensly's book now trumped by the ecstasy of Schechter's finds, that the twins made their way down the Red Sea. The boats of the Khedival Steamship Company now stopped at Tor on the Sinai peninsula's east coast, cutting the overland trip to the convent from seven days to three. Agnes still could not quite bend her knees well enough for camel riding, so they walked most of the way but, as she had predicted, the steady exercise eased the rheumatic hold on her limbs.

The normally barren peninsula had received plentiful rain that year. Fresh milk and mutton were available: they were roused one day from their tents by shouts of 'Fat! Fat!' from a Bedouin with two marketable sheep trailing behind him. It was touching, wrote Agnes, 'to see how the trustful creatures followed him about all unwitting of his nefarious designs upon them'. At St Catherine's they found the top of Mount Sinai covered in snow and the convent garden a mass of almond blossom.

On every visit Agnes and Margaret had noticed changes to Sinai's apparently ageless landscape, with each year's wind and weather sculpting the wadis anew. This year the mosque inside the convent walls had fallen down, leaving only its tower standing, prompting Father Polycarp to observe that the church was the only solid building in the whole place. (Agnes thought this a parable for the whole world.) The palimpsest was found safely in its box and still wrapped in the stripy silken cover donated by Mrs Bensly.

The visitors were as varied as ever. One hundred Russian pilgrims, mostly peasants, were set to depart, and camping in the garden were two Italian gentlemen, Cavaliere Emilio Silvestri and his secretary. They were on a photographic expedition, commissioned by a professor from Milan, but had not so far succeeded in seeing a single manuscript. Agnes and Margaret interceded for them, translating between Greek and Italian, and Agnes even directed them to the most important pages of the palimpsest, holding the manuscript open as they operated their camera. They were shortly joined by another Roman Catholic party, that of the Archbishop of Montevideo. When he visited the library the monks told him, 'It was all in confusion until the ladies came here.'

In isolated circumstances, social courtesy must triumph over sectarian difference, and the twins soon hosted a tea party in their tent for the two Italians and the Uruguayan archbishop. 'The story of the Israelites was discussed in racy Italian, and with a freedom which I would not have believed possible among Roman Catholics,' wrote Agnes. All present were in gratifying agreement that anyone who has viewed the Plain of Er-Rahah from the height of Râs Sufsafah must know this to be the scene of the giving of the Law, and the archbishop compared the roads of Uruguay favourably with those of Sinai.

Agnes was much restored. She read the Bedouin the story of the Prodigal Son. They liked the Christian Scriptures, they told her, because the Prophet says that 'it is good for us to know both the Torah and the Angeel [Gospels]'; however, they thought this particular parable would be enhanced if the father had killed a lamb, rather than a fatted calf, for the feast at the end.

On the journey back they met violent weather. Sand, rain and hail followed each other in blasts across the desert flats. Wind-blown columns of sand played havoc with their broad-brimmed pith helmets and ripped Margaret's parasol out of her hands. Even with veils down, sand filled their eyes and mouths. Once in the felucca, the wind was still so wild as to blow the waves over their knees, yet the trip had the effect of restoring Agnes's strength, spirits and power of locomotion.

They returned to Cambridge in time for a great celebration. On

25 May 1897 the twins laid the foundation stone for the new college they had worked so hard to have built. It was to be called Westminster College, after the Presbyterian Church's historic confession of faith. The timing of this event held an accidental irony: only four days earlier the Senate of the university had, in the culmination of a heated campaign, decisively rejected the proposal that Cambridge degrees be awarded to women.

A debate on the question had been simmering for around thirty years, sometimes coming to a boil, with a vocal minority arguing that women were both fully capable of higher education and in need of university degrees. As a small but inconsistent concession, since 1881 women had been permitted to sit all the same examinations as men, but without any entitlement to the degree. It was not long before the university was faced with embarrassingly impressive results. A survey of lecturers, which asked 'what problems had been caused by the presence of women' drew the response that the women, getting to lectures early, got all the good seats. Two colleges for women (Girton and Newnham) were established, even though their students could not be awarded degrees; this included in 1887 the only candidate in the university to achieve first-class marks in Classics, a 'Miss' Ramsay. In 1890 Miss Philippa Fawcett was top of the Mathematical Tripos – widely regarded as the gold standard of Cambridge qualifications – to similar effect. In addition to the patent injustice there was (as the principal of Newnham College, Mrs Eleanor Sidgwick, noted) the disastrous practical consequence for many women of being unable to get jobs by which to support themselves. Fifty per cent of the women in the educated classes, Mrs Sidgwick observed, did not marry, a much higher figure than in the population at large, and the daughters of these homes, unless provided with an inheritance by their parents, were left stricken without the qualifications for remunerative employment.[6] Mary Kingsley was precisely one of these women who, having had no formal education at all, and nursing two elderly parents until their deaths, was left with virtually no means with which to support herself.

The newer British universities and all the Scottish ones began awarding women the degree in 1895, but still Cambridge held out, convinced that the admission of women to full membership in the University would fray the fabric of undergraduate life and that giving them a vote in the Senate, the university's governing body, would allow them a means to manipulate the institution, if not national politics. The undergraduates were in violent opposition – the most common reason being that, if young ladies were too evident about the place, then young men would have to cut back on their drinking,

Cambridge, 21 May 1896. Students throng the streets
outside the Senate House on the day of the great vote

gaming and carousing, and other pleasures that made undergraduate life so sweetly memorable.

The matter had been put to a vote before the Senate on 21 May 1896. Those 'against' degrees for women arranged for special trains from London to Cambridge to take 'old boys' (who, as alumni, were entitled to vote) back to the alma mater for the occasion. Outside the Senate House undergraduates buoyant in boaters and blazers thronged the streets from an early hour. An effigy of a woman on a bicycle – deemed a wicked and immoral species of modern conveyance for women – was suspended from a student room above the heads of the crowd.

When news of the result came – those in favour of awarding women the degree, 662; those opposed, 1,713 – the cheering was so vociferous and prolonged as to make the reporter for *The Times* declare that it was the 'most memorable division [vote] in the history of the University' and wonder whether there would now be consideration of withdrawing some of the privileges already accorded to women.

Not all the press was amused. Writing for the *Cambridge Independent*, the anonymous 'Pertilote' observed that it was a strange coincidence that only four days after the historic vote in Senate, 'two ladies – so learned that had they chanced to be men they would have received Honorary Degrees from this University long ago . . . should lay the stone for a college for men. I think there are not many women who could be so magnanimous, and I hope their conduct made its due impression on the members of the Senate who were present.' What Agnes and Margaret might have thought of this, they were too discreet to say.

CHAPTER 27

Castlebrae

Solomon Schechter returned in triumph from Egypt and was given an honorary degree (the first given by Cambridge University to a Jew), as well as a large room in the University Library for his sacks of manuscripts. Some of these ran to full volumes, others were merely fragments. Many sheets had been 'palimpsested', sometimes two or three times over – an analogue for the world from which they had emerged: one Syriac Christian text had been overwritten in Arabic, then effaced to bear a Hebrew text, before finally finding its way to the sacred rubbish heap.

Schechter recruited a team of scholarly volunteers to help him spin the ancient straw into gold: Charles Taylor, Master of St John's and the friend who had underwritten his expenses, was to handle the post-biblical *Hebraica* and Hartwig Hirshfield of the Jews' College, London was to do the Arabic. Francis Burkitt dealt with the Greek items and identified some important Syriac palimpsests, but the honour of editing and deciphering these, along with the other Syriac texts, was given to Mrs Smith and Mrs Lewis, working in consultation with Dr Nestle, Professor Ignazio Guidi of Rome, and Rendel Harris.[1]

Castlebrae was humming, alive with scholarship and sociability. One bathroom served as a dedicated dark room, and a room above the porte cochère, well away from all others, was dedicated to use of the noxious-smelling reagent. Except when cleared for meals, the huge dining-room table was covered with notes, books, proof sheets and photographs.[2]

The twins held frequent dinner parties and, in the summer, garden parties. In winter the dining-room table was decorated with small dried fruits from Sinai and with silver bowls of musty-looking chocolates that no one ever ate. Summer garden parties were adorned with a small replica of the biblical Tabernacle, which was placed just outside the French doors leading to the dining room. On these occasions a Scots piper supplied northern airs and, as he was inclined to 'avail himself of the refreshments' too freely, was remembered by guests as often resting in a flower bed at the party's end.

Grace Blyth, now in her late sixties, was once again a frequent visitor to Castlebrae. She frustrated the twins with her idiosyncrasies. She refused to sleep in the same bedroom for two nights in succession and insisted on having the chimneys swept whether there had been fires in them or not, 'to clear the foul air'. She also had an obsessive devotion to her lapdog, Lappie. Grace believed that this dog had been knighted and insisted that the gardener and household servants, whether at

Solomon Schecter with *genizah* treasures, in the Cambridge University Library

home or at Castlebrae, address him as 'Sir Lappie'. She commissioned a
miniature bed with blankets from a furniture-maker. In Trumpington
Road, Sir Lappie always sat with Grace at table and was served first.
Grace was incensed that Agnes refused to follow this practice at
Castlebrae, and that she bristled at having the dog sit at table. When
Lappie died, he was wrapped in a Persian rug and buried in her lawn
under a marble pillar bearing the inscription: *'May his pure spirit return
to the realms from which it came.'* Agnes and Margaret thought this
preposterous.

Agnes's *Palestinian Syriac Lectionary* was published in October 1897 as
volume VI of their series, *Studia Sinaitica*. In the same year Margaret
edited and published *El Cid and other Ballads*, a posthumous collection
of James Gibson's translations of Spanish and German verse, which
was widely and favourably reviewed. Agnes's lectionary did not, she
said in her introduction, strictly come from Mount Sinai as she had
bought it in Cairo while on her way there. Its inclusion in the *Studia
Sinaitica* was warranted, however, by the close comparison it bore to
two Syriac lectionaries she and her sister had photographed at the
convent. The importance of all three lay in the fact that they were in
the same, extremely rare dialect of Syriac known as Palestinian Syriac.
'No other form of Syriac,' wrote Agnes, 'comes so near to the language
in which the Targums were written, and of these one at least was in
oral use in Palestine in the first century of our era.'[3]

In her lectionary Agnes discovered a variant reading that especially
touched her. In standard texts of St Matthew's Gospel, Jesus says that,
at the time of judgement, you will have to give account of every
careless word you have uttered, 'for by your words you will be justified, and by your words you will be condemned'. Agnes's lectionary
had something rather different. In it Jesus says that men will at the day
of judgement be called to give account of every *good word* which, for
whatever reason, they *did not* speak. Agnes reflected that by this
reading the famous British 'stony stare', or the particular Cambridge
custom of passing even one's friends in the street without a sign of
recognition, stood condemned. She was bound to admit that this
variant could scarcely be considered authoritative, being otherwise

unattested and found in a lectionary copy dated AD 1118. But, she observed, all sorts of twaddle had been attributed to Jesus or to apparitions of Mary at Lourdes, and as this at least had the simple ring of truth, it did not seem a sacrilege to attribute it to Jesus.

Eberhard Nestle, now professor at Ulm, hailed Agnes's *Palestinian Syriac Lectionary* as one of the richest contributions thus far to this little-known literature and language, which prompted 'Pertilote', the author of the women's column of the *Cambridge Independent*, to ask:

> is there anything in the Statutes of our University to prevent Mrs Lewis and Mrs Gibson from having Honorary Degrees conferred upon them? These highly prized titles are reserved for distinguished persons who have contributed to the sum of human knowledge to a conspicuous extent. Many men who have received them are far less distinguished than these ladies . . . It is not a question of sex, but of scholarship, and many men as well as many women here are loudly pleading for Honour to whom Honour is due.'[4]

Such formal recognition would come instead from Germany, where the University of Halle-Wittenberg announced its intention to award Agnes the degree of Honorary Doctor of Philosophy in the summer of 1899. With the possible exception of Cambridge, no institution's acknowledgement could have been more welcome. Halle had for almost a century been a world leader in the study of oriental languages. The twins' first mentor, Robertson of Irvine, had been a student of there, as had Professor Bensly, William Robertson Smith and Margaret's own husband, James Gibson. Its Protestant lineage was impeccable.

Agnes was proposed for the Halle degree by Friedrich Blass, scholar of Greek and friend of Rendel Harris. He wrote to her in great excitement, addressing her (in anticipation of future status) as 'Dear Doctor' Lewis. The vote, he told her, had been unanimous at a well-attended faculty meeting, and 'unanimity was needed in this case . . . one dissentient vote being sufficient for the rejecting of the motion'. Only one woman had received the Halle honorary doctorate before.

He added the hope that she would not reject 'what we offer as a token – the greatest we can bestow – of the high esteem in which we hold your learning and your splendid scientific merits'.[5]

It was planned that in March, prior to the awarding of the degree in the summer of 1899, Blass would visit Cambridge bringing his two daughters, Magdalene and Editha, both in their teens, with him.

The professor was to stay at Clare College and his daughters at the home of Rendel and Helen Harris. Nena and Dita (as they were known) had never travelled outside of Germany before and knew of English oddities only from their father's stories, and from observing a succession of English excavators and archaeologists who had passed through their home in Germany.

At the Cambridge train station Rendel Harris rushed forward to meet them. The girls had imagined he would be a large man, but he was average in height and slender, with a great shock of hair 'and friendly eyes. He certainly did not look like a Quaker,' wrote Nena in her diary.[6] She described the strange elements of English life as though she were a visiting anthropologist: the purgatorial fires in hearths that roasted your outside 'until one looked like a crab, without ever giving any inner warmth', and the challenging breakfast menu: porridge with milk and cold cream, followed by 'bread, toast, eggs, fried bacon, pies, butter, marmalade and "jam", a substance which could be compared with our home-made stuff but is not quite the same'. With all this one drank coffee . . . 'Father had already prepared us for the fried bacon. The smell of it at home makes me completely full so I couldn't bring myself to eat any, especially so early in the morning! In the course of the 6 weeks in England, I got so used to it that I surprised myself. A human being can accustom himself to anything.'

Dita and Nena were shocked to discover that Helen Harris road a tricycle, which she called 'her horse'. They saw this as an indication that 'even in the strongly Christian circles to which the Harrises belonged, there is nothing of the "pious shuddering" about bicycles which is so widespread amongst pious men and women in Germany. Not that I want a bicycle, of course!'

Agnes and Margaret had left them an invitation to dinner, and a notice that they would call round to the Harrises' one day before that event so as to introduce themselves.[7] In the meantime there was an English Sabbath to negotiate. 'One hears so many unpleasant things about English Sundays, that we viewed the day with some trepidation,' wrote Nena. They elected to go with Rendel Harris to the Friends' Meeting House, and on the way had their first sight of the 'famous ladies' whom they had heard so much about.

The streets were slushy and the twins, who always walked to church so as not to violate their coachman's Sabbath, were picking their way through the puddles, umbrellas aloft. Nena had very exalted, not to say confused expectations of Agnes and Margaret – she understood them to be very rich and widows, who had made 'the biggest biblical discovery of the century'; that they had a beautiful house, did many good works and lived for their scholarship.

But on their first meeting in the slushy streets Nena was taken aback; she found Mrs Lewis fairly stout, 'wrapped around two or three times with fur', with all her learning inside of her, like the English houses. They exchanged only brief pleasantries before continuing on to their respective places of worship.

It was the first time the Nena and Dita had been to a Quaker meeting house: a bare, bright-green whitewashed hall, with simple wooden pews. Opposite the door was a platform with seats on it for 'members of the congregation whom the spirit moved to speak'. Rendel Harris sat here, alongside an elderly lady in a great Quaker bonnet.

There was no music but instead, said Nena, 'Deepest silence reigned in the whole gathering, in which everyone reverently concerned themselves with their inner thoughts . . . At last, after a period which seemed to us uninitiates painfully long, Mr Harris arose, cleared his throat and gave a very pleasing address about a psalm.'

Nena very much wished that the Holy Spirit would inspire the lady in the Quaker bonnet to speech, but she sat motionless throughout. Later they learned that she was Miss Caroline Stephen, sister of the famous philosopher and atheist Leslie Stephen, and thus the aunt of Virginia Woolf and Vanessa Bell. Miss Stephen prayed daily for her brother's conversion, 'continually and faithfully'.

On Monday afternoon Agnes and Margaret paid the promised courtesy call. Nena recorded that she was sketching the view from the drawing-room window and Dita was writing in her diary, 'when I suddenly noticed a carriage stop before the garden door. Out of the coach alighted, or rather rolled, Mrs Lewis and Mrs Gibson, completely wrapped up in fur.' Agnes sat alone on a sofa, 'enthroned in her furs', and said little more than 'yes, yes'. Margaret tried to engage Nena in conversation, but Nena scarcely understood a word 'because Scots barely open their mouths when speaking'. After a hearty yawn, Agnes ('unspeakably learned' and 'unspeakably dignified') rose to leave. Her sister followed, leaving Nena and Dita standing in reverent silence until the door had closed behind the two august ladies.

Dinner at Castlebrae took place on the eve of the German guests' departure. Mrs Harris helped the girls dress, but confessed that she herself never went to such gatherings, having no time for fancy dresses, wine-drinking and worldly chatter: 'That is the strict Quaker view, wrote Nena.'

Entering the drawing room at Castlebrae on the arms of their father and Rendel Harris, the girls were received by the two 'learned sisters in their full glory': 'Mrs Gibson wore a dress of red velvet with black stripes. Mrs Lewis wore one of light grey silk, also with black stripes, half-length sleeves, and valuable jewellery marked out by its enormous size. Huge rings, a huge brooch – but as it was all real, it did not look bad. Large items of jewellery are now back in fashion again.'

The drawing room gradually filled with guests, a number of whom – despite apparent indifference to Dita and Nena on first meeting – had clearly been chosen by the twins to pay attention to the girls and put them at ease. There was Eleanor Sidgwick, principal of the 'Girls college', Newnham, and Professor Alick Macalister, who had brought his daughter, Edith. There was also an undergraduate, invited in the belief that he had studied German. Dita, seated next to him at dinner, found little evidence of it.

A meal of great variety was served with startling efficiency by two servants. 'There was much to eat, but I would lie if I said I could remember what,' wrote Nena. No sooner was one plate finished than another was set before them, so that, despite its many courses, the dinner was concluded swiftly, clearing the way for the intellectual exchange that was the true purpose of the evening. The ladies withdrew, to be joined in turn by the men, who looked as if they longed for cigars but were not offered any. Nena noted that one gentleman familiar with the ways of his hostesses – probably Rendel Harris – was 'clever enough to bring one with him, which he lit on his way home'.

The young women found the post-prandial conversation heavy-going. Mrs Lewis sat next to Dita and told her a number of stories that the young woman only imperfectly understood as she concentrated on trying to laugh at the appropriate moments. Nena concluded, 'It had been – without any irony – a very interesting evening for us. Despite this, I had come to understand Mrs Harris's point of view better.'

In July of 1899 Agnes and Margaret travelled to Halle. Dita recollected that, at a dinner party in her honour, Agnes brought to table with her a piece of radium that she had recently acquired, and requested that all the lamps be turned down low so that its glowing properties might be apparent as it was passed round the guests. At one stage she lost sight of it and made a lunge at the distinguished historian sitting next to her, mistaking his gleaming watch-chain for her radium in free fall. (The same glowing stone also featured at dinner parties back at Castlebrae, where Agnes kept it in the airing cupboard just off the dining room, so that guests could inspect it in the dark and be informed that it had been discovered by a lady scientist, Madame Curie.)[8]

The grand opening of Westminster College was to be that October and the twins invited Dita Blass, who aspired to be an artist, to return to Cambridge to paint their portraits, with an eye to making them gifts to the new college. Dita arrived at Castlebrae on a foggy autumn morning: 'As I stood in the hall of their house, doors opened from both sides [from their two respective studies] and the sisters, startled by my coming, hurried in like ships in full sail. They had not expected me until afternoon, they told me: "We have to work now, but we'll meet at lunch." '

Dita was shown to a comfortable room and, with a big house full of books and curiosities to explore, did not mind this temporary neglect at all, 'Until the learning and painting began, that is . . .' For, along with portrait-painting, the twins determined that Dita should undertake some studies parallel to their own curriculum. She was given regular instruction in Greek and Syriac, and sometimes was even shut up in her room to learn declensions in which she was to be quizzed later ('I was just young enough to put up with this madness,' wrote Dita). Every day was entirely filled. Breakfast was dominated by *The Times*, to which both sisters regularly wrote letters. This was the only full meal of the day, the others being very puritanical, 'so as not to weary our minds', the twins told her, and quite often Dita 'crept off to the attic, like a child, to fill up with apples'.

In the afternoon the twins sat for their portraits, but there was a full round of lectures, church services and social engagements to fit in. Their elderly maid, Bessy, bustled Dita about 'like an object', in haste to bath, groom and dress her. But even while on the move scholarship was not to be neglected; as soon as their coachman, Eastwell, drew up with the carriage ('he has got no brains at all,' said Agnes), the sisters pulled the Syriac grammar out from under the seat and ignored their young guest until they reached their destination.

The twins had definite views about the portrait. Both wanted to be painted in full evening dress until Dita dissuaded them. They were fifty-four years old at the time and, although biologically identical, Agnes had aged less well than Margaret: she was more wrinkled and more rounded as a result of her bouts of rheumatism and bed rest. To the nineteen-year-old artist, her subjects were 'old' ladies who were 'defeated on the battlefields of beauty, and had retreated with lowered flags to the academic arena, to salvage some success there instead'. But whatever their fate on the 'battlegrounds of beauty' (photographs from the opening of Westminster College show them to be quite presentable), the twins were at the height of vigour for travel and transcription. Dita found her sitters rather vain about their small hands, and quite insistent that the paintings be varnished until almost black, 'to make them shinier'. They were fond of telling her 'grotesque anecdotes, which made the dark romance of their homeland [Scotland] seem strangely vivid. When you looked long and steadily into the depths of those strange, twinkling, mischievous eyes, you might catch sight of a solemn melancholy.' Yet as the days of sittings passed, she saw that these were 'genuine and very superior people'.

They were also very active ones. In the few months she spent at Cambridge, Dita Blass recalled meeting at Castlebrae various members of the families of Dr Stanley, the African explorer, and of General Kitchener, famous for his Sudan campaigns at the time. She met Charles Darwin's sister – 'a grumpy old spinster' whom she none-theless liked – and one of Darwin's sons. She met the Catholic historian Lord Acton, Mrs Flinders Petrie, wife of the famous Egyptologist (who came attired as an *Égyptienne*) and the polyglot Madame de Bunsen, whose 'charm and elegant femininity' were the subject of some sceptical Scots comment at Castlebrae. Dita met so many famous people, she said, that she was 'almost weary of it', yet her abiding memory of the twins and their friends 'was the constant sense of rounded human personality, of whole and full humanity'.

Despite the oddities of the regime at Castlebrae, Dita's views softened from her harsh appraisal of the previous spring so much that when two elegant nieces from London (probably Samuel Lewis's relations) took Dita aside at a Castlebrae party to ask whether she did not find everything in the house 'appallingly Scottish' and the party 'absolutely exhausting' – and, further, 'How could you stand it so long?' – she could not quite agree. In the end, Dita wrote, '. . . I found it very hard to take leave of the twins, because of their genuine friendliness. After their stern tellings-off, which I had to face so often, there would always be a twinkle of apology, as they pressed on to some new project.'

The twins declared themselves pleased with the portraits – 'Very nice, the little hands,' said Margaret, although they were never presented to Westminster College and have since disappeared.[9] Dita Blass left laden with presents for her family, a great facsimile edition of the Sinai Palimpsest, and her fee sewn into the lining of her coat lest she lose it on the way home. 'I can scarcely remember such a carefree period in my whole life.' The next winter she was studying in Paris and the twins, en route to Egypt, invited her to dinner. Dita brought along a French lady journalist who wished to write an article about the two impressive women. But the twins were tired and spent the whole meal bickering between themselves as to whether the wall murals in the restaurant, depicting Athens and Constantinople, actually resembled those places or were just an artist's fantasies. Little was said of scholarship or adventure, and the final straw, for the journalist, came when at the end of the meal Agnes and Margaret dropped the dessert fruit and chocolates into their handbags for later consumption. 'The article,' Dita wrote, 'was abandoned at that moment.' But as the twins departed, Dita had this exchange with Agnes:

> 'O dear me,' said Mrs Lewis, 'I have something else for you. For the little picture of Ellison that you painted for me.' I was taken aback and refused: the picture didn't bear mentioning. 'O dear me, no, it was very nice,' said Mrs Lewis. She was already very weary and yawning sleepily, but she didn't forget to hand me the envelope. 'Don't lose it!' And Mrs Gibson entreated me 'Don't lose it!' They rolled their R's a little, with their unmistakeably Scottish way of saying 'girl'. They kissed me, and disappeared.

When Dita opened the envelope she found the surprisingly generous sum of 400 francs.

CHAPTER 28

The college's opening

The opening of Westminster College took place on 17 October 1899, a clear, still autumn day. Apart from its proximity to a number of gin palaces, the new college was elegantly situated, presiding over a broad new avenue that ran close the River Cam and the Backs of the ancient colleges.

The building was set back from the road behind wrought-iron gates. Like Castlebrae, it stretched horizontally across its plot and was only one or two rooms deep, giving from the front a grand impression while remaining, inside, pleasingly domestic in scale. Two stone-dressed wings projected from its red-brick body, and the inside glowed with warm oak panels. No expense had been spared.

The twins had chosen the architect, Henry Hare, whose design – like so much British architecture of the day – harkened back to the past, but in his case to the Elizabethan and Protestant past, not the medieval Gothic and its popery. There were several discreet bows in the direction of the significant lady benefactors. The tower to the left of the front door leaned slightly backwards, hinting at the entarchic entry gates of an Egyptian temple. The coffered plasterwork of the dining hall's ceiling bore the emblems of all the Presbyterian churches in the land, the motif of the burning bush predominating. The same symbol – emblematic around the world of the Reformed Church, but especially resonant for the twins – surmounted the front gates, with the motto beneath it: *Nec Tamen Consumebatur* ('Nor was it consumed'). The reference was to the burning bush at Sinai, but with the distinctive Scottish understanding that their Church was evergreen in faith, despite the obstacles put in its way (by the English).

The opening was an entirely genial occasion, civic as well as religious. There was a formal handing over of the keys to the principal, Dr Oswald Dykes, and a succession of speakers throughout the day supplied the huge Presbyterian appetite for speeches, followed by a lunch for 650 guests in the Guildhall and the Lion Public House.

The Master of Trinity gave an address. Only thirty years ago no Presbyterian could hold a position at Cambridge, but today the vice-chancellor, professors, Members of Parliament and the Mayor of Cambridge were all present at this inauguration of a Presbyterian college. And of course in the midst of it all were the twins, at whose mention the Guildhall burst into applause. The 'Pertilote' column of the *Cambridge Independent* noted, 'I was glad the Master of Trinity spoke of Mrs Lewis and Mrs Gibson as he did. He has earned the gratitude and respect of every woman who listened to his eloquent address . . . The sisters must have felt radiantly happy all day; indeed they looked it.'

The vice-chancellor, underlining the recent abandonment of bigotry, said that he welcomed Westminster as he welcomed the new Catholic College, established in the same year just a little further up the same hill. Maybe one was the poison and the other the antidote, as nature puts docks and nettles near each other, but he wouldn't like to say which was which (roars and applause).[1]

Guests returning to Westminster College were met by boy pipers from the Caledonian Asylum, a Presbyterian orphanage in London, who marched up and down playing Scottish airs; and they listened to an ode written by Agnes for the occasion. All in all it was a day full of ponderous corporate rejoicing.

It may be that, from Dita Blass's youthful perspective, the twins had been 'defeated on the battlefields of beauty' and were now drawing solace from scholarly success, but this was not the view of the sisters themselves. They had been happily if briefly married, and to princes amongst men. They had rejoiced at being called 'Mrs', but were equally delighted to be called 'Doctor'. After the publication of another book on their travels by Agnes (*In the Shadow of Sinai*, 1898), Margaret's edition of her late husband's translations of Spanish and German verse, *El Cid and Other Ballads* (1898), and in the following year Margaret's edition of 'The Arabic Version of the Acts of the Apostles' (1899), their own nation honoured them. In April 1901 the University of St Andrews made both sisters Doctors of Law (LLD): the terms 'Ph.D' and 'LLD' subsequently adorned their many letters to the editor of *The Times*.

As the nineteenth century turned into the twentieth, Agnes and Margaret continued their life of manuscript-hunting with undiminished vigour. They visited monasteries and other communities where documents might lurk. They travelled to foreign capitals – once as far as St Petersburg – to examine and photograph manuscripts for comparison with those they were working on at home. Once back in Cambridge, they turned their photographs into lantern slides and verified uncertain readings with the aid of an electric lamp. The same lantern slides were used in their many public-speaking engagements – usually with Agnes in the lead, but with Margaret making interjections.

CHAPTER 29

To the monasteries of the Nitrian desert

The year 1901 saw the twins off again to Egypt, this time to visit the Coptic monasteries of the Nile.[1] It was from a monastery in the Nitrian desert, to the north-west of Cairo, that Archbishop Tattam had recovered the Curetonian Syriac and, although Egypt's monastic libraries had been combed many times, the twins were hopeful that their kind ways with the monks and their keen eye for neglected, discarded and palimpsested texts would avail them of something yet.

They headed upriver first. Leaving the Nile at Beni Suef, some seventy-five miles to the south of Cairo, they travelled five days east by camel over sand strewn with black and grey flints to Egypt's most ancient monastery, St Anthony's (Deir Mar Antunyus) in the Red Sea mountains. This was the birthplace of monasticism, for it was here that St Anthony lived, in solitude, in a cave in the early fourth century. No woman had entered the monastery in its 1,600-year history, but perhaps no woman had come armed with a letter from the Patriarch, as did Agnes and Margaret. They were greeted warmly. Agnes's rheumatism did not prevent their making the climb up the steep chalk hill to St Anthony's cave, and entering it by means of a narrow aperture in the face of a cliff, leading to a passage so narrow they had to wriggle through it. Another fifteen camel-hours south brought them to the Monastery of St Paul of the Desert (Deir Mar Bulus). This, like all Egypt's monasteries, was a fortress built to resist attack, with high, thick walls that could only be surmounted by being hauled up over with windlass and rope. The twins devised a winch-basket improvised out of the rope-netting that normally protected their camel equipment.

Once inside, they found themselves joining a small procession laid on in their honour (with crosses and banners), which took them to the church for a two-hour service. A lengthy address in Arabic from the *hegumenos* expressed delight in their visit, praise for Lord Cromer (the generally unpopular British Consul-General of Egypt), grief at the death of Queen Victoria in January and certainty in the final triumph of the Cross. Despite their privileged access, Agnes and Margaret found nothing to interest them, either here or at St Anthony's.

Returning to the Nile, they went back to Cairo and struck out north-west to visit four monasteries of the Nitrian desert. At Deir Abu Makar (St Macarius) there was a hermit of great sanctity who, after living as an ordinary monk for thirty years, had lived alone in a cave for the last six, eating only bread and water. Acting as their guide round the monastery, he proved surprisingly sociable. The hermit of Deir el-Suryani (the Monastery of the Syrians) was even more austere, living for twelve years in a desert cave on just desert herbs and the charity of the Bedouin. Later an older and wiser Agnes, in her account of this visit to the Cambridge Antiquarian Society, would forbear to make any judgement on this very different foreign Christianity, concluding only that we must never forget their constancy under the trials to which the Coptic Church had been subject over many centuries.[2] There were no Syriac manuscripts worth retrieving, but they found and photographed an important Christian Arabic text at St Mary Deipara in the Wadi Natron. This manuscript was to lead to a broadening of their publishing and editing endeavours.[3]

The *Studia Sinaitica* series proceeded under the twins' general direction. Most of the manuscripts that were included had been discovered by the sisters themselves and were of Sinaitic provenance. Rendel Harris recruited additional editors and translators, including Eberhard Nestle and Schechter's Oxford rival, David Margoliouth, to edit some of the texts that Agnes and Margaret did not do.[4] These men also involved Agnes and Margaret in their own projects. A second series under the twins' editorship, *Horae Semiticae*, was begun to cope with non-Sinai-related materials.

Rendel Harris and his associates were a scholarly vanguard,

convinced that the study of ancient Near Eastern folk-tales could shed
light on the origins of biblical material. Harris roped Agnes into an
immense project editing the stories about Ahikar, Grand Vizier of
Sennacherib. A character in Aesop's Fables and the Arabic *One
Thousand and One Nights*, Ahikar, it had recently been demonstrated,
also makes an appearance in the apocryphal biblical book of Tobit as
Tobit's nephew. Harris was keen to bring together all the various
Ahikar stories (which existed in the Syriac, Arabic, Armenian,
Ethiopic, Greek and Slavonic languages) for comparative purposes. As
he himself was competent in fourteen ancient and modern languages,
he needed only two other scholars for back-up; Frederick Conybeare,
from Oxford, for the Armenian, and Agnes for the Syriac.[5]

It was a move beyond biblical literature for Agnes, but of biblical
interest all the same. Where previously it had been thought that the
books of the Old Testament represented an isolated literary eminence,
it now appeared that the writers of Israel's holy books were conversant
with a wide range of other writings, anecdotes and legends. Apparently
the story of Ahikar had been treasured by Israel's scribes long before
the book of Tobit crowned Ahikar's glory by turning him into a Jew.

'Startling as it seemed at first,' wrote Eberhard Nestle in his review
of the Ahikar stories, 'that a story from the *Thousand and One Nights*
should have connexions with our Bible, not as the offspring of a biblical
book, but as an ancestor of it, it is no longer incredible, and this is
reason enough for anyone who has his eyes wide enough open to say
"Century, what a joy to live!" '[6] Agnes and Margaret were amongst
those with 'eyes wide enough' to see that hunts for the origins of the
biblical books might lead one to unexpected places. Having piqued the
interest of her friends and readers, Agnes even edited as Volume 9 of
Studia Sinaitica the 'Select Narratives of Holy Women', whose risqué
antics were described in the overwriting of the famous palimpsest that
had started the sisters on their way.

Agnes and Margaret were now famous and, in Cambridge,
famously eccentric, a status enhanced by their possessing one of
Cambridge's first motor cars. (They were less conspicuous in their

active help of the poor one of their good works by stealth was to buy property and let it at low rents to those in need.) Within their own congregation they were ponderous and regular Sunday School teachers: 'Now which one of you children can tell me how to spell "Ur"?' More than one visiting preacher at St Columba's received a note subsequent to delivering his sermon, which pointed out his failure to mention a salient cross-reference from the Syriac text. Fellow Presbyterians marked the annual advance of winter by what they called 'moth-ball Sunday' – the first, odoriferous Sabbath on which the twins brought their heavy furs out of storage for winter wear.

They would squabble, even publicly, almost as a form of entertainment. Those who walked to church with them recalled being spoken to by both twins simultaneously, on different erudite topics but in the same heavy Ayrshire accents, and being expected to follow both at once. Since Samuel's death, Margaret had slept in Agnes's room at Castlebrae, but they set a line of string down the middle of the big double bed to avoid border disputes.

In the observance of protocols they could be quite as firm with others as they were with themselves. Allan Whigham Price, who interviewed a number of elderly Cambridge residents with youthful memories of Agnes and Margaret, records one such occasion:

The guests of honour at one of her dinner parties were Dr Alexander Wood – fellow of Emmanuel and University lecturer in Physics – and his young bride, then newly returned from her honeymoon. Mrs Wood, attired as was the custom of those days in her wedding dress minus the train, was given the place of honour on Agnes' right, the young physicist . . . on her left. Shy and nervous, Mrs Wood was dismayed to observe, at the far end of the table and seated next to Mrs Gibson, the wife of the Master of one of the Colleges. As a matter of course, this important lady assumed priority rights as 'leader of the lady guests'; and, after dessert, began to collect her bag, gloves and wrap in readiness for the first sign from her hostess that the meal was ended and the time had come for her to lead the withdrawal to the drawing-room. Agnes observed these preparations with a cold eye, and called out, 'Mistress Wood firrrst, if you please!' The young don's bride wished that the floor might open and engulf her; but, avoiding the furious looks of the Master's wife, she obediently led the company into the other room.[7]

CHAPTER 30

The active life

By the turn of the century the sisters who had struggled so long for acceptance in the insular world of Cambridge seemed, to many, its permanent fixtures. Some of their friends, however, were finding (as had Ecclesiastes) that 'of making many books there is no end; and much study is a weariness of the flesh'. Important though the *genizah* and the recovery of the rabbinic past were for him, Solomon Schechter wanted to throw himself into education for the Jewish future. Cambridge had proved intellectually stimulating, but religiously isolating. He was, for most of his twelve years there, the only obser-vant Jew in a community almost wholly unfamiliar with the robust Jewish orthodoxy he espoused. On high days and holy days when the Jewish students were not around there was not even a quorum for services. Convinced that the future of Judaism was in the United States, he accepted an invitation to be president of the Jewish Theological Seminary of America and moved, with his family, to New York in 1902.[1]

It was a difficult move for him – Schechter, at the height of his fame as a text scholar, effectively threw it all over for a new career – and for his family, who were happily settled in Cambridge, but it was a move altogether consistent with his deepest ideals. Judaism was not a museum piece but a living faith, and the young needed scholarly and imaginative training. The Jewish Theological Seminary had been founded in 1887 as a conservative reply to Reform Judaism, but its hold on life in the first years of the twentieth century was still very fragile. Meanwhile thousands of Jews from Eastern Europe, mostly Orthodox, were arriving in the United States every year. The leaders of Conservative Judaism saw the urgent need for someone vital to head a modern seminary for historical and traditional Judaism, and Schechter was just the man. Agnes and Margaret found a characteristically thoughtful leaving gift for the Schechters – a silver kiddush cup for use on the Sabbath, inscribed with a verse from one of the leaves of Ben Sira, which had brought their lives together so dramatically: 'Blessed is the man who meditates on wisdom and who reasons intelligently.' (Ben Sira 14:20).[2]

Their good friend Rendel Harris meanwhile had held a series of fellowships at Clare College: a six-year term was renewed for four years, a four-year term was then renewed for two. In 1903, saying that he understood what Arithmetical Progression was, he left.[3] He was offered a prestigious professorship at Leyden, but instead accepted the invitation of a fledgling Quaker study house near Birmingham, called Woodbrooke.

It was a move that paralleled Schechter's, from the security and prestige of an ancient academy to something new and risky, but promising. Woodbrooke had been the home of George Cadbury, of the Quaker chocolate-making family, who had recently donated it as a house of training for Quaker lay-ministry. Rendel Harris was the new establishment's first Director of Studies. This is not to say that he abandoned his work on ancient texts in obscure languages – he simply expected that his Woodbrooke students, men and women of very mixed educational backgrounds and abilities, would *want* to learn Hebrew and Greek, and to study the Septuagint or early Church fathers in the original languages; and in his company they did.

From his semi-rural retreat at Woodbrooke, Harris continued with undiminished energy: teaching and playing tennis with his students, researching in his enormous private library and, at night, playing cards indefatigably. He fired ideas for new projects at the sisters, in the first decade of the twentieth century involving Margaret in a multi-volume set of commentaries on the wonderfully named ninth-century Syriac bishop, Ishodad of Merv.[4]

In New York, Schechter had thrown himself into the transformation of the Jewish Theological Seminary. He recruited new professors and courted new benefactors. In April 1903, a year after his arrival in Manhattan, the seminary opened two new buildings. He invited his old friends, Agnes and Margaret, to be amongst to first give a lecture in these new premises. On 17 October 1903 the *New York Tribune* reported that a 'hall of appreciative listeners' at the Jewish Theological Seminary had the previous evening listened to a lecture, 'Mount Sinai and its Manucripts' by Mrs Gibson and Mrs Lewis, women 'whose discoveries of old manuscripts have given them fame as paleographic scholars'.[5] It was an illustrated talk, and by means of slides Agnes explained what palimpsests were, how the ancient scribes worked and how discrepancies could creep into their ancient writings, providing the grist for modern scholarship.[6]

The sisters' renown also put them in touch with others in the New World, including some distant Dunlop relations (their mother's side) in Canada and Virginia. They now visited these relatives (of whom little is known other than that they appear to have been the repository for the ill-favoured portraits painted by Dita Blass), giving public lectures as they progressed between Montreal, Toronto, New York, Philadelphia and Richmond, Virginia.

Their most extravagant press coverage was in *The North American* of Philadelphia of 8 November 1903. In a double-page spread surrounded by an Egyptian frieze, banner headlines proclaimed 'Twin Sister Explorers turn new Light on the 4 Gospels', 'Sister Explorers Have Unearthed a Manuscript of Wonderful Value in an Ancient Monastery in the Shadow of Mount Sinai'. An attractive head-and-shoulder portrait of both sisters in academic dress (done realistically from photographs) was accompanied by a vivid artist's reconstruction of the scene at Sinai: a fine lady in riding hat and cape, camera in one hand and riding gloves in the other, gives instructions to a cowboy in a Stetson (presumably the dragoman) holding a map – and a Roman Catholic priest in a skullcap holding a torch the whole tableau owing more to Nevada than to Egypt.

It was stirring stuff. The copy was similarly vernacular, but in substance more accurate:

> From the dark recesses of an abandoned cell in the monastery of St Catherine on Mount Sinai – the very cradle of the gospel – two English [*sic*] women, twin sisters, inspired by a Philadelphia theologian [Rendel Harris's stint as a professor at Haverford not forgotten], have just brought to light a document that antedates all other scriptural records by two and a half centuries . . .
>
> The favourite contention of agnostics – it was Thomas Paine's trump card – that four centuries had elapsed after the death of Christ before His followers were able to present any authentic record of His teaching, has thus been overcome by these two women, after a struggle that would have appalled the strongest men.
>
> Now the gap between the Crucifixion and the record has been reduced to 150 years at most . . .

The American papers, under headlines like 'Gifted Twin Sisters', 'The First Lady Doctors of Theology', were quick to note that although the twins were 'themselves inhabitants of an English university town', it had been left to foreign seats of learning to recognise their research. Only three months previously the University of Heidelberg had followed Halle in awarding both ladies Doctorates of Divinity, 'an honor', wrote the Philadelphia journalist:

> which they are the first women in Europe to receive . . . 'We didn't know anything about it until afterwards,' said Mrs Gibson, discussing the new honor. 'The first time we heard that the University had conferred the degree upon us was one day while we were at Newnham College. Someone saw a paragraph in a newspaper stating what had been done. Of course, we got an official letter a few days later.'

'These sisters, Mrs Agnes L. Lewis and Mrs Y. L. Gibson [*sic*],' continued *The North American*, 'whose work has gained for them the highest honors and degrees by the chief universities of Europe, have just returned home to England after a visit to Philadelphia, and will immediately equip another expedition to Sinai in search of further revelations.'[7]

With another of Germany's most prestigious universities joining in the laurelling, some in Cambridge must have been embarrassed by that university's apparent neglect. Cambridge's difficulty was that it could not award honorary degrees to women, for it did not award any degrees to them.[8] By way of convoluted indirect recompense, the list of those 'honoured' in the following year, 1904, included Archbishop Porphyrios of St Catherine's Monastery.[9] The archbishop stayed as a guest at Castlebrae for the occasion and Agnes was lauded by proxy in the Latin speech of the University Orator:

> We rejoice that to a man so learned should be given charge not only of so much else but particularly of the library hidden in so remote a fold of the mountains, which so many Cantabrigians, distinguished for learning in oriental languages, have recently visited. Entrusted to the care of such a man, no doubt that most ancient palimpsest of the sacred Gospels translated into the Syriac tongue will be kept safe, whose discoveress [*inventrix*] is a Cantabrigian and has more than once been deservedly honoured with honorary academic titles at home and abroad.[10]

There is no sign that Agnes and Margaret resented this constipation of compliments. What did bother them immensely was what they perceived to be Francis Burkitt's persistence in downplaying the importance of the palimpsest and of Agnes's role in its discovery.

In 1904 the long-promised Bensly and Burkitt *Old Syriac Gospels* came into print. Begun in theory by Professor Bensly, it was in the end almost entirely Burkitt's work: it is a sign of his immense generosity, which he seemed to apply to everyone except Agnes, that he did not take the full credit. Burkitt had used the Curetonian as the primary text, supplementing this with footnote references to the Sinai Palimpsest. Agnes was firmly convinced that the primacy should be the other way around: the Sinai Palimpsest was both more complete than the Curetonian and, by all indicators, an earlier transcription.[11] But a seemingly trivial matter in Burkitt's introduction galled her almost as much: in a congratulatory but also corrective note she wrote to Burkitt to say that it was 'not quite scientific' to state, as he had, that she and her sister had found the palimpsest. She alone had been responsible, since Margaret had no Syriac at the time. Burkitt, nonetheless, continued to infuriate both sisters on this point, in his talks and writings repeatedly crediting them both equally. While it might seem a trivial imprecision on Burkitt's part, it had the effect of suggesting the old canard that the twins had somehow just 'stumbled upon' the palimpsest in their travels, whereas Agnes knew – and Margaret would not disagree – that the discovery was very much a conscious achievement by someone looking for ancient Syriac manuscripts. The twins' suspicions that Burkitt was never quite sound were corroborated when he was barracked at the Church Congress of 1908 for saying that Adam and Eve 'belonged to Asiatic folk-lore (Cries of dissent).' And for suggesting that men could no longer accept St Paul's doctrine of sin and death, closely tied as it was to the story of the eating of the forbidden fruit. (Cries of 'Yes, we can.').[12]

Cambridge, for centuries a sleepy medieval town, had expanded with the railways, and speculative builders ran up new streets over its fields and grazing lands. A new citizenry had appeared in a few decades whose lives were mostly sharp and poor – amongst the names of the new streets were Brew House Lane, Gas Lane and Occupation Road.

Margaret was asked by a young Sunday School teacher to visit a pupil about whom she was anxious. Margaret went at once, and reported back 'You are quite right. The father *does* drink. If I lived in a house like theirs, I should drink too.'[13]

St Columba's Church had run a mission for several years near the railway station. York Street, in which it stood, was an even meaner and narrower street than most, with the house fronts like two opposing parallel walls, pierced at regular intervals by doors and small windows. In the 1890s its occupants were mostly railway employees, college servants, bricklayers, general labourers and large numbers of children.

In 1905 Agnes and Margaret bought the building and presented it to the Church as a permanent mission. The twins would arrive for the Sunday evening service in their chauffeur-driven car (a concession to the fact that they were now in their sixties) and would also take the women's meeting on Friday afternoons. They hung a large coloured relief map of the Holy Land in the women's room and gave illustrated talks on their travels, as well as arranging summer bible-class outings and tea at Castlebrae. During the week there were activities every day: carpentry, gymnastics, and band playing.

It was important, the twins and their friends believed, to provide these young people with proper trades that could carry them through life. Otherwise lads fell into a short-term and scrounging existence of odd jobs at the colleges, work as barrow boys, carrying suitcases or picking up tennis balls. This was a listless way to spend the few valuable years when they might have learned a trade and avoided an adulthood of temporary work and poverty, relieved only by visits to the public houses – one of which, Miss Eglantyne Jebb had calculated, could be found at thirty-six-yard intervals in the Newmarket Road.[14] Slightly different, but equally wretched lives awaited girls who were bundled into service in the many Cambridge homes that were too small to provide a properly ordered household training; they would be overworked as junior domestics and shop girls in hot, unventilated rooms with unnourishing meals. Without guidance, the brief intervals of freedom were squandered, especially by the shop girls, and their funds were wasted on hats and showy clothes, with too little left for sensible underclothes and durable shoes. The answer to this was to capture the young with activities, instilling shape and discipline through sport and busy evenings of woodwork, talks and debating clubs. Among some of the societies that were formed were the Young Women's Christian Association, the Girls' Friendly Society and the Free Church Girls' Guild. For the boys a bit more salesmanship was required, producing the Boys' Brigade, the Church Lads' Brigade, the Naval Crusaders and the Band of Hope. As Henry Drummond, a popular religious writer, wrote, 'Amazing and preposterous illusion!

Call these boys "boys", which they are, and ask them to sit up in a
Sunday class, and no power on earth will make them do it; but put a
five penny cap on them and call them soldiers which they are not, and
you can order them about till midnight.'[15]

Although the stream of manuscripts to be found in monasteries was
drying up, the first decade of the twentieth century saw wondrous
biblical finds dug out of the dry sands of Egypt. Since the late 1890s two
Oxford scholars called Bernard Grenfell and Arthur Hunt ('excitable
young men,' thought Dita Blass, who had met them) had been digging
in the sandy soil of Egypt searching for papyri from Egypt's Greek and
Roman periods.[16] At the site of the abandoned city of Oxyrhynchus –
though virtually nothing remained above ground – they found layers
and layers of papyrus manuscripts. It was an ancient rubbish dump, not
unlike the Cairo *genizah* except that these manuscripts were, many of
them, much older. In 1897 the men had found a previously unknown
'Saying of Jesus', apparently dating from the early second century
(subsequently identified as part of the apocryphal Gospel of Thomas)
and a portion of the Gospel of St Matthew. Over six seasons ending in
1907 Grenfell and Hunt recovered 700 boxes of papyri, an estimated
500,000 separate pieces, and shipped them back to England in biscuit
tins.[17] Restored in this way were many whole works previously lost:
the *Paens* of Pindar, the only known comedy of Sophocles and the
'New Comedy' of Menander. The significance of the biblical papyri
only became apparent with the passing decades and improved
analytical methods. One, possibly from Oxyrhynchus, is a tiny, though
recognisable fragment of John's Gospel, which may be dated to the
first half of the second century. Since John was judged by the sceptical
most likely of all the Gospels to be 'late', this material proof of early
circulation was the final nail in the coffin for the sceptical view,
expressed by Thomas Paine in *The Age of Reason*, that the Gospels did
not make their appearance until more than 300 years after Jesus had
lived.[18]

A photograph from January 1906 shows the twins, bundled in furs, with the by now elderly Grace Blyth similarly swathed and Sir Lappie in attendance. The occasion was the wedding of one of the Gibson nieces whom Agnes and Margaret had taken under their wing. The 'Stevenses' were married from Castlebrae. In a letter dated 3 January Margaret informs her brother-in-law that the wedding has gone well and that, much as she and Agnes would like to visit him in Edinburgh, they could not for the time being because they were departing immediately for Mount Sinai. It would be their sixth and last trip to St Catherine's.

They travelled, as usual, by camel. Agnes overheard one Bedouin say to another, referring to her rheumatic constraints, 'which one do you want, the good one or the broken one?' The twins were sixty-three. As if by way of indicating that the journey was as important as the arrival, the significant discoveries of this trip were made at Port Tewfik at the southern end of the Suez Canal, as the twins were on their way back from St Catherine's in April 1906. Agnes purchased two Syriac palimpsests. Only once they had reached Castlebrae did she realise that one of these was the remainder of a manuscript she had recently purchased from a dealer in England. Its upper writing was a copy of a spiritual text written at St Catherine's, *The Ladder of Divine Ascent* by St John Climacus. The manuscript underwritings included fragments of the Gospels, the Letters of Paul, the Acts of the Apostles and some parts of a lectionary, all in Palestinian Syriac.[19] These could be dated to the sixth century, before the rise of Islam and the spread of Arabic had extinguished this dialect. Her other purchase was a theological dispute between a Christian and a non-believer in a rare specimen of Christian Arabic, dating from about the tenth century. The underwriting in Syriac contained the story of a massacre of forty of the monks of the Sinai desert at the hands of Saracen tribesmen and a legend of an early saint named Eulogios. These stories were both known from other sources, and the paramount importance of this manuscript was linguistic: they were the only non-biblical documents of any length in Palestinian Syriac to have survived.

CHAPTER 31

The darkening to war

Throughout the years of the twins' eastern travels the region had been dangerously unstable. Already in 1893 as they returned from St Catherine's with the Burkitts and the Benslys, the party had been alarmed to hear cannon fire as they approached the Suez Canal. Their first thought was that hostilities had broken out – the question was, between whom? As it turned out, the explosions were just to celebrate the end of Ramadan. The declining Ottoman Empire staggered from one opportunistic political alliance to another, and indulged in periodic blood-lettings of its minority populations.

In the first decade of the twentieth century the normal jostling in Jerusalem between the Russians (as protectors of the Orthodox), the French (as protectors of the Catholics), and the English (as protectors of the Protestants) was joined by the Germans. In 1898 the German kaiser, Wilhem II, and his wife, Augusta Viktoria, visited Jerusalem. The ostensible purpose was to dedicate the newly built Lutheran Church of the Redeemer, but it was political theatre from first to last, aimed to show that the kaiser was the leader of both his German Protestant and his German Catholic subjects in the Holy Land (who might otherwise come under the jurisdiction of the English and French respectively), and to consolidate his friendship with the sultan. He wanted to enter the city gates on horseback, like a 'pacific' Crusader knight. Since Muslim tradition accorded this honour only to a conqueror, his Ottoman hosts breached the wall near the Jaffa Gate so that he could enter mounted – but not through a gate. The Russian and French press covered the event with undisguised hostility.

When, several years later, the Ottomans began the construction of a railroad linking Damascus to Medina, to facilitate the passage of pilgrims to Mecca and meet other commercial needs, the British did not fail to note that it was being built with German technical assistance and that it was capable of carrying German troop trains and provided the means of neatly circumventing the Suez Canal. The Ottoman Empire was drifting into the alliance that would entail, with the defeat of its German allies, its final dismemberment. The young T. E. Lawrence would abandon his budding career as a Near Eastern archaeologist to blow up the Hijaz railroad instead.

For Agnes and Margaret, the academic rivalry with 'the Germans' was more symbolic than anything else. The build-up to war meant separation from dear friends and certain knowledge of hardship for others. When Eberhard Nestle died in 1913 the twins bought his library, possibly as a way to channel funds discreetly to his widow. Dita Blass last saw them in the same year when they visited her in Germany. They had hired a car and driver to take them right across Europe to Breslau in Poland, only to discover that the ancient manuscript they sought was not there, but in a monastery of the same name near Stuttgart (hundreds of miles south and west). They found it on their way back.

After the outbreak of hostilities the students of Westminister College were moved up to Birmingham and the buildings used to house Croatian troops. Although it must be said that her earlier poetic efforts did not pose much competition, Agnes wrote some of her best verse at this time. There is genuine feeling in 'Christmas, 1914':

> O How can ye think of Christmas,
> If your sky is black with smoke?
> If ye dwell in a trench, and breathe in the stench,
> Where the shell of the lyditte broke?
> While ye look on the Belgian homesteads,
> Where the bairns were wont to play,
> Now blackened and lone, while the doggies moan
> For their masters far away.[1]

At Woodbrooke, Rendel Harris, a lifelong pacifist and witness to the horrors of the Armenian massacres, was strained and white. The place itself was under suspicion as a Quaker institution, and was raided in a search for fugitive conscripts. Harris was exercised by the fate of conscientious objectors who, in the early days of the war, were being sent to France and even faced the death penalty for their refusal to fight. He threw all his influence behind the efforts – in the end successful – of some Members of Parliament to get these men back from France and, at least, into English prisons.

In the vastness of Castlebrae, Agnes and Margaret decided to take in some refugees; the first were a Belgian doctor with his wife and two small children. Emily Free, the twins' housekeeper, recalled the stay years later. It was a great mismatch. The children banged the dinner gong at inopportune moments, and their mother infuriated Agnes and Margaret by going on about the furs and jewels she had been forced to leave behind, while at the same time treating the twins as 'upper servants' of sorts in their own house. When the Belgian lady came across Agnes knitting some coarse, thick socks, she hazarded 'For the troops?' and was told, 'No. For meself'.[2]

The next refugee was altogether more suited to the twins' dynamic work ethic. She was a Belgian hat-maker, keen to get on with restoring her fortunes. Agnes and Margaret arranged for their friends a show of the hats, using wine bottles as hat stands posed about the house, and modelling some themselves. In the end they helped her take quarters in central Cambridge and set her up in a small shop in the centre of the town.

Also as part of the war effort Agnes and Margaret determined to breed rabbits. They purchased nine does and a buck for the purpose, but no offspring appeared. Agnes had read that anxious rabbits might be soothed by music and so acquired a wind-up gramophone, which was placed near their hutch to assist romance, but again with no results. Some of their friends surmised that, in their innocence, the sisters had been sold ten does. Emily Free, on the other hand, disclosed that their driver, Eastman, who had responsibility for the rabbits, hated them. He had read that the creatures were alarmed by abrupt and loud noises, so he pounded on the top of their hutch every time he passed. Either way, there were no young – prompting this exchange, remembered from a Castelbrae dinner party by one of their friends: 'Agnes, how are the rabbits?' Agnes – 'Acch they're all right, but they've no been very familiar yet.'[3]

In the November of 1916 Rendel Harris, sixty-four years old and two years a widower, declared he was wearied by the prospect of another long English winter and set out for India (sailing second-class) to join his friends J. H. Moulton and T. R. Glover, who were lecturing there for the Bible Society. The boat was torpedoed in the Mediterranean. After three hours in icy rowing boats the passengers were rescued, with some loss of life, and Harris went on to Alexandria. There he was effectively marooned, frustrated in his attempts to communicate with Moulton, but he did still manage to buy some manuscripts at Fayum, near the excavations of Grenfell and Hunt. Eventually he arranged to meet his friend on the way back from Port Said.

Harris favoured staying on in Egypt until the submarine dangers had subsided, but Moulton, weakened by boils and anaemia from his time in India, was anxious to get back to England as soon as possible. They set out on 31 March and their ship was torpedoed and sunk on 4 April, within sight of land, but on heavy seas in darkness. There were twenty-eight people crammed into a leaking boat and they had to lie in the freezing water, with the strongest taking their turns at the oars. Fourteen died, including Moulton, much weakened by his travels, and were buried at sea. On the fourth day they came in sight of a town, but were blown out to sea again. Harris thought his end had come, but they had been seen from shore. He was scarcely conscious when he became aware of a young French-speaking curé bending over him (they had landed in Corsica) to ask his name. Harris replied and added, in French, 'I believe I am known in France' – at which the young man turned to the onlookers and said, 'C'est l'Orientalist!' Then, said Harris, 'I knew I was not among barbarians.'[4]

Agnes and Margaret were now in their seventies. Agnes confessed to Rendel Harris in 1911 that a small stroke had made concentrating on palimpsests a bit more difficult, but it did not stop her from publishing

Light on the Four Gospels in 1913, a popular account of the theological significance of her famous palimpsest, and receiving with her sister an honorary degree from Trinity College, Dublin.

Their lifelong fondness for travel now suffering from the constraints of war, they continued nevertheless to broaden their intellectual horizons: in 1914 Agnes edited some early fragments of the Koran, which she had found palimpsested amongst other of their discoveries, and wrote in her introduction that she hoped Muslim readers would find as much to delight and as little to fear from the application of textual science to their scriptures as she had done.[5]

The darkness of their war years was briefly lightened by the award to them, in 1915, of the Triennial Medal of the Royal Asiatic Society, 'the blue ribbon of Oriental research.'[6] This was the first time it had been awarded to a lady – or rather to two, since (also for first time) two persons were jointly honoured for their labours in Syriac and Arabic studies. Margaret thanked the society in her speech for associating her with her sister in this signal award: 'I came into this world as a supplement to her, and have always recognised that its was mine to take a second place. But you will agree with me that it is better to be second in a good cause than first in a bad one.'

As Agnes grew increasingly rheumatic, Emily Free (who was with the twins for twenty-five years, first as house-maid, then table-maid, then personal maid) would take her in a bath chair to the University Library and the University Press. On the way back they would stop to visit their friend, the Belgian milliner, at her shop in Rose Crescent for a glass of milk.[7] Mentally Agnes was undiminished and in 1917 both sisters appended their names, along with those of several female Darwins and other Cambridge notables, to a letter to *The Times* urging the vote for women. When Grace Blyth died in March of that year, victim of her own eccentric intersection with a gas fire, the twins dispatched cogent letters dealing with her estate. Agnes fired off a few as well to the Cambridge newspapers for good measure, detailing the gas company's negligence. One of their first acts on Grace's death was to remove the pillar with the heretical epitaph for Lappie. They used the £10,000 they had settled on Grace during her lifetime, and now released, to establish a lectureship in modern Greek at the university.

After the war, the students returned to Westminster. The memoir of P. Carnegie Simpson, a professor at the college, recalled the sisters from his Cambridge days, by which time they were known by most of Cambridge as 'the Giblews':

> . . . They were staunch friends of Westminster College . . . and were never absent from its public or social functions. The Students' Theological Society elected them to be honorary members; and they attended its meetings with embarrassing frequency. I recollect one evening there was a debate on Pacifism, at which they were present. The discussion was prolonged; and it was late when one member arose and began his speech by saying, 'Mr President, the fundamental question is, "What is Christianity?"' Whereupon Mrs Lewis turned to her sister and said, in very audible tones, 'Maggie, if at this hour of night they are going to begin to ask what Christianity is, we must go'; and go they did.[8]

Margaret had noticed her sister slipping in small ways, giving, for instance, a Bible study two times running on the same text. Sometime around 1919 Agnes descended into a state of confusion from which she never fully recovered. The old Agnes was still there; at times she would rise in the night and declare that she must get on with editing some manuscripts, but she had lost her awareness of the way the world held together. Margaret, who couldn't accept this loss, doggedly conducted Agnes about in her bath chair, taking her to tea with friends: 'I know Agnes does not add much to conversation, but it's good for her to go out.' Soon Margaret herself, under the strain and anxiety of her worry for Agnes, began to decline, and one cold day she appeared unannounced on a friend's doorstep, with no proper coat on.

It was Margaret who left first, on the twins' seventy-seventh birthday, 11 January 1920. She had suffered a stroke the day before and never regained consciousness. Apparently there had been some agreement between them that Agnes, as the eldest by half an hour, would die first. Their friends and servants were at a loss as to how to tell Agnes of Margaret's death. When, on the day of her funeral, they finally did so, Agnes replied simply, 'How inconsiderate of Maggie!' Agnes would be found wandering around the house in the months to come, calling her sister's name.

She lived for another six years, with moments of lucidity, as Castlebrae grew dark and damp around her. A companion related that when she lay very near death, almost paralysed, no one knew how far she was conscious or could make out what she said in those rare moments when she spoke. But one day her companion said loudly, 'Mrs Lewis, Mrs Lewis! I met Dr Burkitt near the Backs this morning.' No response. She repeated, 'I met Dr Burkitt near the Backs this morning.' Slight lifting of the head. 'And he said to me, "Mrs Lewis is the most learned lady in England." ' Agnes suddenly answered, 'And so I am.'[9]

Agnes died on 29 March 1926. She was eighty-three. Principal Oman of Westminster's funeral address at St Columba's began by saying it was a strange thought that there may 'be many here who never saw her' to whom Agnes Lewis was no more than 'a name of a distinguished person'.

CHAPTER 32

Palimpsest

The twins had outlived many of their friends and allies. Mary Kingsley had died in South Africa in 1900, nursing Boer prisoners of war in atrocious circumstances. Solomon Schechter had died in 1915 after delivering a lecture on Jewish philanthropy. (Having collapsed, he agreed to lie down to await the doctor, but insisted that Mathilde give him a book to read – 'But I can't just lie here doing nothing' – and left this life reading one of his favourites, Walter Scott's *The Antiquary*.)

Agnes Lewis and Margaret Gibson were gradually forgotten in Cambridge. Perhaps, if their achievements had been in a less recondite field, their fame might have endured better, but even Mr Austen Chamberlain, MP, the Secretary of State for India who presented the sisters with the Gold Medal of the Royal Asiatic Society, admitted that he could not really understand or fully appreciate their remarkable achievements in Arabic and Syriac. Certainly the Gibson nieces and great-nieces who came down to clear out Castelbrae after Agnes's death, destroying boxes and boxes of the twins' personal papers, did not.

Castlebrae was sold to Clare College and converted to student lodgings, its great bright rooms divided into small dingy ones by partition walls and fire doors. The brackets that held the twins' exercise ropes in the tower staircase were removed, and the Greek inscriptions over the doorways painted over. (But not before they puzzled Nikos Kazantzakis, the author of *Zorba, the Greek*, who stayed in the house briefly while visiting Cambridge just after the Second World War.[2] No one could enlighten him as to why these Greek inscriptions were there.) An Arabic proverb on the shortness of this life and the preferability (to the wise man) of the next has remained over the fireplace in Agnes's former study.

Agnes always felt that Francis Burkitt wanted to take away the credit of the palimpsest from her. On the face of it this seems improbable, and those in the Cambridge academic community who were interviewed by Allan Whigham Price were in agreement that Burkitt was 'too great a scholar to have any need of pinching anything'. Yet when, after her death, Burkitt wrote Agnes's entry for the authoritative *Dictionary of National Biography*, he said of the twins' first visit to St Catherine's, 'One manuscript especially struck them: it was written in AD 778, but underneath the eighth century script older effaced writing was visible here and there . . . Thinking that so ancient a manuscript *might* be interesting, Agnes Lewis photographed *several pages*.' [author's italics] Agnes had in fact photographed almost 400 pages, on which Burkitt himself had worked extensively. The faultless memory for which he was renowned seem to have failed him at this point.

In Cambridge it seems that, even while alive, the twins had been better known for their eccentricities than their achievements. Today the one thing known by those who have heard of Agnes and Margaret at all is that they found the Sinai Palimpsest by accident when a page of it was put before them as a butter dish. The *textus receptus* here is Allan Whigham Price in *The Ladies of Castlebrae*:

> . . . their notable discovery was not to be the result of diligent burrowing: it was to be the result of one of those curious accidents which look so improbable in the pages of fiction. Hospitality in an all-male community, though cordial, is apt to be of a somewhat rough-and-ready kind. At St Catherine's, meals tended to be served on the firm principle that one eats to live, and no more. Butter dishes, for instance, were scorned: when, at breakfast, butter was required, it was simply plonked down on an old sheet of discarded manuscript, and put thus on the table. After all, vellum is a tough material, and will resist grease for at least the period of one meal; and its use reduces the washing-up. Such, at any rate, was the monks' normal custom, and they saw no

reason to vary it for their feminine visitors. They had been so long out
of the world that they had forgotten that women attach considerable
importance to such trifles. So the butter for the twins' meals appeared
on the same ersatz tableware. Our heroines were somewhat discon-
certed but, as well-bred women, naturally made no comment. Agnes,
indeed, saw in such unusual arrangements an excellent opportunity to
combine study with eating, to blend intellectual refreshment with the
somewhat clumsy methods prescribed by the Lord for refuelling
the human frame. Hence it soon became her custom to scrutinise the
'butterdish' with an unobtrusive scholarly eye, to see whether it offered
anything of interest. As a rule it did not; but one morning the grubby
sheet proved to be a fragment of a palimpsest, and at the edge of the
'dish', disappearing under the lump of butter, was a line or two of the
underwriting clearly visible – which she at once recognised as a verse of
the Gospels. This happened to be in Syriac, Agnes' newly acquired
language (and therefore one in which she happened to be especially
interested at that moment). Tactful and casually-worded enquiries,
after the meal, led her to a certain basket in the glory-hole where they
had been working. There she found a complete Syriac palimpsest of
three hundred and fifty-eight pages . . .[2]

Charming though this tale may be, it entirely lacks plausibility.
Agnes and Margaret described the moment of Agnes's great discovery
many times over and never once gave anything even remotely like this
story of the butter dish. Their account did not vary: on arrival at St
Catherine's they asked to be shown to the dark cupboard of which
Rendel Harris had written, and soon afterwards Agnes set eyes upon
the palimpsest.[3]

To accept 'the butter-dish' account – a story with affinities to von
Tischendorf's claim that the monks were just about to burn the Codex
Sinaiticus when he seized upon it – one would have to believe the
following: that just at the moment the twins turned up at St
Catherine's, the monks, having guarded this palimpsest intact for
hundreds of years, were taking it apart, piece by piece, to avoid dish-
washing. Despite having thousands of decrepit printed books on paper

and loose leaves of parchment at their disposal, their monastic hosts chose to go to the obscure dark, basement cupboard containing Syriac manuscripts in a basket and remove a sheet from a palimpsest that was otherwise, as Whigham Price himself says, 'entirely complete'. (Even this would not at all have been easy, because the palimpsest's pages were glued together by time and not yet prisèd apart using the steam kettle.) We must add to this refutation the fact that Agnes and Margaret did not eat breakfast or any other meal with the monks: they ate in their own dining tent in the garden, off their own china plates and cups. Finally, the monks did not eat butter but olive oil.

Whigham Price left no record of where he heard the butter-dish story. Possibly it was a reminiscence of one or more of the Cambridge ladies such as Mrs Keynes, whom he was able to interview in the 1950s when she was in her nineties, and who in their young days had known – or known of – the sisters.[4] But it is interesting to note that a great-niece of Rendel Harris also recalls that, as a child, she had been told he made one of his important manuscript discoveries, *The Odes of Solomon*, when it was in use as a butter dish.[5]

Agnes's discovery of the Syriac Gospels was, along with Rendel Harris's 'Apology of Aristides', the most important manuscript find since von Tischendorf's recovery of the Codex Sinaiticus in 1859. The palimpsest pushed back the Gospels to a date earlier than the Codex Sinaiticus, as the Greek text on which it was based could be presumed to antedate that of von Tischendorf. It demonstrated with near-certainty that the last verses in Mark's Gospel were not original, but added at a later date. From Agnes's point of view, it was also an echo-chamber for the Aramaic-speaking world of Jesus. In one of her last books, *Light on the Four Gospels from the Sinai Palimpsest* (1913), she asks: is 'it not possible that this version [from Greek into Syriac] was made by men who had either been themselves eye-witnesses of the events recorded, or in whose ears were still ringing certain phrases or expressions heard by them in the synagogue from the lips of those who had been eye-witnesses?'[6] This would, she admitted, be claiming a very early date. But if not eye-witnesses, the Syriac translators might well have been familiar with the stories of Jesus from their own oral traditions, and would have detected places where the Greek was misleading. The variants in the Sinaitic Syriac might enable us, Agnes believed, 'to get behind the oldest of Greek texts, and to detect its slight corruptions'.[7]

The twins' two series of editions of manuscripts for the Cambridge University Press, *Studia Sinaitica* and *Horae Semiticae*, ran to twelve and nine volumes respectively – all but two of which were edited, or joint-edited, by one of the twins. These do not include Agnes's edition of the transcription of the palimpsest, her subsequent translation of it or her own full edition of *Old Syriac Gospels*, published in 1910 to rival that of Bensly and Burkitt. This list of publications is all the more remarkable, given that the sisters did not even begin this kind of work until they were in their fifties.

Agnes and Margaret were remarkable in their ability to grow intellectually with the material that was coming before them. Although the Bible was their first best love, they also threw themselves into editing lectionaries, commentaries, lives of martyrs and folk-tales, bringing back to life lost texts from the early days of Christianity. The treatise 'On the Triune Nature of God', which Margaret edited in Volume VII of *Studia Sinaitica*, is now thought to be the earliest extant Christian Arab apology for Christianity, dating to about AD 750.[8] And now, in a time of increased interest in the relations between Islam and Christianity, the twins' Arabic editions are being revisited and their names are once again in circulation amongst grateful scholars.[9]

The contribution the twins made in cataloguing the Arabic and Syriac manuscripts at St Catherine's is literally incalculable: we cannot know when another scholar might have been entrusted with the task by the monks, or how many manuscripts might have gone missing in the interlude.

The same conjectural element attends the sisters' role in the recovery of the Cairo *genizah*. The horrible possibility is that what is now the world's foremost archive of medieval Jewry might instead have been lost, leaf by leaf, sold as souvenirs. Agnes and Margaret were always insistent that they deserved no credit for its discovery, other than recovering the documents that led Schechter to his Aladdin's cave of Judaica, but how many travellers would have known how to buy ancient fragments, or been able to help Schechter edit them once home? The twins were convinced that a Greater Providence had led them.

It was their fierce commitment to the truth that most impresses. At a time when many feared that new manuscript finds would destroy the trust of the faithful in their Scriptures (Gladstone said of the reception of the Revised Version of the Bible, 'You will sacrifice truth if you don't read it, and you will sacrifice the people if you do'), Agnes and Margaret were convinced that, if the Bible was God's truth, then no scientific finds could damage its fundamental integrity.[10]

Of course one had to grow and that, in their view, was part of God's plan. Considering the question of why God should allow variants and scribal errors to creep into biblical manuscripts, Agnes (again in *Light on the Four Gospels*) drew upon Darwinist reasoning: 'man becomes a nobler animal through his effort to supply his own wants'. We are not flawless automatons, and generations of scribes were bound to make

The twins with the Stevenses

mistakes, but 'the very variants which frighten the weak-minded amongst us act as a stimulant to others, inciting them to search the Scriptures more diligently . . .'[11] It was this openness to truth, and thirst to get at the truth behind tradition, that endeared Agnes and Margaret to the great scholars with whom they worked and corresponded, and which excites us still today.

The last family photo of the twins that we possess, dated around 1914, shows them posed in a mock studio biplane with the Stevenses and their daughter, the couple who had married at Castlebrae in 1906. The twins always liked new technology and deployed each novel technique as it came along, yet it could be said that, by the end of their lives, this new technology was at the point of dissolving the world into which they had been born. With cinema and radio available, hell-fire sermons (even in Presbyterian Scotland) became less an occasion of the keenest concentration and the topic of discussion for the week, and more an obligation. However, in recent decades, advances in technology (especially in computing and digital imagery) have once again transformed the world of textual scholarship. Ancient manuscripts are still being discovered today – lost, unlisted or undetected because bound in with other writings – in Moscow, Bucharest, on Mount Athos, even in the library of Corpus Christi College, Oxford, by the sharp-eyed intellectual descendants of Agnes and Margaret.[12]

Solomon Schechter never forgot his debt to his Scottish friends and, when searching for a motto for the Jewish Theological Seminary, chose 'And the bush was not consumed'. This symbolised, he said, both the Eternal Light of the Torah and his 'belief that Judaism was a living thing, a plant that never stopped growing'.[13] Transplanted to Presbyterian terms, it was the twins' own philosophy. In Cambridge Mrs Gibson and Mrs Lewis are remembered fondly in Westminster College, where their disconcertingly similar 'founder portraits' hang in the dining hall. Their memory is kept, too, with reverence by the monks of St Catherine's at Mount Sinai, where a hundred years is as a day, and the Syriac palimpsest of the Gospels rests in the library in the wooden box that Agnes had made for it.

CODA

Rendel Harris made his last visit to Sinai in 1922–3. An elderly man with a long, silvery beard and the same intense blue eyes, he was stirred into action by a report that the object of his long-standing desire, the Diatessaron of Tatian, had turned up in the convent library. He spent October in Constantinople, November in Jerusalem and December in Cairo (visiting the monasteries of the Nitrian desert), before heading

Rendel Harris in the library at St Catherine's

for Sinai and Jerusalem. As the days went on, Harris became so impatient to get to Sinai that his friend, H. G. Wood, kept him calm with endless games of bezique. They travelled from Tor to St Catherine's with forty-seven camels and a mixed party that included several ladies photographing manuscripts, a student of icons, a lady physician who was also an artist and copied manuscript illustrations, and an American producer intent on making a film about Moses. But once at St Catherine's, the manuscript that Harris hoped would crown his researches turned out not to be the Diatessaron or a Gospel harmony of any kind, but rather an ordinary copy of the Gospels whose pages had been bound out of order. Within the half-hour Harris had put them straight. The American film producer said, 'It was worth while coming here, just to see the way the old man took his disappointment.'[1] Harris died in 1941 and is beloved of his Quaker community and the academy at large.

In 1933 Joseph Stalin contacted the British authorities with an unusual offer – he wanted to sell them a Bible. Soviet Russia needed hard currency. Having already sold off many treasures of the Hermitage to Andrew Mellon, who was forming the core collection of America's new National Gallery of Art, the Russians were now prepared to part with the Codex Sinaiticus which had remained in Russian possession since von Tischendorf conveyed it to the Tsar. The asking price was £100,000, at the time the largest sum ever fixed for a book or manuscript. The book was bought for the British Museum, with half the money raised by public subscription, despite concerns about pouring so much money into the coffers of an atheistic regime. The Codex is now in the British Library, and is still 'beyond price'.

In 1975, in the course of general repair works at St Catherine's, the monks discovered a collapsed and hidden room in the northern wall of the monastery. Archimandrite Sophronios, the *stevophylax*, or wall-keeper, of the monastery saw a small piece of parchment removed by one of his Bedouin assistants. Over the next days, working by oil lamps in darkened daylight, he collected four boxes of parchments. Amongst these were some missing leaves of the Codex Sinaiticus. The world has still not had a full edition of this, the most important Bible known, but as this book goes to press, monastic editors are working together with officials of the British Library and scholars in Germany and Russia (where a few leaves still remain) to produce one. At St Catherine's itself, the most important manuscript of their great collection is that discovered in a dark cupboard by Agnes Smith Lewis.

A note on sources

My primary sources throughout are the writings of Mrs Lewis (Agnes) and Mrs Gibson (Margaret) and especially, in the early years, those of Agnes, who kept travel diaries and wrote them up into books. Margaret's writings appear mostly in letters and in scholarly publications which often – as with those of Agnes – had lively and incident-filled introductions. It seems clear that both twins worked on books, like *The Shadow of Sinai*, which were published under Agnes's name. Agnes's hand-written manuscript account of their trips to Sinai is held by Westminster College, Cambridge (WGL6), as are a number of letters from both twins to Rendel Harris (WGL3). The University of Birmingham Archive holds a wealth of materials on Rendel Harris, including the letters he wrote to Helen Harris from Sinai (DA21) that I have used here.

I am also indebted to Allan Whigham Price whose labour of love, *The Ladies of Castlebrae*, kept these two remarkable women from falling into total obscurity. His notebooks, held in Westminster College (WGL7/1) include interviews taken in the 1950s with Cambridge residents who had living memories of Agnes and Margaret – not perhaps, in every case, accurate ones.

The twins catalogues of the Arabic and Syriac manuscripts of St Catherine's remain, according to Professor Sebastian Brock of Oxford University, a useful guide though now surpassed by others.

Notes

Chapter 1 – Cambridge, 13 April 1893

1   See Owen Chadwick, *The Victorian Church*, Part II (London, 1970), pp. 43–4.

2   Sir Frederic Kenyon, *The Story of the Bible* (London, 1936), p. 87. The text was published simultaneously by the Oxford and Cambridge University presses.

3   Chadwick, op.cit., p.43.

4   The letter writer was Maud Du Puy and was in due course to marry George Darwin, despite his being an 'argonaist'. Gwen Raverat, *Period Piece: A Cambridge Childhood* (London, 1954), p. 11.

Chapter 2 – The birth and upbringing of the lady Bible-hunters

1   James Brown, *The Life of William B. Robertson, D.D.* (Glasgow, 1888), pp. 83–4.

2   Council minutes of Irvine, cited in John Strawhorn, *The History of Irvine* (Edinburgh, 1985), p. 128.

3   Robert Service, *Ploughman of the Moon* (London, 1946).

4   This is surely the model for the parish church in one of Agnes's novels of which, when a lightning strike caused a mass of debris to fall into the pulpit, its detractors observed that the pulpit had not been so well filled for a long time.

5   An unnamed correspondent, cited in Arthur Guthrie, *Robertson of Irvine: Poet Preacher* (Ardrossan, 1889), pp. 43–44.

6   Arthur Guthrie, *Robertson of Irvine* (Ardrossan, 1889), p. 115. The Burgher Church was part of the Secession tradition, whose branches came

together in 1847 to become the United Presbyterian Church.

7   My main source of information about the early days of John Ferguson is M. S. Tait's *The Ferguson Bequest* (Glasgow, 1883), written for the Trustees of his estate, which includes a small biographical sketch of the benefactor.

8   Ibid.

9   His income was £40,000–£50,000 a year, in the money of the time. To give some perspective, this meant that Ferguson made *every day* twice the annual salary of the best-paid schoolmasters; *four times* the annual wages of the least well-paid teacher.

10   Agnes Smith, *Effie Maxwell* (London, 1876).

Chapter 3 – The journey to the Nile

1   Agnes Smith, *Eastern Pilgrims* (London, 1870), pp. 1–2.

Chapter 4 – The boat

1   Agnes Smith, *Eastern Pilgrims* (London, 1870). Unless otherwise indicated, all the quotes in this chapter and in Chapters 5 and 6 are from this work.

Chapter 5 – The perfect dragoman

1   Amelia Edwards, *A Thousand Miles up the Nile* (London, 1888), pp. 4–6.

2   Stephen Olin, *Travels in Egypt, Arabia Petraea and the Holy Land* (New York, 1843), Arno Press reprint, p. 155.

3   Mary Whateley, *Ragged Life in Egypt* (London, 1863), p. 10.

4   Edwards, op. cit., pp. 1–2.

5   *The Times*, 18 February 1869.

6   Although Agnes does not say so, this is probably a pseudonym, playing on the Italian for 'certainty' (*certezza*).

7   Herodotus, *Histories*, Book II, 109.

8   Florence Nightingale, February 11, 1850 in ed. Anthony Sattin, *Letters from Egypt* (London, 1987), p. 139.

9   Piers Brendon, *Thomas Cook* (London, 1991), p. 125.

Chapter 6 – The search for the perfect mate

1   David Cornick, 'Cambridge and Sinai', in David Cornick and Clyde Binfield (eds), *Cambridge to Sinai* (London, 2006), p. 6.

2   Unless otherwise stated the details of Gibson's life come from his sister-in-law's memoir, included in Gibson's *El Cid and Other Poems* (London, 1887), a work edited by Margaret Gibson and published after her husband's death.

3   George Eliot in the Prelude to *Middlemarch* (1871–2).

4   Agnes Smith Lewis, *Margaret Atheling and Other Poems* (London, 1917), p. 104.

5   J. S. Blackie, *Notes of a Life* (Edinburgh and London, 1910), p. 175.

6   Cited in A. H. Sayce, *Reminiscences* (London, 1923), p. 103.

Chapter 7 – Greece

1   Agnes Smith, *Glimpses of Greek Life and Scenery* (London, 1884). Unless otherwise indicated, all quotes in this chapter come from this work.

2   Cited by Agnes Smith in her 'Memoir' of James Gibson, included in his *El Cid* (London, 1887).

3   James Y. Gibson, 'Tout Va Bien! Written on Receipt of a Telegram from Aigion', included in his *El Cid* (London, 1887)

Chapter 8 – The estate of marriage

1   Agnes Smith, *Through Cyprus* (London, 1887). Unless otherwise indicated, all quotations in this chapter are from this work.

2   Miss E. Jane Whateley (sister of Mary Whateley, who began the school in 1861), writing in the *Presbyterian Churchman*, Vol. III (1879), pp. 169–70.

3   Cited in Mary Roussou-Sinclair, *Victorian Travellers in Cyprus* (Nicosia, 2002), p. 42.

4   Mary Roussou-Sinclair, in a private conversation.

5   See Roussou-Sinclair, op. cit., p. 142.

6   Both verses were printed in Agnes Smith Lewis, *Margaret Atheling and Other Poems* (London, 1917).

7   The 'broken column' was a common symbol used on memorial stones

of the time to indicate a life cut short in its prime.

8   Agnes Smith, 'Memoir', in James Y. Gibson, *El Cid* (London, 1887), p.54–5

Chapter 9 – The Cambridge antiquarian

1   Editorial, 'Cambridge', in the *Presbyterian Churchman*, Vol. IX (1885).

2   Patrick Bury, *The College of Corpus Christi* (Cambridge, 1952), p. 219.

3   Agnes Smith Lewis, *The Life of the Rev. Samuel Savage Lewis* (Cambridge, 1892), p. 124.

4   *Presbyterian Churchman*. Vol. IX (1895), p. 35.

5   Ibid, p. 36.

6   Lewis, op. cit., pp. 65–6. Unless otherwise indicated, all quotes in this chapter are from Agnes's life of her husband.

7   Jeffrey Spier and Eleni Vassilika (lately Curator of Antiquities at the Fitzwilliam Museum, Cambridge) have written an informative article on Lewis's collection and Lewis as a collector from which I have gathered a great deal of what follows, assisted by other curators at the Museum. J. J. Spier and E. Vassilika, 'S. S. Lewis: Notes on a Victorian Antiquary and Contemporary Collecting', in *Journal of the History of Collections* (1995).

8   Mrs Florence Ada Keynes, *Gathering Up the Threads* (Cambridge, 1950), p. 56.

9   Martin Henig, 'The Lewis Collection of Gemstones', in *British Archaeological Reports (Supplementary Series 1)* (1975), p. 1. Lewis's gemstones are now on loan, from Corpus Christi College, to the Fitzwilliam Museum in Cambridge, as are his coins and antiquities.

10   To give an idea of how the trade worked, this coin had been found in a hoard near Jericho in 1874, taken up by a British dealer in Smyrna, brought by another to Paris and purchased by Lewis in 1875.

11   Gwen Raverat, *Period Piece* (London, 1954), p. 57.

12   I have only Allan Whigham Price's evidence for this. He conducted interviews with those who knew, or knew of, Agnes and Margaret at this stage, but many years after the twins' deaths. His interview notes are held at Westminster College Archives, Cambridge, Gibson-Lewis papers (hereafter WGL), WGL 7/1.

13   WGL 7/1. Christopher Brooke notes that the ideal academic wife of the

time was 'highly intelligent, but deliberately unacademic'. *A History of the University of Cambridge* (Cambridge, 1993), p. 255.

Chapter 10 – Heresy and mortality

1   For instance, Robertson Smith also gave a concise refutation of the Hegelian 'Tübingen School', whose insistence that the Gospel of St John was written many decades after the death of the Apostles had driven von Tischendorf into the desert thirty years earlier.

2   William Robertson Smith, *The Old Testament and the Jewish Church*, cited in Matthew Leitch's review in the *Presbyterian Churchman* (1881), p. 253.

3   Dr A. H. Charteris in the *Edinburgh Evening Courant*, 16 April 1876, cited in J. S. Black and G. C. Chrystal, *Life of Robertson Smith* (London, 1912), p. 189.

4   Black and Chrystal, op. cit., p. 197.

5   Cited in John Rogerson, *Bible and Criticism in Victorian Britain* (Sheffield, 1995), p. 59.

6   Cited in Alec C. Cheyne, 'Bible and Confession', in William Johnstone (ed.), *William Robertson Smith* (Sheffield, 1995), p. 34. Cunningham's *Theological Lectures*, published right in the midst of Smith's trial.

7   From A. T. Innes, *Chapters of Reminiscence* (London, 1913), p. 193. Cited by Cheyne in Johnstone, op. cit., p. 40.

8   Published as *The Old Testament in the Jewish Church* (Edinburgh, 1881).

9   Cited in S. Reif, 'Giblews, Jews and Genizah Views', *Journal of Jewish Studies* (2004), No. 55. Mathilde Schechter once told Francis Burkitt that her husband 'liked to read 365 novels a year, and that she had the greatest difficulty in providing a supply for him!' F. C. Burkitt in the foreword to *Solomon Schechter* by Norman Bentwich (London, 1931), p. 15.

Chapter 11 – Sinai and von Tischendorf

1   In the Eastern Church, religious houses are called 'convents' whether they comprise men or women. As this term is generally used in the West for religious houses of women, I sometimes refer to St Catherine's, an all-male establishment, as a 'monastery'.

2   Constantin von Tischendorf, *Codex Sinaiticus* (London, 1934), p. 22.

3   *Journal of Sacred Literature* (April, 1863), cited in Elliot, *Codex Sinaiticus and*

the Simonides Affair (Thessalonika, 1982).

4   Agnes Smith Lewis, in her introduction to *In the Shadow of Sinai* (Cambridge, 1898), p. iii. Agnes does not mention where she first heard of Harris's book, but it was discussed at length in an article by the Reverend Professor Leitch in the *Presbyterian Churchman*, Vol. XV (1892). She may also have read Helen Harris's account of the find, *The Newly Recovered Apology of Aristides* (London, 1891).

5   This descriptive detail is provided in the book written by Helen Harris, with her husband Rendel. See Harris, op. cit.

6   Bliss was himself a distinguished archaeologist of the Holy Land, brought up in Beirut, where his father was the founder of the American College.

Chapter 12 – The perils of Bible-hunting

1   I John 5: 6–10.

2   Irene Pickard, *Memories of J. Rendel Harris* (Quaker publication, 1978), p. 3.

3   Ibid.

4   Agnes Smith Lewis, Westminster College Archives. This remark is from Agnes's Draft Account of the First Visit to Sinai, WGL 6/1.

Chapter 13 – The story von Tischendorf did not tell

1   Constantin von Tischendorf, *Codex Sinaiticus* (London, 1934), pp. 23–4.

2   This amnesia was evidently selective, since a Russian scholar called Porfirij Uspenskij was able to inspect the manuscript at St Catherine's in 1845 and again in 1850, although without realising its significance.

3   Ludwig Schneller and Dorothee Schröder, *Search on Sinai* (London, 1939), p. 50.

4   By von Tischendorf's own account, his patronage aroused a jealous and fanatical opposition in St Petersburg. The Russian people 'were astonished that a foreigner and a Protestant should presume to ask the support of the Emperor of the Greek and Orthodox Church for a mission to the East. But the good cause triumphed.' Tischendorf, op. cit., p. 26.

5   Ibid., p. 27.

6   Ibid., pp. 27–31.

7   According to the present Keeper of Manuscripts at the British Library, Dr Scot McKendrick. The fact that the manuscript sheets, when von Tischendorf first saw them, were in a basket tells us nothing. The monks kept many manuscripts in baskets rather than on bookshelves, perhaps a relic of the days when scrolls were most easily stored this way.

8   Ihor Sevcenko, 'New Documents on Constantin Tischendorf', *Scriptorium* 18 (1964), p. 62. But, in Tischendorf's defence, see also Kurt Aland, *Konstantin von Tischendorf* (Berlin, 1993).

Chapter 14 – Setting out for Sinai

1   Procopius of Caesarea, *Buildings*, V, p. viii.

2   Niccolò da Poggibonsi, *A Voyage Beyond the Seas* (Jersualem, 1945), p. 98.

3   Margaret Dunlop Gibson and Agnes Smith Lewis, *How the Codex Was Found* (Cambridge, 1893).

4   Ibid., p. 22.

5   Ibid., pp. 16–17.

6   Ibid, p. 26.

7   H. V. Morton, *Through the Lands of the Bible* (London, 1938), p. 299.

Chapter 15 – The treasure in the dark closet

1   Margaret Dunlop Gibson and Agnes Smith Lewis *How the Codex Was Found* (Cambridge, 1893), p. 37.

2   Agnes Smith Lewis, *In the Shadow of Sinai* (Cambridge, 1898), p. vi.

3   Ibid., p. vii.

4   The manuscript is, as Agnes said, clearly dated but that dating is not entirely clear. There is a hole in the MS towards the end of the number. Some scholars date the manuscript to 697, but other authorities favour 779. The second is the preference of Professor Sebastian Brock of Oxford University, to whom I am grateful for clarification on this and other matters.

5   Gibson and Lewis, op. cit., p. 52.

6   Ibid., pp. 42–3. Although Agnes did not know it, this must have been the Feast of St Tryphon, 1 February in the Julian Calendar, the day when the

monks in procession bless their garden.

7 Arthur Stanley, *Sinai and Palestine in Connection with Their History* (London, 1881), p. 53.

8 The *semantron*, a type of wooden gong, was used when, under Ottoman rule, the ringing of bells was prohibited.

9 Gibson and Lewis, op. cit., p. 55.

10 Egeria's diary was translated and included by Margaret in *How the Codex Was Found*. For this extract, see Gibson and Lewis, op. cit., pp. 112–13.

11 Due to the inaccessibility of the site, the first detailed photographic study was done by the Alexandria-Michigan-Princeton Expedition to Mount Sinai between 1958 and 1965. They determined that only very minor repairs had ever been made to the mosaic. See Kurt Weitzmann, 'The Mosaic in St Catherine's Monastery on Mount Sinai', in *Proceedings of the American Philosophical Association*, Vol. 110, No. 6 (December, 1966), pp. 392–405.

12 Gibson and Lewis, op. cit., p. 40.

Chapter 16 – The Cambridge party

1 Mark 5:41.

2 Mark 15:34.

3 Agnes Smith Lewis, letter to Rendel Harris, 29 July 1893. WGL 5/3.

4 Agnes Smith Lewis, *In the Shadow of Sinai* (Cambridge, 1898), p. x.

5 Ibid., p. xi Persis Burkitt's note is a bit confusing and confused. The palimpsest was not, strictly speaking, a 'copy' of the Curetonian. The Syriac text in the palimpsest was the same as that borne by the Curetonian, which hitherto was the only known manuscript to carry this, the very oldest Syriac translation. Mrs Bensly later recalled seeing her husband and Mr Burkitt work on the photographs that weekend: 'I sat in the room where the two scholars, with their heads together, were deciphering some of the underwriting, and I well remember their exclamations of gladness and triumph where they found it to contain the earliest Syriac translation of our Gospels, made in the second century . . .' Mrs R. L. Bensly, *Our Journey to Sinai* (London, 1896), pp. 12–13.

6 The Cambridge University Press had given him a contract for an edition of the Curetonian Syriac, with an English translation, only in May of that year, 1892. Minutes of the Syndics of Cambridge University Press, 1892.

7   Whigham Price research notebook, WGL 7/1.

8   This was ninth-century Arabic manuscript of some of the Epistles of Paul.

9   R. Buick Knox in his *Westminster College, Cambridge: Its Background and History* (Cambridge, 1978) laid out the arguments on both sides beautifully, and here I am following him.

10 Exodus 23:8.

11 Agnes Smith Lewis: 'The three gentlemen who undertook to transcribe it, and among whom I divided some 350 photographs, Professor Bensly, Mr Rendel Harris, and Mr Burkitt, volunteered to go with my sister and me on a joint expedition to Sinai, Mrs Bensly and Mrs Burkitt accompanying us.' Margaret Dunlop Gibson and Agnes Smith Lewis, *How the Codex Was Found* (Cambridge, 1893), p. 125.

    Mrs Bensly: 'The ladies above mentioned volunteered to go a second time, to assist the party with their experience in Eastern travel and with their knowledge of modern Greek, the language of the monks on Sinai.' (Mrs Bensly, op. cit., p. 13.)

Chapter 17 – The disjoint expedition

1   Agnes Smith Lewis, *In the Shadow of Sinai* (Cambridge, 1898), p. 32. Unless otherwise mentioned, all references from Agnes in this chapter are from this book.

2   Mrs R. L. Bensly, *Our Journey to Sinai* (London, 1896), p. 61.

3   I am indebted to Persis's present-day descendants, Miles and Caroline Burkitt and Caroline Barwise, both for permission to use family photographs and for confirmation of this story.

4   Rendel Harris to Helen Harris, 5 February, 1893. University of Birmingham Archive, Special Collection, DA21. All the letters quoted from Rendel Harris to Helen Harris are from this collection.

5   Ibid. Harris followed the Quaker practice of using the archaic second person singular, 'Thee', in his correspondence.

6   Rendel Harris to Helen Harris, 19 February 1893.

7   Ibid.

8   Agnes Smith Lewis, WGL 6/1. Although this is listed as Draft Account of the First Visit (to Sinai), it contains a treatment of the second trip, with the Benslys, the Burkitts and Harris, and some subsequent trips.

9   Agnes Smith Lewis, letter from Sinai, 15 February 1893, in Lewis, *Two Unpublished Letters* (Cambridge, 1893), p. 9.

10   Margaret D. Gibson, Introduction, *Catalogue of the Arabic MSS in the Convent of S. Catherine on Mount Sinai* (London, 1894), p. viii.

11   All this was quite without foundation. Harris's letters to Helen make it evident that he had no personal ambitions in joining the expedition, and did so to assist Agnes and Margaret.

12   Rendel Harris to Helen Harris, 23 February 1893. Birmingham University Archive, DA 21.

13   Mrs R. L. Bensly, *Our Journey to Sinai* (London, 1896), pp. 125–6. All the citations from Mrs Bensly are from this work.

14   Agnes Smith Lewis, introduction to *A Translation of the Four Gospels from the Syriac of the Sinaitic Palimpsest* (London, 1894), p. xx.

15   John was not to know that posterity would be more interested in the Gospel text he had scrubbed out than in the lives of the saints he laid down, which was, in any case, not an original work. Agnes drew a moral from this: 'Here we find in sober fact what happened only meta-phorically in the middle ages – the Word of God completely obscured by the legends of the saints.' Ibid., p. xix.

16   Ibid., pp. xv–xvi.

17   Margaret Dunlop Gibson and Agnes Smith Lewis, *How the Codex Was Found* (Cambridge, 1893), p. 73.

18   Professor Bensly, it turns out, was in the right. All of these reagents damaged the manuscripts. WGL 6.

19   Agnes Lewis, introduction to *A Translation*, op. cit., p. xx.

20   Mrs Bensly, op. cit., p. 120.

21   Mrs Bensly, op. cit., p. 110. Few Westerners, even art historians, had any sensibility for icons much before the mid-twentieth century, so Mrs Bensly cannot be faulted on this matter. Those at St Catherine's are the oldest in existence, having escaped a widespread destruction of icons during the iconoclast controversy of the eighth and ninth centuries.

Chapter 18 – The final falling-out

1   Lagrange was actually French, not Belgian, but it was almost certainly he to whom Rendel Harris was referring.

2   The Dominicans, however, recorded their visit slightly differently,

writing that, since it was not possible for them to celebrate Mass in the church at St Catherine's, the monks had permitted them to celebrate it in their own quarters. The walls of division were not quite so fallen as Mrs Bensly imagined. See P.-M. Séjourné, 'Chronique – II. Le Sinai', in *Revue Biblique* (1897), p. 107.

3   In Agnes's manuscript account of the visit. WGL 6/1.

4   Mrs R. L. Bensly, *Our Journey to Sinai* (London, 1896), p. 124.

5   Ibid., p. 157.

6   Ibid., p. 158.

7   WGL 6/1.

8   WGL 6/1.

Chapter 19 – The devilish press and the Highland Regiment

1   The *Daily News*, or its Berlin correspondent, had got the name wrong – it was Professor *Harnack*.

2   Nestle was later most famous for his edition of the New Testament in Greek, which became the standard basis for the British and Foreign Bible Society translations.

3   Rendel Harris to Eberhard Nestle, Suez, 30 March 1893. Published as the appendix to Agnes Smith Lewis, *Two Unpublished Letters* (Cambridge, 1893).

4   Agnes later believed that the letter had reached *The Times*, but had not been published due to 'the pressure of parliamentary reports'. She had this letter, and another like it sent from Sinai that had met the same fate, published privately as *Two Unpublished Letters*.

5   Margaret Gibson to Rendel Harris, 10 April 1893. WGL 5.

6   Agnes Lewis to Rendel Harris, reporting on earlier exchange, 13 April 1893. WGL 5/5.

7   WGL 5. Mary Kingsley now lived in rooms in London. She was a house guest of the twins at the time, in the final stages of planning her trip to the Congo.

Chapter 20 – The Cambridge cold shoulder

1   Agnes to Helen Harris, 8 June 1823. WGL 5/5.

2   Independent corroboration from Burkitt's side of the row between the
     scholars comes from this diary entry made by the young Cambridge
     scholar T. R. Glover for 6 March, 1896: 'I went away and called on the
     Burkitts. Was surprised to find how very violent the row with Rendel
     Harris had been – Bensly's quarrel – getting so far as suggestion to
     publish the Sinai Codex in 2 vols separately each's leaves by themselves.'
     Diaries of T. R. Glover, St John's College, Cambridge.
3   Agnes to Rendel Harris, undated letter. WGL 5/5.
4   Agnes to Rendel Harris, 26 July 1893. Ibid.

Chapter 21 – A lightning course in text scholarship

1   In due course Kennett would rise to be a distinguished Professor of
     Hebrew, but in August 1893 he was twenty-nine years old, an Anglican
     of evangelical tendencies and a spirited example of late nineteenth-
     century manly Christianity.
2   Agnes to Rendel Harris, 11 August 1893. WGL 5/5.
3   Agnes to Rendel Harris, 21 August 1893. Ibid.
4   Agnes to Rendel Harris, 30 August 1893. Ibid.
5   T. R. Glover, *Cambridge Retrospect* (Cambridge, 1943), pp. 70–1.
6   Agnes Smith Lewis, introduction to *Old Syriac Gospels* (London, 1910), p.
     iii.
7   Agnes to Rendel Harris, 10 December 1893. WGL 5/5.
8   A letter from Burkitt to Robertson Smith, undated but probably from
     early in 1894, indicates his progress, and his unhappiness with Agnes's
     involvement:

> I have finished revisiting SS Luke and John and S. Mark is more than half
> done, so I shall certainly be ready with my share of the MS as soon as it
> will be needed. As you say, it will be well for me not to see Mrs Lewis'
> Introduction until it has satisfied you. I hope it will not be very long. I do
> most sincerely trust that some of the Englishmen who will be set loose
> upon the book will understand Syriac, and that they will not all be
> dependent on the Introduction! (MS, Cambridge University Library).

9   Report of the Church Congress, *The Times*, 10 November 1895.
10   A good modern translation of the Bible, like the New Revised Standard
     Version, will usually provide all twenty-one verses, but will indicate in a

note that some ancient authorities end the Gospel after verse 9.

11   Agnes Smith Lewis, *In the Shadow of Sinai* (Cambridge, 1898), p. 108.
12   Agnes Smith Lewis, *Light on the Four Gospels from the Sinai Palimpsest* (London, 1913), p. 17.
13   Ibid., p. 12.

Chapter 22 – In the company of Orientalists

1   Margaret wrote in her introduction of her indebtedness to Professor Robertson Smith, 'the great scholar who first suggested this publication, who watched it with eager and helpful interest, till increasing pain and weakness made work impossible'. Margaret Dunlop Gibson, *An Arabic Version of the Epistles of St Paul to the Romans, Corinthians, Galations with part of the Epistle to the Ephesians from a ninth century MS. in the Convent of St Catherine on Mount Sinai* (London, 1894), p. 8.
2   Although it is still a matter for debate, direct borrowing of the psalm from the Hymn of Aten seems less likely than the possibility that both the author of the Psalms and the pharaoh Akhenaten (who is thought to have written the Amarna version) drew on the same pool of ancient Near Eastern literature.
3   Max Müller, *Address Delivered to the Opening of the Ninth International Congress of Orientalists* (London, 1892), pp. 33–4.
4   On this, see Edward Said's *Orientalism* (London, 1978), a book that has made the term a byword for imperial appropriation, but which is not beyond criticism for caricaturing 'the Orientalists' in much the same way as he accused them of caricaturing 'the Orient'.
5   Müller, op. cit., p. 63.
6   Ibid., p. 14.

Chapter 23 – Burying the hatchet

1   *The Times*, 28 November 1893.
2   Ibid.
3   Margaret to Rendel Harris, 29 January 1895. WGL 5.
4   Agnes Smith Lewis, *In the Shadow of Sinai* (Cambridge, 1898), p. 78.
5   The source of this piece of information is the present brethren of St

Catherine's, who still speak of this room as having been a gift of Mrs Gibson and Mrs Lewis.

6 There were some new variants, and she was especially proud of one she found for John 4:27, which she believed cast new light on the story of Jesus's meeting with the much-married Samaritan woman at the well: the disciples had left Jesus to go and buy food and returned to find him speaking to a Samaritan woman – exceptional enough, since Jews did not associate with Samaritans, and nor did men speak privately with unknown women in this way. A brush of reagent, whose smell she had actually begun to like, revealed that the palimpsest added the further detail that Jesus was *standing* while speaking to the Samaritan woman, and Agnes picked up on this change: why was Jesus now standing? He was tired and earlier on in the passage had been described as sitting. She reflected that '. . . sitting is the proper attitude for an Eastern when engaged in teaching. And an ordinary Oriental would never rise of his own natural free will out of politeness to a woman . . . I like to think that His great heart, which embraced the lowest of humanity, lifted Him above the restrictions of His race and age, and made Him show that courtesy to our sex . . .' Agnes Smith Lewis, *In the Shadow of Sinai* (Cambridge, 1898), p. 98.

7 Margaret to Rendel Harris, 17 February 1895. WGL 5/5.

Chapter 24 – Keepers of manuscripts

1 They nowhere disclosed the identity of this person.

2 Agnes Smith Lewis, *In the Shadow of Sinai* (Cambridge, 1898), pp. 148–9.

3 Agnes Smith Lewis, *Light on the Four Gospels* (London, 1913), p. 92.

4 Agnes Smith Lewis, *In the Shadow of Sinai* (Cambridge, 1898), p. 167.

5 Lewis, *In the Shadow of Sinai*, op. cit., p. 167.

6 Lewis, *In the Shadow of Sinai*, op. cit., p. 170. Agnes and Margaret, while still in Jerusalem, must have anticipated difficulties as they had consulted Frederick Bliss, and took the precaution of binding the Yemeni Pentateuch in covers misleadingly stating '1896'. Letter from Agnes Lewis to Oswald Dykes, 6 September 1896.

7 J. Rendel Harris,, *Letters from the Scenes of the Recent Massacres in Armenia* (London, 1897), p. 110.

Chapter 25 – Solomon Schechter and the Cairo genizah

1   There is a lively note of this in the diaries of Terrot Glover, later in life a distinguished professor of classics, but at the time a young research student eking out a penurious existence by tutoring: 'Great event of the day was lunch with the Heavenly Twins. An Oriental gathering. Professor Rieu, Professor Cowell, Dr Sinker, Schechter & Kennett, Mrs Kennett, Mrs Schechter . . . An amusing time. The twins go east on Sunday.' Glover walked back to his house with Schechter – 'a most wonderful man, a Roumanian Jew of broad sympathies' – and met his children, the dark-haired Ruth and the red-haired Frank, who told Glover he got his hair 'from God'. Diaries of T. R. Glover, 10 February 1896, St John's College, Cambridge.

2   Agnes Smith Lewis, *In the Shadow of Sinai* (Cambridge, 1898), pp. 174–5.

3   Margoliouth's father, Ezekiel Margoliouth was said to have been a rabbi before becoming an Anglican missionary to the Jews.

4   Although Schechter was right, the thesis of Margoliouth was only finally refuted by discoveries of ancient Hebrew copies of Ben Sira at Masada in 1964. Stefan Reif, *A Jewish Archive from Old Cairo* (Richmond, Surrey, 2000), p. 76.

5   Mrs R. L. Bensly, *Our Journey to Sinai* (London, 1896), p. 13.

6   Ibid., pp. 166–7.

7   *Cambridge Chronicle*, 8 October 1896. It is typical of Agnes's forthright style to make superfluous mention of the fact that Surur died soon afterwards at Suez of excessive beer-drinking – 'He drank, said Ahmed, until the beer ran out at his nose.'

8   Mrs R. L. Bensly, op. cit., pp. 104–5.

9   *Cambridge Chronicle*, 8 October 1896. Mary Kingsley later said that she had been concerned about misrepresentation of her own travels by the tenor of Mrs Bensly's remarks about Agnes.

10 *Cambridge Independent*, 26 October 1896.

11 Stefan Reif, *A Jewish Archive from Old Cairo* (Richmond, 2000), p. 19.

12 *The Times*, 3 August 1897.

13 Ibid.

14 Ibid.

15 Agnes Smith Lewis, *In the Shadow of Sinai* (Cambridge, 1898), p. 183.

Chapter 26 – In Cairo with Schechter

1 Agnes Smith Lewis, *In the Shadow of Sinai* (Cambridge, 1898), p. 185.
2 In fact it was more than 140,000 and still, more than 100 years later, not fully catalogued.
3 Solomon Schechter, *The Times*, 3 August, 1897.
4 All of this is beautifully presented in Stefan Reif, *A Jewish Archive from Old Cairo: The history of Cambridge University's Genizah Collection* (Richmond, Surrey, 2000). Reif himself is drawing on S. D. Goitein's five-volume *A Mediterranean Society* (Berkeley, 1967).
5 Agnes Smith Lewis, *In the Shadow of Sinai* (Cambridge, 1898), p. 192.
6 Rita McWilliams-Tullberg, *Women at Cambridge* (London, 1975), p. 114.

Chapter 27 – Castlebrae

1 See Stefan Reif, *A Jewish Archive from Old Cairo* (Richmond, Surrey, 2000), p. 83.
2 Much of the information about this aspect of their lives in later years is taken from Allan Whigham Price's interview notes, held at Westminster College.
3 Introduction to Agnes Smith Lewis, *A Palestinian Syriac Lectionary, Studia Sinaitica* VI (London, 1897), p. vii.
4 'Pertilote' in the *Cambridge Independent*, April 1897.
5 Printed in the *British Weekly*, July 1899.
6 Nena's diary of the Cambridge visit, translated by Andrew Thompson, is to be found in David Cornick and Clyde Binfield (eds), *From Cambridge to Sinai* (London, 2006), pp. 87–108.
7 It being best manners to present yourself to previously unknown guests before having them to dine.
8 Dita Blass originally from the *Schweizer Frauenblatt*, April 1934. This translation, by John Proctor, is in Cornick and Binfield, op. cit. Editha became a painter and was married to the artist Felix Klipstein. This document and others by the Blass sisters were sent to Westminister College by Mr Rolf Haaser, Vice-President of the Klipstein Society, from the Klipstein Archives in Laubach/Hessen. All the citations that follow are from Dita, as translated by John Proctor.
9 It seems they may have been given to some distant cousins in America.

Chapter 28 – The college's opening

1   *Cambridge Independent.* David Thompson writes of the 'half-joking half-serious view of dissent in late nineteenth century Cambridge'. Thompson, *Cambridge Theology in the Nineteenth Century* (Aldershot, 2008), p. 169.

Chapter 29 – To the monasteries of the Nitrian desert

1   This seems to be the trip on which they saw Dita Blass in Paris.

2   Agnes Smith Lewis, 'A Visit to the Coptic Monasteries of Egypt', in *Proceedings of the Cambridge Antiquarian Society* (25 November 1901), p. 215.

3   Some of their photographs of this MS failed, so they returned the following year to the Nitrian desert to photograph it again. It became *Horae Semiticae* , No. III.

4   The series' twelfth and final volume was published in 1907.

5   The edition of the tale they produced in 1898 had to be revised in 1913 after excavations on an island in the Nile at Aswan, the Elephantine, disclosed a hoard of Jewish documents, the leavings of a Jewish military colony established by the Persians in the Upper Nile. This contained a fifth-century BC version of the life of Ahikar. F. C. Conybeare, J. Rendel Harris and Agnes Smith Lewis, *The Story of Ahikar* (Cambridge, 1913).

6   Eberhard Nestle, Review of *The Story of Ahikar* in *The Expository Times*, March, 1899.

7   Allan Whigham Price, *Ladies of Castlebrae* (London, 1985), p. 169.

Chapter 30 – The active life

1   Norman Bentwich, *Solomon Schechter* (London, 1931), pp. 84–5, 97.

2   Letter from Agnes to Francis Jenkinson, 24 January 1903. Cambridge University Library, Add 6463 (E) 5309.

3   T. R. Glover, *Cambridge Retrospect* (Cambridge, 1943), p. 70.

4   Between 1903 and 1913 the prodigious Harris also published, amongst other things, three volumes (one running to some 490 pages) on twins and twin cults in the ancient world. This may bear no relation to his

friendship with Agnes and Margaret, but he did call one of these books *The Cult of Heavenly Twins*, a name by which they were known in Cambridge.

5 Scrapbook of press cuttings kept by Agnes Smith Lewis and Margaret Dunlop Gibson, University of Birmingham Archives.

6 The same newspaper, two days later, reported that the two lady travellers and explorers, now the guests of Mrs Samuel van Vechten Huntingdon of East Seventy-Eighth Street, were persons whose names were known to 'every philologist, antiquarian and Biblical critic in the world'.

7 *The North American*, 8 November 1903.

8 Germany was in this respect, as in so many others in academic life, greatly in advance. Heidelberg had its first female student successfully promoted to a doctorate in 1895. Halle had awarded a woman a doctorate in 1754. These, it should be noted, were doctorates achieved by studies in the university, and not honorary degrees like those awarded to Agnes and Margaret.

9 Not the Porphyrios first met by the twins in 1892, but a successor of the same name.

10 From the Latin of the Cambridge University *Reporter*, June 14 1904, translated by Professor David Armstrong of Austin, Texas.

11 Agnes brought out her own edition of the Syriac Gospels in 1910, reversing the priority. The two contesting volumes sit on the shelves of the Cambridge University Library today, their historic rancour separated by only a couple of feet of books.

12 *The Church Times*, 9 October 9 1908. They were also annoyed by the residual scepticism which lead him to put late dates on manuscript finds. See, for instance, Agnes's introduction to *Horae Semiticae* IX, p. xi.

13 Edith MacAlister, *St Columba's Church Cambridge: Some Recollections and a Chronicle* (Cambridge, 1950), p. 36.

14 Eglantyne Jebb, *Cambridge: a brief study in social questions* (Cambridge, 1906), pp. 96–7. Jebb went on to found the charity 'Save the Children'.

15 Henry Drummond, cited in. Jebb, *op. cit.*, p. 162.

16 Roughly the 1,000-year period between the conquest of Alexander the Great and the Arab invasion, during which Upper Egypt was part of the Greek-speaking diaspora and, from the first century A.D. until the rise of Islam in the seventh, largely Christian.

17 Peter Parsons, *City of the Sharp-Nosed Fish* (London, 2007), p. 17. These

are still to be fully identified and published.

18 This fragment, known as P52, is in the John Rylands Library of the University of Manchester. It is the earliest known fragment of the New Testament.

19 Published by Agnes as *Codex Climaci Rescriptus*, *Horae Semiticae*, VIII, 1909.

Chapter 31 – The darkening to war

1   Agnes Smith Lewis, *Margaret Atheling and Other Poems* (London, 1917).

2   Allan Whigham Price, *The Ladies of Castlebrae* (London, 1985), p. 213 and also his interview notes, WGL 7/1.

3   Ibid., pp. 214–15.

4   Irene Pickard, *Memories of J. Rendel Harris* (Birmingham, 1978), pp. 44–5.

5   Alphonse Mingana and Agnes Smith Lewis, *Leaves from Three Ancient Qurans* (Cambridge, 1914).

6   Austen Chamberlain, M.P., in presentingte Gold Medal for oriental Research to Agnes and Margaret. *Journal of the Royal Asiatic Society for 1915*, p. 617.

7   Whigham Price, notes from interviews, Westminster College Library. WGL 7/1. All the unreferenced quotes in this chapter are from this source.

8   P. Carnegie Simpson, *Recollections* (London, 1943), p. 67.

9   WGL 7/1.

Chapter 32 – Palimpsest

1   I am grateful to Professor David Holton, current holder of the post in Modern Greek established by Agnes and Margaret at Cambridge University, for this piece of information.

2   Allan Whigham Price, *The Ladies of Castlebrae* (London, 1985), pp. 125–6.

3   Whigham Price acknowledges that the twins themselves never mentioned finding the palimpsest as a butter dish, but surmised that they did not wish to humiliate the monks any further after von Tischendorf's mistreatment. Agnes, especially in her earliest accounts, was not nearly so sensitive to monastic feelings. She was, however,

ruthlessly honest and, had she wished to cover something over, she would have done so by saying little, not by devising an elaborate counter-narrative.

4   At least one of Whigham Price's handwritten memos of such an interview mentions butter purchased warapped in a leaf of old manuscript, though not at Sinai, but in Palestine.

5   Personal communication from Alessandro Falcetta, who is writing a book on Rendel Harris.

6   Agnes Smith Lewis, *Light on the Four Gospels from the Sinai Palimpsest* (London, 1913), p. 6.

7   Ibid., p. 141. John O'Neil believes that Agnes can be defended on this point. He discusses a variant in the Syriac palimpsest for John 20:15–17. Mary Magdalene here meets the risen Christ in the garden. Mistaking him for the gardener, she says (in the Revised Standard Version) ' "Sir, if you have carried him away, tell me where you have laid him, and I will take him away;" Jesus said to her, "Mary." *She turned and said to him in Hebrew, "Rabboni!"* (which means Teacher).' Agnes's Syriac variant for the italicised passage translates '*And she understood Him, and answered, saying unto him, Rabbuli.*' O'Neil writes, 'In place of *she turning*, the Syriac has *she understood*, surely the correct rendering of the underlying Semitic original: she changed her mind about the man she mistook for a gardener.' John O'Neil, 'Agnes Smith-Lewis as a textual critic', in David Cornick and Clive Binfield (eds), *From Cambridge to Sinai* (London, 2006), p. 49.

8   See Samir K. Samir, SJ, 'The Earliest Arab Apology for Christianity', in S. K. Samir and J. S. Nielsen (eds), *Christian Arabic Apologetics During the Abbasid Period, 750–1258* (Leiden, 1994). With the aid of infra-red lamps and other accoutrements of the modern text scholar, Samir was able to add at least ten pages to the MS.

9   Of the twins' textual work, Professor Sidney Griffith, an authority on Christian Arabic texts, says, 'I have the highest regard for the work of Gibson and Lewis. Their inventories and their editions of texts are still the best access we have to a number of important texts preserved in the monastery library at Mt Sinai. I have used their work many times . . . But the twins' importance was not just limited to the access they afforded later scholars . . . their own work displays a considerable erudition and a high scholarly quality. My admiration for them increases when I recall that they were largely self-taught . . . Their work is still very important

to scholars of the biblical text and the history of Christian communities in the middle East, well into Islamic times.' Personal communication of 30 August 2008.

10 In this they could be said to stand in the Cambridge tradition. In 1855 J. B. Lightfoot had written that 'the timidity, which shrinks from the application of modern science or criticism to the interpretation of the Holy Scriptures evinces a very unworthy view of its character . . . From the full light of science and criticism we have nothing to fear.' Cited in David M. Thompson, *Cambridge Theology in the Nineteenth Century* (Aldershot, 2008), p. 107; and see this work throughout for interesting insights on scholars and dissenters of the period.

11 Lewis, op. cit., pp. 15–17.

12 See D. C. Parker, *An Introduction to New Testament Manuscripts and Their Texts* (Cambridge, 2008), pp. 1, 45–6.

13 Azriel Eisenberg, *Fill a Blank Page* (New York, 1965), p. 114.

Chapter 33 – Coda

1 Irene Pickard, *Memories of J. Rendel Harris*, (Quaker Publication, 1978), p. 59.

Select bibliography

Bensly, R. L., J. Rendel Harris and F. Burkitt (1894). *The Gospels in Syriac, with an introduction by Agnes Smith Lewis.* Cambridge, Cambridge University Press.

Bensly, Mrs. R. L. (1896). *Our Journey to Sinai: A Visit to the Convent of St. Catarina.* London, The Religious Tract Society.

Bentwich, N. (1931). *Solomon Schechter.* London, George Allen & Unwin.

Black, J. S. and G. Chrystal (1912). *The Life of William Robertson Smith.* London, Adam and Charles Black.

Blackie, J. S. (1910). *Notes of a Life.* Edinburgh and London, William Blackwood and Sons.

Brendon, P. (1991). *Thomas Cook: 150 Years of Popular Tourism.* London, Secker & Warburg.

Brooke, C. (1993). *A History of the University of Cambridge.* Vol. IV. Cambridge, Cambridge University Press.

Brown, J. (1888). *Life of William B. Robertson, D.D.* Glasgow, James Maclehose & Sons.

Bury, P. (1952). *The College of Corpus Christi and of the Blessed Virgin Mary.* Cambridge, Cambridge University Press.

Chadwick, O. (1970). *The Victorian Church.* Chatham, Kent, W. & J. Mackay & Co. Ltd.

Cornick, D. and Clyde Binfield, Eds. (2006). *From Cambridge to Sinai: the worlds of Agnes Smith Lewis and Margaret Dunlop Gibson.* London, URC History Society and the United Reformed Church.

Edwards, Amelia. (1888). *A Thousand Miles Up the Nile.* London, G. Routledge and Sons.

Eisenberg, A. (1965). *Fill a Blank Page: A biography of Solomon Schechter*. New York, United Synagogue Commission on Jewish Education.

Elliott, J. K. (1982). *Codex Sinaiticus and the Simonides affair: an examination of the nineteenth century claim that Codex Sinaiticus was not an ancient manuscript*. Thessalonike, Patriarchikon Hidryma Paterikon Meleton.

Gibson, James. (1887). *The Cid ballads: and other poems and translations from Spanish and German / by James Young Gibson; edited by Margaret Dunlop Gibson; with memoir by Agnes Smith Lewis*. London, Kegan Paul, Trench, Trubner and Company.

Gibson, Margaret D. (1893). *How the Codex was Found; a narrative of two visits to Sinai, from Mrs. Lewis's journals 1892–1893*. Cambridge, Macmillan and Bowes.

Gibson, Margaret D. Ed. (1894). *An Arabic Version of the Epistles of St Paul to the Romans, Corinthians, Galatians with part of the Epistle to the Ephesians from a ninth century MS. in the Convent of St. Catharine on Mount Sinai. Studia Sinaitica*. London, C. J. Clay and Sons.

Gibson, Margaret D. (1894). *Catalogue of the Arabic mss. in the Convent of S. Catharine on Mount Sinai*. London, C. J. Clay and Sons.

Gibson, Margaret D. and Agnes Smith Lewis (1893). *How the Codex was found: a narrative of two visits to Sinai from Mrs Lewis's journals, 1892–1893*. Cambridge, Macmillan & Bowes.

Glover, T. R. (1943). *Cambridge Retrospect*. Cambridge, Cambridge University Press.

Guthrie, A. (1889). *Robertson of Irvine, Poet Preacher*. Ardrossan.

Harris, J. R. and Helen B. Harris. (1897). *Letters from the Scenes of the Recent Massacres in Armenia*. London, Nisbet & Co.

Harris, J. R. (1891). *The Apology of Aristides on behalf of the Christians: from a Syriac ms. preserved on Mount Sinai*. Cambridge, Cambridge University Press.

Jebb, E. (1906). *Cambridge: a brief study in social questions*. Cambridge, Macmillan & Bowes.

Johnstone, W., Ed. (1995). *William Robertston Smith: essays in reassessment*. Journal for the study of the Old Testament supplement series. Sheffield, Sheffield Academic Press.

Kenyon, F. G. (1936). *The Story of the Bible: a popular account of how it came to us*. London, John Murray.

Keynes, F. A. (1950). *Gathering up the Threads: a study in family biography*. Cambridge, W. Heffer & Sons Ltd.

Knox, B. (1978). *Westminster College, Cambridge: Its Background and History*. Cambridge, University Library and Westminster College.

Lewis, Agnes Smith, see also Smith, Agnes (1887). *Through Cyprus*. London, Hurst and Blackett.

Lewis, Agnes Smith (1892). *Life of the Rev. Samuel Savage Lewis M.A., F.S.A.: Fellow and Librarian of Corpus Christi College, Cambridge*. Cambridge, Macmillan and Bowes.

Lewis, Agnes Smith (1893). *Two Unpublished Letters of Agnes Smith Lewis*. Cambridge, Printed for Private Circulation, Trinity College, Cambridge.

Lewis, Agnes Smith (1894). *A translation of the Four Gospels from the Syriac of the Sinaitic Palimpsest*. London and New York, Macmillan and Co.

Lewis, Agnes Smith (1894). *Catalogue of the Syriac mss. in the Convent of S. Catharine on Mount Sinai*. London, C. J. Clay and Sons.

Lewis, Agnes Smith, Ed. (1897). *A Palestinian Syriac Lectionary containing lessons from the Pentateuch, Job, Proverbs, Prophets, Acts, and Epistles*. Studia Sinaitica. London, C. J. Clay and Sons.

Lewis, Agnes Smith. (1898). *In the Shadow of Sinai: A story of travel and research from 1895 to 1897*. Cambridge, Macmillan & Bowes.

Lewis, Agnes Smith. (1900). *Select narratives of holy women from the Syro-Antiochene or Sinai Palimpsest*. London, C. J. Clay and Sons, Cambridge University Press.

Lewis, Agnes Smith. (1904). *The Mythological Acts of the apostles: translated from an Arabic ms. in the Convent of Deyr-es-Suriani, Egypt, and from mss. in the Convent of St. Catherine on Mount Sinai and in the Vatican Library: with a translation of the palimpsest fragments of the Acts of Judas Thomas from Cod. Sin. Syr. 30*. London, C.J. Clay and Sons.

Lewis, Agnes Smith. (1910). *The old Syriac gospels, or, Evangelion da-Mepharreshe, being the text of the Sinai or Syro-Antiochene palimpsest, including the latest additions and emendations, with the variants of the*

Curetonian text, corroborations from many other MSS., and a list of quotations from ancient authors. London, Williams & Norgate.

Lewis, Agnes Smith. (1913). *Light on the Four Gospels from the Sinai Palimpsest.* London, Williams & Norgate.

Lewis, Agnes Smith and Alphonse Mingana (1914). *Leaves from Three Ancient Qurans.* Cambridge, Cambridge University Press.

MacAlister, Edith. (1950). *St Colomba's Church Cambridge: Some recollections and a Chronicle.* Cambridge, Cambridge University Presso.

Macdonald, L. O. (2000). *A Unique and Glorious mission: women and presbyterianism in Scotland 1830–1930.* Edinburgh, John Donald.

McJannet, A. F. (1938). *Royal Burgh of Irvine.* Glasgow, Civic Press.

McWilliams-Tullberg, R. (1975). *Women at Cambridge: a Men's University – though of a mixed type.* London, Victor Gollanz Ltd.

Metzger, B. M. (1977). *The early versions of the New Testament: their origin, transmission and limitations.* Oxford, Clarendon Press.

Milne, H. and T. T. C. Skeat (1955). *The Codex Sinaiticus and the Codex Alexandrinus,* British Museum.

Murray's (1875). *A Handbook for Travellers in Egypt.* London, John Murray (see also Wilkinson).

Nightingale, Florence. (1987). *Letters from Egypt: a Journey on the Nile (1849–1850).* Ed. Anthony Sattin. London, Barrie & Jenkins Ltd.

Olin, S. (1977 (reprinted from 1843 edition)). *Travels in Egypt, Arabia Petraea and the Holy Land.* New York, Arno Press.

Parker, D. C. (1997). *The Living Text of the Gospels.* Cambridge, Cambridge University Press.

Pickard, Irene. (1978). *Memories of J. Rendel Harris.* Birmingham, Edward Cadbury Trust.

Poggibonsi, Fr. N. (1945). *A Voyage Beyond the Seas (1346–1350).* Jerusalem, Franciscan Press.

Raverat, Gwen. (1954). *Period Piece: A Cambridge childhood.* London, Faber and Faber.

Reif, S. (2000). *A Jewish Archive from Old Cairo: the history of Cambridge University's Genizah Collection.* Richmond, Surrey, Curzon.

Robinson, E. (1977). *Biblical Researches in Palestine, Mount Sinai and*

Arabia Petraea. New York, Arno Press.

Rogerson, J. (1995). *Bible and Criticism in Victorian Britain*. Sheffield, Sheffield Academic Press.

Roussou-Sinclair, M. (2002). *Victorian Travellers in Cyprus: A Garden of Their Own*. Nicosia, Cyprus Research Centre.

Samir, S. K. (1994). The Earliest Arab Apology for Christianity. *Christian Arabic Apologetics during the Abbasid Period (750–1258)*. Samir K. Samir and J. S. Nielsen. Leiden, Brill: 57–114.

Sayce, A. H. (1923). *Reminiscences*. London, Macmillan and Co.

Schneller, L. (1939). *Search on Sinai; the story of Tischendorf's life and the search for a lost manuscript*. London. The Epworth Press (E.C. Barton).

Simpson, P. Carnegie (1943). *Recollections: mainly ecclesiastical but sometimes human*. London, Nisbet & Co.

Smith, Agnes – see also Agnes Smith Lewis. (1870). *Eastern Pilgrims: the travels of three ladies*. London, Hurst and Blackett.

Smith, A. (1884). *Glimpses of Greek Life and Scenery*. London, Hurst and Blackett.

Smith, A. (1887). *Through Cyprus*. London, Hurst & Blackett.

Stanley, A. P. (1881 (new edition)). *Sinai and Palestine in Connection with their history*. London, John Murray.

Strawhorn, J. (1985). *The History of Irvine: Royal Burgh and New Town*. Edinburgh, John Donald Publishers Ltd.

Tait, M. S. (1883). *Report to the Trustees of the Ferguson Bequest Fund*. Glasgow, Robert Maclehose & Sons at the University Press.

Thompson, D. M. (2008). *Cambridge Theology in the Nineteenth Century: Enquiry, Controversy and Truth*. Aldershot, Ashgate Publishing Limited.

Tischendorf, C. von (1934). *Codex Sinaiticus: the ancient biblical manuscript now in the British Museum*. London, Lutterworth Press.

Whigham Price, A. (1985). *The Ladies of Castlebrae*. London, Headline Book Publishing.

Wilkinson, Sir Gardner, 1797–1875. (1843). *Modern Egypt and Thebes: being a description of Egypt, including information required for travellers in that country*. London, John Murray (this became the first Murray's guide).

Index